COMMUNITY POWER AND POLITICAL THEORY

# Community Power and Political Theory

*A Further Look at Problems of Evidence and Inference*

Second, enlarged edition

# Nelson W. Polsby

Yale University Press
New Haven and London, 1980

Set in Linotype Caledonia type.
Printed in the United States of America by
The Murray Printing Co., Westford, Mass.


Published in Great Britain, Europe, Africa, and
Asia (except Japan) by Yale University Press,
Ltd., London. Distributed in Australia and
New Zealand by Book & Film Services, Artarmon,
N.S.W., Australia; and in Japan by Harper & Row,
Publishers, Tokyo Office.


First edition published as volume 7 in the Yale
Studies in Political Science.

*Library of Congress Cataloging in Publication Data*

Polsby, Nelson W
    Community power and political theory.
    Second, enlarged edition

    Includes bibliographical references and indexes.
    1. New Haven—Politics and government.   2. Municipal
government—United States—Case studies.   3. Community
power—Case studies.   4. Social classes—United States.
I. Title.
JS1195.2.P6 1980      301.44'92'0973   79-22966
ISBN 0-300-02445-2 (cloth)
ISBN 0-300-02528-9 (paper)

For E.W.P. and in memory of D.P. II

# Contents

# Preface to the Second Edition

> Meddling with another man's folly is
> always thankless work.
>
> Kipling, *Plain Tales*

Mr. Justice Holmes once wrote that "all books are dead in 25 years, but luckily the public does not always find it out."[1] No doubt in this, as in so much, Holmes was at least half right, which means that on an optimistic timetable this book has only a few years to go. It was not my intention that *Community Power and Political Theory* in its first edition should last even this long. And yet the hopeful and becomingly modest expectations, expressed in the final pages of Chapter 7, for the sort of intellectual progress that would put this book out of business do not seem to have been realized.

The decade and a half since the publication of the first edition have not been altogether edifying either in the theory or practice of politics. I think it is an indication of a lack of progress in the study of politics that it should seem a good idea—to me and to Yale University Press—to give renewed life in a second edition to a book like this. *Community Power and Political Theory* endeavored to summarize and criticize the literature on community power as things were years ago and, if possible, to set work on community power upon a new track. The continued usefulness of this book suggests that, at the least, in this last ambition it has failed. If it had not failed, presumably the original contents would now be of only cursory interest, as a road map to an intellectual ghost town. But as someone once observed of an Oxford college, "These ruins are inhabited."[2]

The literature on community power, no exemplar of clarity or intelligence when I first wrote this book, has since its publication become even more dense with misunderstandings of all kinds, while burgeoning in nearly every direction—every direction, that is, except toward the resolution of empirical problems about the shape and scope of power in American communities. Thus, anybody who returns to this field does so at the haz-

---

1. Letter to Frederick Pollock, July 9, 1912, in Mark D. Howe, ed., *Holmes-Pollock Letters*, vol. I (Cambridge, Harvard Univ. Press, 1941).
2. According to K. C. Wheare, it was said of Exeter College. See the delightful book by Muriel Beadle, *These Ruins are Inhabited* (London, Robert Hale, 1961), p. 83.

ard of augmenting a scholarly morass and, in the fine figure of Thomas Brackett Reed, subtracting from the sum total of human knowledge. The passing years have added, so it seems, to the conceptual and theoretical debris, and the task of clearing away this debris may not take us as far as we would like toward the goal of understanding power and its exercise in the local community.

A pessimistic view of the last decade and a half would surely call attention to the fact that not all the debates and disagreements on display in this literature have been conducted with the utmost of scholarly decorum. In fact, this has been so much the case that the lack of decorum in the field has itself become the subject of pious comment.[3] Self-appointed peacemakers and ecumenical movements have come and gone.[4] Bibliographies,[5] symposia,[6] and books of readings have flourished,[7] and there has even grown up a small scholarly offshoot that takes as its subject matter quantitative analysis of the relationship in studies between certain conclusions about community power on the one hand and the formal disciplinary affiliations of their authors on the other.[8]

3. See, for example, Harry M. Scoble, "Where the Pluralists Went Wrong," in Frederick M. Wirt, ed., *Future Directions in Community Power Research: A Colloquium* (Berkeley, Institute of Governmental Studies, 1971), p. 110; or Frederick W. Frey, "Comment: On Issues and Nonissues in the Study of Power," *Am. Pol. Sci. Rev.*, 65 (Dec. 1971), 1081.

4. See, for example, Lawrence J. R. Herson, "In the Footsteps of Community Power," *Am. Pol. Sci. Rev.*, 55 (Dec. 1961), 817–30; Peter H. Rossi, "Community Decision-Making," *Administrative Science Quarterly*, 1 (March 1957), 415–43; Frey, "Issues and Nonissues," pp. 1081–1101.

5. The two largest recent bibliographies of which I am aware are both published as separate volumes: Willis D. Hawley and James H. Svara, *The Study of Community Power* (Santa Barbara, ABC Clio, 1972), which goes on for 123 pages and includes (on pp. vi–vii) a list of other bibliographies of community power, seven in number; and Irving P. Leif, *Community Power and Decision-Making* (Metuchen, N.J., Scarecrow Press, 1974), listing 1,196 items, including seven other bibliographies (on pp. 157–58) but not the same seven as Hawley and Svara. A combined tabulation gives twelve bibliographies.

6. For example, Bert E. Swanson, ed., *Current Trends in Comparative Community Studies* (Kansas City, Mo., Community Studies, Inc., 1962); *Southwestern Social Science Quarterly*, 48 (Dec. 1967); *The New Atlantis*, 2 (Winter 1970); Wirt, *Future Directions*.

7. Here are a few examples: Terry N. Clark, ed., *Community Structure and Decision-Making: Comparative Analyses* (San Francisco, Chandler, 1968); Michael E. Aiken and Paul E. Mott, eds., *The Structure of Community Power* (New York, Random House, 1970); Charles M. Bonjean, Terry N. Clark, and Robert L. Lineberry, eds., *Community Politics: A Behavioral Approach* (New York, Free Press, 1972); Willis D. Hawley and Frederick M. Wirt, eds., *The Search for Community Power* 2nd ed. (Englewood Cliffs, N.J., Prentice Hall, 1974).

8. Two manifestations of this literature are the following doctoral dissertations: Claire W. Gilbert, "Community Power Structure: A Study in the Sociology of Knowl-

There has been a powerful resurgence of interest in the application of quasi-Marxian insights such as I criticize herein to all manner of American settings, not least the local community. So what I earlier identified as one tendency among social scientists blossomed in the 1960s as very much the intellectual fashion. Since I continue to doubt the veracity and the competence of much American political analysis that is written à la this particular mode, I still wonder if it is something other than its empirical persuasiveness that compels the belief of true believers in the stratification approach to the study of community power.

This sense of wonder is given some fortification by a recent general account of intellectual activity which makes the arresting claim that persuasion by means other than empirical demonstration is not especially uncommon in presumably scientific endeavor. Thomas Kuhn's discussion of the structure of scientific revolutions, if it had been available when I first wrote, might have alerted me to the stark improbability that anything as slender as the weight of evidence would swiftly triumph even in purportedly scholarly discourse.[9] And severely—and justly—as Kuhn has been beaten about the ears by assorted philosophers of science,[10] there is, I believe, a core of empirical validity—at least in the contemporary, soft, social sciences—to his view that scientific arguments are frequently fights about what questions to ask masquerading as disagreements about the answers to agreed-on questions.

This is meant to suggest that the volume you have before you can be viewed at least in part as an occasion for epistemological reflection rather than as a tract about community politics. I have no doubt that this unlooked-for dimension of the work I have done is what has kept it alive since the early sixties. To the recent upsurge of interest in problems of the local community, in urban political activity—legal and illegal, mass and elite—and in the impact of demography and policy upon the lives of city dwellers, the study of community power has contributed little or nothing in the way of knowledge. It should have been plain enough a decade ago, but at any rate it bears repeating, that the academic study of community power is not much about urban politics. Rather, our subject is the writings of scholars, and what they say they have found, and whether we ought to

edge" (Ph.D. diss., Northwestern Univ., 1966) and John Thomas Walton, "An Analysis of Methods and Findings in Studies of Community Power Structure" (Ph.D. diss., Univ. of California, Santa Barbara, 1966). Published works arising from these dissertations and other contributions to this subfield are discussed in Chapter 8.

9. Thomas S. Kuhn, *The Structure of Scientific Revolutions* (Chicago, Univ. of Chicago Press, 1962).

10. See, for example, Imre Lakatos and Alan Musgrave, *Criticism and the Growth of Knowledge* (Cambridge, Univ. Press, 1970).

believe them or not, and why. How satisfactory is this literature as a forum for the contemplation and debate of issues in democratic theory, epistemology, and evidence and inference in social research? On this point, the vote of social scientists seems to be overwhelmingly favorable, despite my own strong misgivings.

These issues are by no means trivial ones, although the level at which the community power literature has debated them has sometimes seemed to trivialize them. At any rate, it is to these issues that I return in the six chapters that I have added as an epilogue to the end of this second edition. I have let the seven chapters of the first edition stand as originally published, corrected only in minor, cosmetic ways. In part, this indicates that what I have said there I continue largely to endorse. Another reason for letting well enough alone in the original seven chapters arises from the unexpectedly pleasant reception the book received upon its first publication and has since enjoyed in spite of the controversiality—indeed, the downright unacceptability in at least some quarters—of many of its conclusions. It is true the original book received some unfavorable notice but, all things considered, not much.[11]

On the positive side of the ledger, people have told me that the original edition was a useful guide to the main studies and issues in the field of community power. This is also what I believed it to be at the time I wrote. Now, the number of studies has ballooned to unmanageable proportions, and so I doubt that this second edition can boast the coverage of the first. I have, however, attempted in the added chapters to deal, to the best of my understanding and ability, with leading issues in the field as they have emerged in the sixties and seventies. Occasionally this has taken the form of explicit dialogue with one or another critic of the New Haven study, to which I am still pleased and grateful to have contributed. And unavoidably, also, because some of the themes that have occupied our critics had already been treated in the first edition, I have sometimes expanded or

11. One reviewer of the book was Robert O. Schulze, whose work I had directly challenged. In a gesture of generosity quite extraordinary for most scholars—but not, I learned, for him—Schulze, while defending his own work, took occasion to praise mine. Robert O. Schulze, "For a Brown Man's Bookshelf," *Brown Alumni Monthly* (Nov. 1963), 22. Other mostly favorable reviews appeared in *Annals, 355* (Sept. 1964), 171–72 (by Joseph LaPalombara); *Am. Pol. Sci. Rev., 58* (June 1964), 415 (by Robert A. Wood); *Am. Soc. Rev., 29* (April 1964), 298–99 (by Phillips Cutright); *Political Science Quarterly, 81* (March 1966), 170 (by Peter Rossi); *Journal of Politics, 26* (Nov. 1964), 939–40 (by M. Kent Jennings); and *Administrative Science Quarterly, 9* (Dec. 1974), 313–15 (by Harry M. Scoble). Mostly unfavorable reviews included: William V. D'Antonio, *Social Forces, 42* (March 1964), 375–76; Thomas J. Anton, *Midwest Journal of Political Science, 8* (May 1964), 212–15; and Warner Bloomberg, Jr., *Am. J. Soc., 70* (July 1964), 102–03.

elaborated on thoughts expressed there, taking what comfort I could from Karl Popper's sage observation that "it is impossible to speak in such a way that you cannot be misunderstood."[12]

Only partly in fun, I once compiled a table listing the various orientations to the study of community power and their multitudinous branches.[13] This table attempted to clarify some of the mysteries of an otherwise impenetrable area of study. I reprint it herewith, in the thought that it may help a reader keep track of at least some of the discussion elsewhere in this book.

### ORIENTATIONS TO THE STUDY OF COMMUNITY POWER

*1. Methodological*
   A. Reputational methodists: People who ask panels of judges to identify community leaders.
   B. Pluralists$_1$: People who use eclectic methods of research, generally anthropological or journalistic in character; collectors of case studies.
   C. Ecumenists$_1$: People who explicitly attempt to compare reputational with other methods.

*2. Empirical*
   A. Community Power Stratificationists:
      1. Elitists. People who claim to have found communities overtly dominated by power elites.
      2. Hidden handites. People who claim to have found communities in which behind-the-scenes power is closely held.
      3. Potential elitists. People who claim to have found communities where an elite does not rule, except it can when it wants to, or could if it wanted to.
   B. Pluralists$_2$: People who claim to have found communities in which power is dispersed in various ways.
   C. Ecumenists$_2$: People who believe that every student's findings are true with respect to his community, regardless of criticisms or evidence.

*3. Theoretical*
   A. General Stratificationists: People who believe that values are distributed hierarchically, that an actor's position on some hierarchies predicts positions on others, etc.

12. Karl R. Popper, *Unended Quest* (Glasgow, Fontana-Collins, 1976), p. 30.
13. Nelson W. Polsby, " 'Pluralism' in the Study of Community Power: Or Erklärung Before Verklärung in *Wissenssoziologie*," *The American Sociologist*, 4 (May 1969), 118–22.

B. Pluralists₃: People who believe that for political purposes community actors may belong to groups, but in America rarely classes; that mostly people do not care about politics; that most resources in the system are not used for political purposes, etc.

4. *Critical*

A. Anti-reputationists: People who believe the reputational method is unsatisfactory.

B. Anti-stratificationists: People who believe findings of community power stratification studies are weakly supported by evidence. (At least one of these lays the blame in part on general stratification theory.)

C. Anti-pluralists:

1. Value-free anti-pluralists. People who believe pluralists (subscript uncertain) are wrong in their methods, or in their conclusions about specific communities, or in their assumptions—sometimes in all three. Occasionally, pluralists are confused with anti-reputationists and anti-stratificationists. This is understandable but harmful, since the invalidation of a critique does not vitiate, e.g., an empirical claim about a local community.

2. Left-wing anti-pluralists. People who believe Pluralist₃ assumptions and/or Pluralist₂ findings are fronts for "The Establishment."

D. Anti-anti-pluralists: A new and promising category. People who believe anti-pluralist critiques of pluralism are wrong.

5. *Wissenssoziologische*

A. People who make up lists classifying students of community power: a growth industry.

What this table suggests, at the outset, is that there are more orientations to the academic study of community power than there are names to label them with. This is bound to cause confusion, although it is not the only source of confusion in this field. If academic confusion were the only thing at stake in the study of community power, there would be ample justification to attempt clarification. But there is also a sense in which the stakes of debate about community power have grown, owing to the fact that ideas central to the study of community power have escaped from their confinement in monographs and professional journals and emerged as a feature of popular culture. For example, here is a report by J. Anthony Lukas in the September 1972 issue of *Esquire* magazine:

In most American cities, power ultimately resides not with the elected Mayor or City Council, but with a group of influential businessmen.[14]

How does J. Anthony Lukas know this? Perhaps it is an unreasonable question to ask outside academic precincts. Presumably, a magazine writer receives his warrant to make statements of this kind not from his personally having checked out "most American cities," but rather from received wisdom that he imagines nobody questions. "Some things," says a psychiatrist in *Science* magazine, "such as 'love' or 'the power structure' . . . are difficult to define but rather easy to recognize."[15] I hazard the guess that if J. Anthony Lukas had anything in mind at all about "most American cities" when he wrote his *Esquire* article, it was quite likely the findings of one or more of the very studies eviscerated in the second and third chapters of this book. This suggests at a minimum the selectivity with which information passes from the academic community into the outside world.

Sometimes the receptiveness of political actors is responsible for the appearance of scholarly or technical terminology in popular discourse. In the early 1960s, especially in the south, community power language had a small vogue.[16] Indeed, as late as 1978, in a speech to civic leaders. Ernest Morial, the newly elected mayor of New Orleans,

> closed by talking about a study . . . on the power structure in New Orleans. "[The] methodology," Morial said, "consisted of asking key individuals which civic leaders were necessary to insure the success of

14. J. Anthony Lukas, "Wanta Buy Two Seats for the Dallas Cowboys?", *Esquire,* 78 (Sept. 1972), 124.

15. William Ryan, "Participant Observer," a book review in *Science, 163* (21 March 1969), 1314. Dr. Ryan is quoted on "the power structure," but not much on "love," in Fred Powledge, *Model City* (New York, Simon and Schuster, 1970).

16. I have not been conscientious in collecting examples of his rhetoric, but I have the impression that Atlanta native Martin Luther King, Jr., frequently used the language of community power analysis, and this may have contributed greatly to its popularity among orators and observers alike in the south. See, for example, Mary McGrory, "Fear in Birmingham: Big Mules' Shun Problem," *Washington Star*, Sept. 20, 1963: "Last spring, when racial disorder boiled in the streets, Burke Marshall of the Justice Department came here, took the power structure by the lapels and made it sit down with the Negro leaders of Birmingham . . . ;" James Reston, "Birmingham: The Big Power Structure in Alabama," *New York Times*, Sept. 22, 1963; Jack Minnis (of Atlanta, Georgia), "Care and Feeding of Power Structures," *New University Thought* (Summer 1964), 73–79; Wallace Turner, "Culture an Issue in San Francisco," *New York Times,* Nov. 29, 1964: "Jeremy Ets-Hokin . . . placed the blame for the situation on the city's 'power structure families.' 'They are imbued with an almost incestuous lethargy,' he said"; Stephan Lesher, "Leroy Johnson Outslicks Mister Charlie," *New York Times Magazine*, Nov. 8, 1970, p. 36: "The white power structure [of Fulton County–Atlanta– Georgia] remained unready for a black legislator."

a project. [The investigator] . . . went to these people and repeated the question, finally coming up with a three-tiered list . . . [A] majority of people failed to mention the mayor."[17]

Community power rhetoric can be found in even more popular places. Consider the following excerpt from Joyce Haber's Hollywood column of August 28, 1968:

"Who are all those people going upstairs?" asked a visiting lady at a back booth at the Bistro. "The Power Structure," said the headwaiter. "They look too old for a rock group," the lady told her husband from Milwaukee. True. The only things they ever rock are industries, political frameworks, social contours and, on occasion, a continent or two.[18]

While it appears to be the case that advocates of some variant of stratification theory have had the greatest success in popularizing their viewpoint, an occasional pluralist voice can be heard. San Francisco columnist Herb Caen complained about an article in the February 1973 *Town and Country* magazine on "the 10 Most Powerful San Franciscans":

as for "power," what is it? The Mayor, as we have found, can't even fix a traffic tag; maybe that's why he isn't on the list. The late Louis Lurie could always get a table at Jack's but he died without being able

17. James K. Glassman, "New Orleans: I Have Seen the Future, and It's Houston," *Atlantic*, 242 (July 1978), 18.

18. Joyce Haber, " 'Power Structure' Goes to a Party," *Los Angeles Times*, Aug. 28, 1968. The "power structure" to Miss Haber turns out chiefly to consist of elderly people in the movie colony. She continues:

"They," the Power Structure, were assembled in force one night last weekend when the Beverly Hills doyens, Harriet and Armand Deutsch, held an elegant black-tie dinner dance for the Philadelphia Power Structures, Lee and Walter Annenberg, their friends of 15 years. "The Annenbergs adore Italian food," sighed Harriet, beautiful in a short white beaded Galanos. So owner Kurt held his first Italian dinner. And everyone was there.

It was that kind of night, the kind of night when a wife (or husband) went, even if the partner was indisposed. Bill was there, but not Edie, Mary without Jack, Fran minus Ray, Jules sans Doris, Bernice missing Sidney, and Roz less Freddie. (Read Goetz, Benny, Stark, Stein, Korshak and Brisson.)

To continue What's My Name of the Power Structure, there together and looking lively were Frances and Sam, Audrey and Billy, Mickey and Paul, Hope and Otto, Denise and Vincente, Ingrid and Jerry, Ruth and Garson, and Tally and Willie.

And, finally, the governor and his lovely lady.

Which governor? Why, Ronnie, with Nancy. And, to fill the other blanks, the Goldwyns, Wilders, Ziffrens, Premingers, Minnellis, Ohrbachs, Kanins and Wylers. Did you score a hundred points?

Well, Harriet did. For a divinely structured evening.

to find a tenant for his Fifth and Market building that is rapidly becoming an eyesore. . . .

Then there are those whose power consists of being able to get you into a box at the opera, or help dismiss a museum director. An odd listing is Richard Gump, who divides his time between Moorea and Florence and spends maybe two days a year here. . . .

Few with real power are on the list, which tilts heavily toward people like a "Vice-Chairman," yet, of the San Francisco Ballet, and a woman who is "On Board of Directors of the Opera Guild." Big deal did you say? Real power in this city is still represented by Big Labor, none of whose leaders are pictured, but maybe they aren't pretty enough. Mr. Bridges can still close down the waterfront and the Teamsters can still close down the city; you'd never know it from reading *Town & Country*, one of whose writers had never heard of Bridges (she's young and is to be forgiven). . . .

Power? Well, if you'd like a stop sign at your corner, you'd better know Myron Tatarian, and if you want a handout from the hotel tax fund, Tom Mellon is The Man. But what availeth it a person if he becomes a millionaire with his photo in *Town & Country* but cannot get a wall table at a moment's notice in the Captain's Cabin at Trader's Vic's? Maitre d'Hotel Mike Gutierrez—now THERE's a man with power.[19]

It is slightly appalling to think how much ink has been spilled in scholarly circles in attempts to convince social scientists of the proposition that fixing a ticket is one thing and getting a tenant at Fifth and Market quite another, that talking about power without specifying power over what is like a bell without a clapper.[20]

In a purportedly serious field of study in which so many custard pies fly about, does not an author needlessly risk his reputation in coming forward with a second edition of a book like this? We are, it appears, no closer today than in 1963 to the establishment of a firmly founded set of empirical propositions about the world which command universal agreement, or indeed even a well articulated sense of what we know and what we do not know. Have we simply been pushing a rock uphill and watching it tumble down again?

In asking where we have gotten after twenty years of study, instead of adopting the metaphor of Sisyphus let us answer as though we were taking

19. Herb Caen, "Here Today, Gone Today," *San Francisco Chronicle,* Jan. 24, 1973.
20. The bell is Bayless Manning's: "The Shareholder's Appraisal Remedy: An Essay for Frank Coker," *Yale Law Journal,* 72 (Dec. 1962), 223–65.

a Gray Line tour, and inquire not where we have gotten but where we have been. For I think that the student of community power these last twenty years would have been in touch with a number of interesting issues that have arisen and drawn the attention of social scientists: the revival, as I mentioned, of Marx-inspired analyses of social systems; the rise of concern among historians for models and methods of the social sciences; the growth of an empirical sociology of scientific knowledge; the problem in political theory of discerning the "interests" of a social group, and distinguishing these interests from "false" interests on the one hand and the preferences of investigators on the other; the myriad issues associated with proper inferences from nonexperimental data unsystematically sampled from a loosely specified universe of "nonissues" and "issues"; problems of inference from elite interviews and case studies; problems of determining when ideological considerations are contaminating the results of investigation.

A large number of these and related problems have come up in the community power literature, and have engaged the efforts of investigators. The fact that those who have written in this field have not reached a consensus about many of these issues is a matter of some disappointment to me, but it does not preclude the possibility that people who have tuned in to the literature at various times might have carried away something of use. I think, in short, that as a source of cumulative knowledge about the governance of local communities, the community power literature is disappointing. As a smallish arena for the ventilation of some of the central metamethodological issues of social research, this literature has some didactic value.

Thus, there seems to me some purpose in continuing the conversation. We can attempt once again, in the light of new work, to shape the intellectual instruments which will guide future empirical study. We can try to aid in the appraisal of work that has recently emerged. Studying the study of community power may have no particular intrinsic merit, but like the humble, unattractive can opener, it may help us get at a number of things of greater interest, including an impressive array of topics in social and political inquiry.[21]

Nelson W. Polsby

Berkeley, California
June 1979

21. I borrow the can opener from somewhere in the voluminous writings of Richard E. Caves.

# Preface to the First Edition

This book grew out of a study of New Haven, Connecticut, but it is not primarily about New Haven at all. In 1957 I was asked by Robert Dahl to join him and Raymond Wolfinger in an exploration of leadership and decision-making in New Haven. Wolfinger, my fellow graduate student, was to go into City Hall for a year's internship with New Haven's Development Administrator and with the Mayor. His job was to keep his eyes open and report what he found. My duties were less clear. A year of prior training as a graduate student in sociology had given me a nodding acquaintance with scholarly literature on the topic we were taking up in New Haven. Slowly I began to reread more carefully the leading community studies, looking for leads and hypotheses which would help us in studying New Haven. Dahl and Wolfinger did the same, and, in the course of a conversation which extended fitfully over perhaps four months, all of us reached the conclusion that previous studies of "community power," as they were usually styled, would not help us as much as we had hoped and expected.

I undertook to discover in detail why this was so, and the book which follows is the result. I attempt here to set the New Haven study into the context provided by previous work, showing explicitly where and how and to a certain extent why the New Haven study diverges from what seems to be the mainstream of community power studies. Hence this book is not principally about New Haven, although it depends in at least three ways on information gathered about New Haven.

First, the demands of doing research in an actual field situation (in which I took part) originally raised the theoretical problems dealt with here. The difficulties of theory which I discuss are not, I think, mere matters of taste but rather have consequences in the real world of research.

Second, the "payoffs" of the alternative research design adumbrated and defended in this volume are made explicitly manifest in the companion volumes reporting the results of the New Haven research: Robert Dahl's *Who Governs? Democracy and Power in an American City* (New Haven, 1961) and Raymond E. Wolfinger's *The Politics of Progress* [Englewood

Cliffs, N.J., Prentice Hall, 1974]. These works describe in detail the operations of the political order of New Haven. I think they lend to my argument for a pluralistic theory a persuasiveness far greater than the words in this book alone could convey.

Finally, I rely heavily on data developed in New Haven to test the theory I found in the literature. Since a major finding of this book is that this theory had not been tested adequately, the New Haven research made possible an attempt to improve on previous efforts at verification.

As befits a reincarnated doctoral dissertation, originally presented to The Department of Political Science at Yale University, this study is addressed primarily to the community of scholars; only they are likely to be familiar with the literature treated here. Some people may feel that my reading of this literature is idiosyncratic, not to say perverse. I have taken the rather tedious but necessary precaution of quoting at length from each of the works I have reinterpreted in order to forestall, if possible, raising the suspicion that instead of having read these works in a new way I have not read them at all. My purpose throughout has been to ascertain the state of "scientific" knowledge about power and policy-making in local communities. I hope the reappraisal I have made will help in future research on this topic, and I trust the pages that follow will be read with this goal in mind.

Nelson W. Polsby

Middletown, Connecticut
August 3, 1962

# Acknowledgments

I owe an especially great debt to Robert A. Dahl. His administrative and personal generosity, creativity, and capacity for bringing order out of chaos are, I fear, only wanly reflected in these pages. Raymond E. Wolfinger gave much to this study as well. His contribution was not confined to the information about New Haven politics which he painstakingly gathered at great risk to life, limb, and sanity, and shared with me, but also included many discussions in which he helped greatly to clarify my thoughts.

Others kept me amply supplied with a running fire of criticism, comment, suggestion, and encouragement. This was especially true of an extraordinarily stimulating group of friends and teachers at Yale, including Charles E. Lindblom, Aaron B. Wildavsky, Fred I. Greenstein, Theodore J. Lowi, Herbert Kaufman, Peter B. Clark, Robert E. Lane, Harold D. Lasswell, Karl W. Deutsch, and David Braybrooke. Two gifted and thoughtful sociologists, Robert O. Schulze and Robert A. Dentler, also contributed their time and talent, as did Francis E. Rourke, George M. Belknap, Newton D. Bowdan, Eugene N. Feingold, Micah H. Naftalin, Norton E. Long, Wallace S. Sayre, and H. Douglas Price. Marian Neal Ash of the Yale University Press helped greatly with her thoughtful and good-natured editorial advice.

This book was written with the help of a Brookings Research Fellowship in Governmental Studies, a Social Science Research Council Fellowship, a Falk Fellowship from the Political Science Department of Yale University, a faculty research grant from Wesleyan University, and gratuitous overpayments for token amounts of research from two indulgent patrons of political science, Peter H. Rossi and Robert Dahl. I also received the valuable stimulus of meeting with others engaged in community studies in all parts of the country at conferences in August 1957 and April 1960, under the auspices of the Social Science Research Council. In addition, I was permitted to work out some of my ideas in public. For permission to repeat a few thoughts here, I am grateful to the editors of

*Social Forces, The American Sociological Review, The Journal of Politics,* and *The Canadian Journal of Economics and Political Science.*[1]

A gesture of thanks is meager acknowledgment for the good humor and interest of members of my family—Edythe Polsby, Allen I. Polsby, and Daniel D. Polsby. This is also true of the occupant of the apex of my own personal power structure, Linda O. Polsby. Her work as research assistant, typist, proofreader, and thesaurus richly entitles her to the hope that I learn to write before Lisa S. Polsby learns to read.

My affection and gratitude for all these people persuades me to credit them with much of the merit of this book. On the other hand, pride of authorship forces me to claim exclusive responsibility for all faults and errors that remain.

Some of the ideas that occur in the new parts of this book have been marinating in my mind for so many years that their origins in a helpful observation or passing remark by someone else are now lost to me. With apologies, I ask all those scholars—and by now there must be a fair number—who have given me stimulation or assistance on the subject of community power over the years, and to whom I have not returned proper thanks by name, to accept a more general expression of gratitude. They, and others whose individual contributions I remember more vividly, are not to be blamed for the idiosyncracies and errors of this edition, any more than for those of the first.

In some cases, I have written preliminary versions of my thoughts, and I would like to thank the original publishers for their permission to draw on this material.[2] A sabbatical from the University of California and a fellowship from the John Simon Guggenheim Foundation gave me the opportunity to enjoy the hospitality of the London School of Economics for a year (1977–78) of reflection, and there I was able to pull together many

1. "The Sociology of Community Power: A Reassessment," *Social Forces,* 37 (March 1959), 232–36; "Three Problems in the Analysis of Community Power," *American Sociological Review,* 24 (December 1959), 796–803; "How to Study Community Power: The Pluralist Alternative," *Journal of Politics,* 22 (August 1960), 474–84; "Power in Middletown: Fact and Value in Community Research," *The Canadian Journal of Economics and Political Science,* 26 (November 1960), 592–603.

2. "The Study of Community Power," *International Encyclopedia of the Social Sciences* (New York, The Macmillan Co. and The Free Press, 1968) vol. 3, pp. 157–63; "On Intersections between Law and Political Science," *Stanford Law Review,* 21 (Nov. 1968) 142–51; 'Pluralism' in the Study of Community Power: Or Erklärung Before Verklärung in *Wissenssoziologie,*" *The American Sociologist,* 4 (May 1969) 118–22; "Community Power Meets Air Pollution," *Contemporary Sociology,* 1 (March 1972) 88–91; "Empirical Investigation of the Mobilization of Bias in Community Power Research," *Political Studies,* 27 (Dec. 1979) 527–41.

scattered ideas about community power. I am especially grateful to Percy Cohen and Donald MacRae, my hosts at the L.S.E. Sociology Department, and to Ann Trowles, the solicitous and efficient departmental secretary. Others in Great Britain who encouraged me with their kindness and interest include Peter Self, George Jones, Elie Kedourie, Huw Wheldon, William Letwin, Ernest Gellner, Thomas Nossiter, and Robert McKenzie at L.S.E., along with Paul Peterson of the University of Chicago, a fellow visitor; Jim Sharpe at Nuffield College, Oxford; Kenneth Newton, then at Nuffield and now at the University of Dundee; Geoffrey Smith of the *Times;* and John Dearlove and Peter Saunders at Sussex.

Early versions of the new material were read—sometimes in full, sometimes in part—and commented upon by a number of colleagues. I am particularly grateful to A. James Gregor, Martin Landau, William K. Muir, Jr., Aaron Wildavsky, David C. Hammack, Andrew S. McFarland, Robert A. Dahl, Raymond E. Wolfinger, Peter Saunders, Jim Sharpe, George Jones, Douglas Yates, Brett Hammond, H. Bradford Westerfield, Felix Oppenheim, Morris Zelditch, Jr., Paul E. Peterson, John N. Gray, Kenneth Newton, and Christopher Achen. Some of these individuals went far beyond the requirements of ordinary friendship in the time and attention they devoted to the careful reading of this work, and I hope they are not too disappointed when, through indolence, obduracy, or inability to grasp what they were saying, I have failed to take full advantage of their help.

I also thank G. William Domhoff and A. Tappan Wilder for their willingness to answer my queries promptly and helpfully, and H. Douglas Price for his encouragement while many of my ideas were stuck at an earlier stage. The Institute of Governmental Studies at the University of California, Berkeley, supplied typing assistance, for which I thank Catherine Winters. The Berkeley Committee on Research and the Department of Political Science have from time to time provided funds for exploratory work directly helpful to this final product. At different times I have enjoyed the research assistance of Bill Cavala, Shai Feldman, Byron Shafer, Steven Van Evera, Sam Kernell, and Philip J. Wilson, and secretarial help from Helen Petit; all have contributed, directly or indirectly, to this new edition.

Finally, I renew my thanks to Linda O. Polsby. In our years together since the first edition Lisa S. Polsby, Emily A. Polsby, and Daniel R. Polsby have come along to make us think that pluralism in some power structures is entirely plausible, at least in practice, and possibly even necessary.

N.W.P.

# Short Titles and Abbreviations

| | |
|---|---|
| Am. J. Soc. | *American Journal of Sociology* |
| Am. Pol. Sci. Rev. | *American Political Science Review* |
| Am. Soc. Rev. | *American Sociological Review* |
| Baltzell, *Philadelphia* | E. Digby Baltzell, *Philadelphia Gentlemen* (Glencoe, Free Press, 1958) |
| Dahl, "Critique" | Robert A. Dahl, "A Critique of the Ruling Elite Model," *American Political Science Review*, 52 (June 1958), 463–69 |
| Dahl, *Who Governs?* | Robert A. Dahl, *Who Governs?* (New Haven, Yale University Press, 1961) |
| Hollingshead, *Elmtown* | August B. Hollingshead, *Elmtown's Youth* (New York, Wiley, 1949) |
| Hunter, *CPS* | Floyd Hunter, *Community Power Structure* (Chapel Hill, University of North Carolina Press, 1953) |
| Lynd, *M* | Robert S. Lynd and Helen M. Lynd, *Middletown* (New York, Harcourt, Brace, 1929) |
| Lynd, *MIT* | Robert S. Lynd and Helen M. Lynd, *Middletown in Transition* (New York, Harcourt, Brace, 1937) |
| Miller, "Industry and CPS" | Delbert C. Miller, "Industry and Community Power Structure," *American Sociological Review*, 23 (February 1958), 9–15 |
| Schulze, "Bifurcation" | Robert O. Schulze, "The Bifurcation of Power in a Satellite Community," in Morris Janowitz, ed., *Community Political Systems* (Glencoe, Free Press, 1961) |

Scoble, "Yankeetown"       Harry M. Scoble, Jr., "Yankeetown: Leader-
                           ship in Three Decision-making Processes,"
                           read at the meetings of the American Polit-
                           ical Science Association, September 1956

Warner, *Jonesville*       William Lloyd Warner et al., *Democracy
                           in Jonesville* (New York, Harper, 1949)

Warner, YC 1               W. Lloyd Warner and Paul S. Lunt, *The
                           Social Life of a Modern Community*, Yan-
                           kee City Series, 1 (New Haven, Yale Uni-
                           versity Press, 1941)

Warner, YC 2               W. Lloyd Warner and Paul S. Lunt, *The
                           Status System of a Modern Community*,
                           Yankee City Series, 2 (New Haven, Yale
                           University Press, 1942)

Warner, YC 3               W. Lloyd Warner and Leo Srole, *The Social
                           Systems of American Ethnic Groups*, Yan-
                           kee City Series, 3 (New Haven, Yale Uni-
                           versity Press, 1945)

Warner, YC 4               W. Lloyd Warner and J. O. Low, *The Social
                           System of a Modern Factory*, Yankee City
                           Series, 4 (New Haven, Yale University Press,
                           1947)

Warner, YC 5               W. Lloyd Warner, *The Living and the Dead*,
                           Yankee City Series, 5 (New Haven, Yale
                           University Press, 1959)

COMMUNITY POWER AND POLITICAL THEORY

# 1. The Relevance of Political Theory to Community Power

It seems to be the unhappy fate of many of those who explore the intellectual roots of current writing in various areas of social science to suffer a certain amount of disillusionment with "old masters" in the field.[1] This book follows the pattern: it was begun as an inventory of knowledge about power in American communities, but now seeks primarily to criticize the approach which currently seems most influential in guiding research and to present an alternative. The literature of community power, which I had hoped would accumulate into a neat set of propositions constituting a reliable body of knowledge, presented unexpected problems.

These problems did not come about because the works I chose to study failed to agree among themselves. The major difficulty was, rather, to account for the extraordinary unanimity that scholars displayed in upholding certain propositions about community power—propositions which, according to a careful reading of the literature and independent research experience, seemed quite wrong.

Let me begin by expressing more precisely the sense in which I shall use the term "community power" and by identifying the body of knowledge under discussion. In its most general meaning, as far as social science is concerned, one can conceive of "power"—"influence" and "control" are serviceable synonyms—as the capacity of one actor to do something affecting another actor, which changes the probable pattern of specified future events.[2] This can be envisaged most easily in a de-

1. See, for example, David Easton, *The Political System* (New York, Knopf, 1953); Lawrence J. R. Herson, "The Lost World of Municipal Government," *Am. Pol. Sci. Rev.*, 51 (June 1957), 330–45; Stanley Hoffmann, "International Relations: The Long Road to Theory," *World Politics*, 11 (April 1959), 346–77; Herbert A. Simon, *Administrative Behavior* (2d ed., New York, Macmillan, 1957); Dwight Waldo, *The Administrative State* (New York, Ronald, 1948).

2. The term "actor" is meant to encompass individuals or groups of individuals acting in concert. Other proposed definitions of "power," most of them equivalent or identical to the one suggested here, may be found in the following sources: Robert Bierstedt, "An Analysis of Social Power," *Am. Soc. Rev.*, 15 (Dec. 1950), 730–38; Karl W. Deutsch, *Nationalism and Social Communication* (New York, Wiley, 1953),

cision-making situation. Where decisions are choices between alternative courses of action leading to outcomes A and B, an actor can be said to possess a certain amount of "power" if, by acting on others, he changes the comparative probability that these outcomes will take place. The amount of power the actor has in this situation is expressed by the magnitude of the changes he introduces.

This is clearly not all one might say about power. But at the moment it is important to observe that power as it is defined above can be applied to a host of social situations. Wherever two or more people engage in making decisions, or attempt to determine an outcome in any area of social life—whether, for example the family will go bowling or swimming, whether the company will promote Smith or Jones to Executive Suite, whether the nation will elect Nixon or Kennedy President—one can analyze the process of decision-making by making use of the notion of power. It is possible to distinguish three kinds of data with respect to decision-making which often serve as indices of the power of actors; one may ask (1) who participates in decision-making, (2) who gains and who loses from alternative possible outcomes, and (3) who prevails in decision-making. Identifying the last of these seems the best way to determine which individuals and groups have "more" power in social life, because direct conflict between actors presents a situation most closely approximating an experimental test of their capacities to affect outcomes. The other criteria are not especially useful in making interpersonal comparisons, though they often help to explain how and why certain alternatives are chosen. These indices make inferences about the exercise of power by actors possible, though hazardous.

This book is concerned primarily with decisions affecting large segments of the population of local communities, hence "community power," rather than "family power," "company power," or "national power." We shall be concerned primarily with local political power, since the political arena is the sector of community life in which large groups in the community make demands upon one another and collectively determine policy

pp. 46–59; Herbert Goldhamer and Edward Shils, "Types of Power and Status," *Am. J. Soc.*, 45 (Sept. 1939), 171–82; Harold D. Lasswell and Abraham Kaplan, *Power and Society* (New Haven, Yale Univ. Press, 1950); James G. March, "An Introduction to the Theory and Measurement of Influence," *Am. Pol. Sci. Rev.*, 49 (June 1955), 431–51; Felix E. Oppenheim, "An Analysis of Political Control: Actual and Potential," *Journal of Politics*, 20 (Aug. 1958), 515–34; Herbert A. Simon, "Notes on the Observation and Measurement of Political Power," *Journal of Politics*, 15 (Nov. 1953), 500–16. See esp. Robert A. Dahl, "The Concept of Power," *Behavioral Science*, 2 (July 1957), 201–15.

outcomes. We shall be examining answers to the question "Who rules?" in various American communities, that is, "who participates, who gains and loses, and who prevails in decision-making?" What criteria shall we use in evaluating answers to this question? It is necessary to consider provisionally the kinds of answers that have been made but are unacceptable, and the kinds of answers to be trusted. One very broad criterion can be stated at once. Findings that pretend to scientific acceptability must be verifiable. By this I mean two things. First, a verifiable answer must refer to events in the real world, accessible to more than one competent observer. Second, this answer must be put in such a form that in principle it is directly or indirectly subject to disproof by an appeal to evidence. If no evidence about the real world can possibly disprove a proposition, it can hardly be called scientific or empirical in character.

These are the essential, formal requirements for any scientific proposition.[3] It is also desirable, of course, that propositions actually be verified by observation—that is, that they be true; but this is an empirical rather than a formal requirement, and the latter concerns us here. Not all statements in science are propositions. Some statements used in scientific discourse propose linguistic conventions (definitions) and others propose provisional prescriptions about the relations between linguistic conventions and the real world (axioms). These statements, along with "primitive" terms, are necessary to scientific discourse. For example, only after stating a definition:

Power is the capacity of one actor to do something affecting another actor, which changes the probable pattern of specified future events,

and an axiom:

American communities may be divided into two groups (classes) which differ with respect to socioeconomic status,

can we arrive at a researchable proposition:

The upper socioeconomic class has more power than the lower class.

For this latter statement to mean anything in a scientific sense, we must, according to the formal requirements postulated above, make refer-

3. See Morris R. Cohen and Ernest Nagel, *An Introduction to Logic and Scientific Method* (New York, Harcourt, Brace, 1934), p. 27: "A *proposition* may be defined as anything which can be said to be true or false." The view that a scientific proposition must be capable of disproof by appealing directly or indirectly to evidence about the real world is now widely accepted. However, the matter is by no means as simple as it sounds. See Karl R. Popper, *The Logic of Scientific Discovery* (New York, Basic Books, 1959), esp. pp. 40–43.

ence to specific decisions in which particular outcomes are affected by members of the classes into which we divide the population,[4] and, secondly, we must state the conditions under which we can take it as demonstrated that the upper class does not have more power than the lower class.

One of the themes of this book is that what social scientists presume to be the case will in great measure influence the design and even the outcome of their research. Suzanne K. Langer states this idea nicely when she says: "The way a question is asked limits and disposes the way in which any answer to it—right or wrong—may be given." [5] Another theme is that empirical presumptions entertained by many researchers in the field of community power exhibit certain characteristics in common. The illusion of unanimity in a large number of community studies is based on these family resemblances among presumptions, I suggest, rather than on adequate, repeated empirical demonstrations of patterns of community power.

I find it convenient to think of the empirical presumptions of researchers in community power as embryonic political theories, though this may stretch somewhat the conventional meaning of theory in science. Theory, as it is conventionally understood, consists of a number of logically ordered statements, asserting relationships among a number of events in the real world. Presumably "good" theory in science describes relationships among a relatively large number of real-world events using a relatively small number of hypotheses.[6] The political "theories" under discussion here can make no pretense to great simplicity, comprehensiveness, or internal consistency. However, they do perform perhaps the most important function of theory in social science; that is, they guide research.[7] It seems unnecessary after expressing this *caveat* to refer to "pseudo-theory," "pre-theory," or some such neologism.

4. Cf. Dahl, "Critique."

5. *Philosophy in a New Key* (New York, New American Library, 1948), p. 1. See also Karl Mannheim's treatment of the "total conception" of ideology: *Ideology and Utopia* (New York, Harcourt, Brace Harvest, 1936), passim.

6. See Cohen and Nagel, pp. 397–99, and Frank A. Pinner, "Notes on Method in Social and Political Research," in Dwight Waldo, ed., *The Research Functions of University Bureaus and Institutes for Government Related Research* (Berkeley, Bureau of Public Administration, Univ. of California, 1960).

7. See Robert K. Merton, "The Bearing of Sociological Theory on Empirical Research," and "The Bearing of Empirical Research on Sociological Theory," in *Social Theory and Social Structure*, pp. 85–117.

The particular political theory that seems to have been most influential in guiding current research on community power will be the primary object of attention in the immediately succeeding chapters. In focusing on this particular theory, and the findings it has produced, several other more or less self-contained bodies of knowledge, all of which deal directly in some way with community affairs, are ignored.[8] The decision to concentrate on contemporary studies of community power structures and their intellectual antecedents is made on the following grounds. First, these studies ask to be considered as "scientific" knowledge. Their authors implicitly accept the standards of verifiability suggested above, and it seems fair to judge them by application of these standards. Second, these studies are widely considered to have contemporary relevance to community affairs. They purport to explain currently observable patterns of community power. Third, these studies include general statements about power in American communities. The community-as-a-whole is taken as the unit of study, and descriptions of intracommunity activities are systematically related to characterizations of the entire community. Thus we have some opportunity to compare units which are similar in the scope of their activities. Conclusions about communities may be regarded as grossly comparable with one another and as useful in interpreting findings in new communities. Finally, the works to be examined here cite one another conscientiously, and later studies give the strong impression that they have been shaped and guided by earlier contributions. Thus this is an on-going, self-conscious "scientific" literature, currently influencing the research concerns of workers in the field of community politics and power.[9]

What is the political theory contained in the literature to be examined in this book? The most general statement of the theory might be as follows: power is a subsidiary aspect of the community's social structure. "The political organization of Jonesville," writes one scholar, "fits the rest

8. Robert T. Daland has given an excellent bibliography of materials on urban politics, in which references to these bodies of knowledge may be found. Daland, "Political Science and the Study of Urbanism," *Am. Pol. Sci. Rev.*, 51 (June 1957), 491–509. See also Wallace S. Sayre and Nelson W. Polsby, "American Political Science and the Study of Urbanization" In Leo Schnore and Philip Hauser, eds., *The Study of Urbanization* (New York, Wiley, 1965), pp. 115–56. Focused more directly upon community power studies are two pamphlets containing, respectively, abstracts and summaries of substantial portions of the literature: Charles Press, *Main Street Politics* (East Lansing, Mich., Institute for Community Development, 1962), and Wendell Bell, Richard J. Hill, and Charles R. Wright, *Public Leadership* (San Francisco, Chandler, 1961).

9. In contrast, current textbooks in the field of city government appear not to exhibit several of these characteristics. See Herson, "The Lost World of Municipal Government."

of the social structure . . . curving or bulging with the *class outlines* of the body politic." [10] I am going to refer to this conception as a "stratification theory" of community power, since it suggests that the pattern of social stratification in a community is the principal, if not the only, determinant of the pattern of power.

Stratification studies make five assertions in common about power in American communities.[11]

The first proposition is:

1. *The upper class rules in local community life.*[12] Stratification studies differ in their descriptions of what constitutes the upper class. Some divide the classes on economic grounds, others according to status ascriptions by community residents. Some authors divide communities into two classes, others into five or six classes. Some authors hold that classes are "real" categories which are understood by citizens of the community and are used in their daily lives; others aver that classes are not real but rather are constructs convenient for analysis.[13] While these differences are

10. Warner, *Jonesville*, p. xviii. My emphasis.

11. There are, of course, occasional deviations from this list in isolated instances. Certainly the great majority of stratification studies uphold most of these assertions. Individual treatment of specific stratification studies, contained in Chapters 2 and 3, will make this clear.

12. Many community studies claim to have found this pattern. See: Lynd, *M* (see Short Titles and Abbreviations), pp. 47, 354, 374, 434; Lynd, *MIT*, pp. 74–75, 97, 377, 456, 459, and passim; Warner, YC 1, pp. 143–44, 168–73; Warner, YC 2, pp. 46–50; Baltzell, *Philadelphia*, pp. 32–35; Warner, *Jonesville*, pp. xviii, 100–02, 209, 294; Hollingshead, *Elmtown*, p. 72 and passim; Hunter, *CPS*, pp. 56, 62, 64, 79, and passim; Miller, "Industry and CPS," pp. 12, 13.

13. See, among other sources: Reinhard Bendix and Seymour Martin Lipset, eds., *Class, Status and Power* (Glencoe, Free Press, 1953); John F. Cuber and William F. Kenkel, *Social Stratification in the United States* (New York, Appleton, 1954); Kingsley Davis, *Human Society* (New York, Macmillan, 1949); Davis and Wilbert E. Moore, "Some Principles of Stratification," *Am. Soc. Rev., 10* (April 1945), 242–49; Hans H. Gerth and C. Wright Mills, *Character and Social Structure* (New York, Harcourt, Brace, 1953); Milton M. Gordon, *Social Class in American Sociology* (Durham, Duke Univ. Press, 1958); Gordon, "A System of Social Class Analysis," *Drew Univ. Bulletin, 39* (Madison, N.J., Aug. 1951); Paul K. Hatt, "Social Stratification in the Mass Society," *Am. Soc. Rev., 15* (April 1950), 216–22; Hollingshead, *Elmtown*; Harold F. Kaufman, Otis Dudley Duncan, Neal Gross, and William A. Sewell, "Problems of Theory and Method in the Study of Social Stratification in Rural Society," *Rural Sociology, 18* (March 1953), 12–24; Kurt B. Mayer, *Class and Society* (Garden City, Doubleday, 1955); Mayer, "The Theory of Social Classes," *Harvard Educational Review, 23* (Summer 1953), 149–67; Harold W. Pfautz, "The Current Literature on Social Stratification: Critique and Bibliography," *Am. J. Soc., 58* (Jan. 1953), 391–418; Pfautz, "Social Stratification and Sociology," *Transactions of the Second World Congress of Sociology, 1953, 2* (London, International Sociological Assn., 1954), 311–20; Baltzell, *Philadelphia*; William Lloyd Warner, Marchia Meeker, and Kenneth

important to the study of social stratification, they are side issues in the present context. *All* students of stratification agree that it is possible to talk about different classes in society. Although many assert that in principle communities can be stratified according to differences in the amount of power held by individuals,[14] all stratify communities on some basis other than power. It is these other bases for stratification that will concern us for a moment. These include income, occupation, housing, social participation, consumption patterns.[15] All of these are considered indices of social or economic standing, so it is proper to refer to the "upper class" as a group in the community of highest social-economic standing, without prejudice to any of the many different ways in which stratification writers arrive at their identification of this group. It is possible to suggest another formulation of this proposition: The group with the highest social-economic standing has the most power. If we can think of a "base" of power as a condition necessary for the exercise of power,[16] then we can state the proposition in still another way: a high social-economic position is the base of most community power.

Social stratification theory organizes individuals for analytical purposes into "strata," stacked one on the other. Thus stratification writers on community power see the upper class as at the top of a ladder of power, with others ranged below them. One of the most significant of the lower groups is composed of civic leaders and politicians, who are not themselves members of the upper class. Of these people, stratification writers assert:

2. *Political and civic leaders are subordinate to the upper class.*[17]

Subordination in two senses is implied or asserted in stratification studies of community power. Political and civic leaders as a group are said to possess less power than the upper class as a group, and in addition (or

Eels, *Social Class in America* (Gloucester, Mass., Peter Smith, 1957); Nelson N. Foote, Walter R. Goldschmidt, Richard T. Morris, Melvin Seeman, and Joseph Shister, "Alternative Assumptions in Stratification Research," *Transactions of the Second World Congress of Sociology, 2,* 378–90; Gerhard Lenski, "American Social Classes: Statistical Strata or Social Groups?" *Am. J. Soc., 58* (Sept. 1952), 139–44; Joseph A. Kahl, *The American Class Structure* (New York, Rinehart, 1957).

14. For example, Mayer, Gordon, Pfautz.

15. See Joseph A. Kahl and James A. Davis, "A Comparison of Indexes of Socioeconomic Status," *Am. Soc. Rev., 20* (June 1955), 317–25.

16. See Lasswell and Kaplan, *Power and Society,* p. 83.

17. For documentation among studies of specific communities, see Lynd, *M,* p. 434, and *MIT,* pp. 89, 321, 329, 334; Baltzell, *Philadelphia,* pp. 35, 364; Warner, Meeker, and Eels, *Social Class in America,* p. 13; Warner, *Jonesville,* pp. 97–101; Hollingshead, *Elmtown,* p. 86; Hunter, *CPS,* pp. 81–87, 93, 100, 162–63, 175; Miller, "Industry and CPS," p. 14; Delbert C. Miller, "Decision-making Cliques in Community Power Structures," *Am. J. Soc., 64* (Nov. 1958), 306–07.

perhaps as a consequence of having less power) they are held to take orders from or do the bidding of the upper class.

A third assertion of the stratification theory is:

3. *A single "power elite" rules in the community.*[18]

This constitutes an extension and elaboration of the propositions already expressed. We may think of an elite as a small group, always less than a majority of the community, and as a group selected by some means other than majority vote.[19] The upper class in every community studied fits these criteria. Another idea suggested by the term "power elite" is that the powers of the elite group are distributed over a large number of significant community decisions, so that stratification writers may say of the power elite that it stands at the apex of a pyramid of "all-purpose" power, dealing with a wide variety of community issues. This group is also held to be homogeneous in its social composition, being made up of members of the upper class.

Each of the various possible outcomes of issues may be said to allocate valued things and events in alternative ways. Stratification writers hold that it is in the interests of each class in society to increase its long-run share of values, but of course rulership implies that only one class possesses the means to accomplish this end. Hence the assertion of stratification writers that:

4. *The upper-class power elite rules in its own interests.*[20]

This arrangement, according to stratification writers, is not or at least should not be acquiesced to willingly by the other classes in society. The final characteristic of community power asserted in stratification studies is therefore that:

5. *Social conflict takes place between the upper and lower classes.*[21]

The reasoning here is that significant social conflicts follow the significant divisions of interest in the community, and these cleavages of in-

18. See Lynd, *MIT*, pp. 74–101; Baltzell, *Philadelphia*, pp. 364–71; Warner, *Jonesville*, p. 101; Hollingshead, *Elmtown*, pp. 72–73.

19. See Dahl, "Critique."

20. See Lynd, *MIT*, pp. 89, 99, 117, 321, 351; Warner, YC 1, p. 372; Warner, *Jonesville*, pp. 195–96; Hollingshead, *Elmtown*, pp. 123–24; Roland J. Pellegrin and Charles H. Coates, "Absentee-owned Corporations and Community Power Structure," *Am. J. Soc.*, 61 (March 1956), 413–19.

21. See Gerth and Mills, *Character and Social Structure*, pp. 339, 341; C. Wright Mills, "The Middle Classes in Middle-sized Cities," *Am. Soc. Rev.*, 11 (Oct. 1946), 520–29; Lynd, *MIT*, pp. 22, 25–44, 72, 91, 93, 329, 340, 360, 451, 452; Warner, YC 4, pp. 10, 66–89, 108–33, and passim; Warner, *Jonesville*, pp. 23, 107–08, 146, 197–98, 204; Hunter, *CPS*, pp. 247–48; Hollingshead, *Elmtown*, 123–24, 135, 451–52.

terest separate the community's upper from its lower social classes rather than divide other groups in the community whose members are recruited on some basis other than class memberships.

The two chapters immediately following present the case for and against these five propositions as it unfolds in the stratification studies of community power themselves. Chapter 4 discusses a separate empirical test of stratification theory, using findings from New Haven. Chapter 5 suggests possible explanations for discrepancies between assertions about community power found in the stratification studies and the facts of power revealed in a re-examination of the empirical materials. In Chapter 6, an alternative method for studying community power is outlined, and Chapter 7 sketches some tentative conclusions and hypotheses about patterns of power and decision-making in American communities.

A final introductory word about the fact that so many studies of community power have been heavily influenced by stratification theory. This is surely an interesting social fact in itself. For a long time, both stratification theory and community power were almost exclusively the province of sociologists. Power is conceived of by sociologists as one dimension of social life along which people may be stratified; hence power is of central interest to those engaged in mapping social structure and social change.[22] Political scientists have also traditionally concerned themselves with power and with the institutional order specialized to the exercise of political power in social life, the state.[23]

In recent years, however, political scientists have largely ignored power in American communities, and sociologists have undertaken to fill the gap in our knowledge about power in community life.[24] Thus, where one might have expected on the basis of disciplinary traditions that both sociologists and political scientists would have been busy analyzing power in American communities, the vast majority of the literature that constitutes current knowledge in the field is in fact the work of sociologists, and very little cross-disciplinary discussion seems to have occurred.

At least this was the case until recently. There are a great many signs of change. Sociologists are, if anything, increasing their research com-

22. Most current theoretical and textbook treatments of social stratification take this position. See the works cited in note 14 above.

23. See Easton, *The Political System*.

24. Several political scientists have made this point. See Herson, "The Lost World"; Daland, "Political Science"; and Herbert Kaufman and Victor Jones, "The Mystery of Power," *Public Administration Review, 14* (Summer 1954), 205–12.

mitments to community studies,[25] though it should be remembered that the community is a social laboratory of interest to sociologists for many reasons irrelevant to the study of power.[26] Political scientists, who seldom profess to a more important interest than the study of power, are now entering the field in force.[27] Most of these researchers seem acutely aware of their debt to recent sociological writings, though, for a variety of reasons, it seems likely that the gingerly acceptance originally accorded by political scientists to sociological findings will in time give way to more vigorous interdisciplinary criticism.[28] The most important factor in this change is no doubt the set of pluralist presumptions entertained by so many political scientists and outlined in Chapter 6 of this book.

It would be a great pity if disciplinary lines were to harden around the alternative political theories generated by stratification and pluralist presumptions.[29] Thus an attempt is made in this book to cross (if not

25. In the January 1959 issue of the *American Journal of Sociology*, numerous studies by sociologists of community leadership and politics were reported as in progress, pp. 405–15. See also Morton Rubin, "Report on 1961 Inventory of Research for the Committee on Community Research and Development, Society for the Study of Social Problems" (the Committee, 1961). This inventory of sociologists lists 63 separate projects, including 15 under the heading "Leadership, Decision-making."

26. There are, for example, ecological-demographic studies of communities (e.g. studies of land use and land values, and migration); studies of various other kinds of intracommunity events (e.g. crime rates); studies of individuals, using place of residence as a control (e.g. rates of student achievement in small-town versus big-city high schools); studies of community social-psychological states and changes (e.g. studies of community reactions to disaster).

27. Some of these studies are still unpublished. However, see Norton E. Long, "The Local Community as an Ecology of Games," *Am. J. Soc.*, 64 (Nov. 1958), 251–61, which draws on his experience in studying Boston; and Edward Banfield, *Political Influence* (New York, Free Press, 1961). Maurice Klain is studying community power and leadership in Cleveland, George Belknap has studied several cities in the San Francisco Bay area, Frederic Cleaveland and his students have re-examined community power in Atlanta, Aaron B. Wildavsky has a study of Oberlin, Ohio, in progress, and Benjamin Walter has studied three North Carolina communities. Benjamin Walter, "Political Decision-making in North Carolina Cities," *PROD*, 3 (May 1960), 18–21. Other efforts, such as Harold Kaplan's study of Newark, are beginning to come out of the Metropolitan Study Program of Columbia University. See Sayre and Polsby for additional bibliographical information about this and other programs.

28. A good indication of the early success of sociological studies of power is the acceptance that Floyd Hunter's book, *Community Power Structure*, received upon its publication in 1953. Only Kaufman and Jones among political scientists expressed reservations about this work. See, in contrast, Daland, "Political Science and the Study of Urbanism," William J. Gore, and Fred S. Silander, "A Bibliographical Essay on Decision-making," *Administrative Science Quarterly*, 4 (June 1959), 106, and reviews of the book by Louis Smith in *Journal of Politics*, 16 (Feb. 1954), 146–50, and Donald S. Strong, *Am. Pol. Sci. Rev.*, 48 (March 1954), 235–37.

29. The temptation to engage in border warfare is perhaps understandable, but

straddle) disciplinary boundaries and to evaluate and compare the general scientific utilities of these alternative theories of community power.

there are at least two reasons why this should be resisted. First, and most obviously, it seems ridiculous for scholars thus to throw away chances to learn from one another. Second, the facts will not justify a general anathema directed across disciplinary lines; there are, as it happens, a goodly number of sociological pluralists, such as Seymour Martin Lipset, *Political Man* (Garden City, Doubleday, 1960); James S. Coleman, *Community Conflict* (Glencoe, Free Press, 1957); S. M. Lipset, Martin Trow, and J. S. Coleman, *Union Democracy* (Glencoe, Free Press, 1958); Peter H. Rossi, "Community Decision-making," *Administrative Science Quarterly*, 1 (June 1957), 415–43; Arthur J. Vidich and Joseph Bensman, *Small Town in Mass Society* (Princeton, Princeton Univ. Press, 1958); James B. McKee, "Status and Power in the Industrial Community: A Comment on Drucker's Thesis," *Am. J. Soc.*, 58 (Jan. 1953), 364–70; Linton C. Freeman et al., *Local Community Leadership* (Syracuse, N.Y., Univ. College, Syracuse Univ., 1960).

There are also some political scientists whose work is heavily influenced by stratification theory. See, e.g., Robert E. Lane, *Political Life* (Glencoe, Free Press, 1959), pp. 256–75; Edwin Hoffman Rhyne, "Political Parties and Decision Making in Three Southern Counties," *Am. Pol. Sci. Rev.*, 52 (Dec. 1958), 1091–1107; Robert T. Daland, *Dixie City: A Portrait of Political Leadership* (University, Ala., Bureau of Public Administration, Univ. of Alabama, 1956); Andrew Hacker, "Liberal Democracy and Social Control," *Am. Pol. Sci. Rev.*, 51 (Dec. 1957), 1009–26; Hacker, "The Elected and the Anointed," *Am. Pol. Sci. Rev.*, 55 (Sept. 1961), 539–49.

Despite this blurring of lines it is undeniably the case that in large measure, each of the social sciences is a relatively independent, boundary-maintaining system, each with its own venerated ancestors, literature, training procedures, professional journals, and standards of relevance. Thus the chances are very much greater that subsequent research in community power will be influenced by stratification theory if the researcher is a sociologist, and by pluralist theory if he is a political scientist.

# 2. Research Consequences
## of Stratification Theory (I)

In the preceding chapter, I presented five key propositions about power in American communities. I also indicated that in many studies of American communities these propositions have been given as presumbly accurate representations of social reality. In the present chapter and the one following I shall investigate the veracity of this claim.

Each of the five propositions is capable of being cast in the form of a hypothesis, of being proven or disproven by empirical evidence. The first question, then, is: Do these propositions correctly describe who rules in American communities—were the hypotheses actually verified by field research or were they, perhaps, empirically unsubstantiated deductions from basic axioms of stratification theory or "necessary" conclusions from the ideologies of researchers? As indications that a proposition has not been properly corroborated we can take the following symptoms: (1) data are given which tend to discredit or disprove a proposition, but the refutation of the proposition is never explicitly formulated; (2) the methods of a study either do not test hypotheses or permit premature confirmation by avoiding or by-passing direct tests; (3) refutations are recognized by authors as occurring in their data, but extraneous, ad hoc explanations are constructed, or extenuating circumstances claimed, so as to evade the necessity of giving up the propositions. The appearance of any single one of these three symptoms is sufficient to throw the findings of research into question. All three need not appear together. In the succeeding pages, I shall attempt to call attention to their appearance in stratification studies of power in eight American communities.

### MIDDLETOWN (MUNCIE, INDIANA)

The oldest still-standing landmark among American community studies is the classic study of Middletown conducted by Robert and Helen Lynd in the middle 1920s and again in the mid-1930s.[1] Today, more than

1. Lynd, *M*, and Lynd, *MIT*.

a quarter-century after the Lynds began their pioneering work, the published reports of their findings repay many times over the attention of those interested in American community culture. The very great debt scholarship owes the Lynds is nowhere more apparent than in the frequency with which the Middletown books are cited in contemporary— even the most recent—research.[2]

This oldest of the stratification studies of community life is in many ways the best, since all five generalizations which seem to characterize stratification analyses of community power are set forth and accompanied by a wealth of circumstantial detail. Indeed, one of the Lynds' greatest contributions is the care and responsibility with which they recorded data that disproves each of the propositions of stratification theory, in spite of the fact that they themselves adhere to these propositions. This is, of course, the ultimate tribute to their skill as reporters.

They observed, for example, in the Middletown of 1925 that the "dominant interests" in the community were those of the "business class."[3] A decade later, the dominance of the business class had hardened into an "inner business control group" centering on, but not limited to, the "X" family. The power of this group was based on the "pervasiveness of the long fingers of capitalist ownership"[4] and "the economic life of the city"[5]—most particularly on the ability of this group to control the extension of credit.[6] Private business, in the Lynds' view, was the dominant institution of society,[7] and a "small top group" of "wealthy local manufacturers, bankers, the local head managers of . . . national corporations with units in Middletown, and . . . one or two outstanding lawyers" comprised the "business control group."[8]

Even in the 1920s businessmen tended to monopolize community prestige, at the expense of city political officials,[9] and when a member of the X family became a leader of the Democratic party in the 1930s,

2. See, for example, Milton M. Gordon, *Social Class in American Sociology* (Durham, Duke Univ. Press, 1958), chap. 3, esp. pp. 71–75; Kurt B. Mayer, *Class and Society* (Garden City, Doubleday, 1959), chap. 6; Miller, "Industry and CPS," pp. 9–15; Robert O. Schulze and Leonard U. Blumberg, "The Determination of Local Power Elites," *Am. J. Soc.*, 63 (Nov. 1957), pp. 290–96; Maurice R. Stein, *The Eclipse of Community* (Princeton, Princeton Univ. Press, 1960), esp. pp. 57–59.

3. *M*, pp. 354, 434, 476. The "business class" consisted of all those who made their living by addressing their activities primarily to *people*: 29% of the population of Middletown in 1920. The working class, those whose occupational activities were addressed to *things*, made up the remaining 71% of the population (*M*, p. 22).

4. *MIT*, p. 97.      5. *MIT*, pp. 74–75.

6. *MIT*, p. 456; *M*, p. 47.      7. *MIT*, p. 377.

8. *MIT*, p. 459.      9. *M*, p. 434.

the Lynds report, "local business control sat astride both parties." [10] The
Lynds describe the typical city official as a "man of meager caliber" [11]
and as "the man whom the inner business control group ignore economically and socially and use politically." [12]

> The professional politician in a city like Middletown occupies in
> reality a position somewhat apart. He is not ordinarily a person ac-
> cepted in the inner councils of the business class, and yet he must
> work with it in order "to get anywhere." And, on the other hand,
> the business class have . . . little respect for local politics and
> politicians, viewing them as a necessary evil which business sup-
> ports and controls only enough to ensure cooperation in necessary
> matters.[13]

The function of the politician, from the standpoint of the business
class, is described still more explicitly:

> The inner business control group may meet and make their de-
> cisions as regards local politics in quite another setting, but it is
> here in these shabby smoke-filled poolrooms and cigar stores . . .
> that the small-time political lieutenants maintain their grip on the
> working class voters year in and year out.[14]

The Lynds report further that "the lines of leadership and the related
controls are highly concentrated." [15]

> Middletown has . . . at present what amounts to a reigning royal
> family. The power of this family has become so great as to dif-
> ferentiate the city today somewhat from cities with a more diffuse
> type of control. If, however, one views the Middletown pattern as
> simply concentrating and personalizing the type of control, which
> control of capital gives to the business group in our culture, the
> Middletown situation may be viewed as epitomizing the American
> business-class control system. . . . The business class in Middle-
> town runs the city.[16]

The Lynds enumerate the categories into which they divide their analysis of the totality of Middletown life: Getting a Living, Making a Home,
Training the Young, Spending Leisure, Religion, Government, Caring

10. *MIT*, p. 329.          11. *MIT*, p. 89.
12. *MIT*, p. 321.          13. *MIT*, p. 329.
14. *MIT*, p. 334.          15. *MIT*, p. 99.
16. *MIT*, p. 77.

for the Unable, and Getting Information, and they find that in each category, the X family and the inner business control group dominated.[17] They quote, at the head of a chapter, this comment by a Middletown man, made in 1935:

> If I'm out of work, I go to the X plant; if I need money I go to the X bank, and if they don't like me I don't get it; my children go to the X college; when I get sick I go to the X hospital; I buy a building lot or house in the X subdivision; my wife goes downtown to buy X milk; I drink X beer, vote for X political parties, and get help from X charities; my boy goes to the X Y.M.C.A. and my girl to their Y.W.C.A.; I listen to the word of God in X-subsidized churches; if I'm a Mason I go to the X Masonic Temple; I read the news from the X morning newspaper; and, if I am rich enough, I travel via the X airport.[18]

The Lynds also observe that: "The control system operates at many points to identify public welfare with business class welfare." [19] In fact, members of the business control group "bother to inject just enough control over the confusion of local politics to insure a tolerable tax rate, support for 'sound' municipal cooperation in maintaining an open-shop town, control over the numerically dominant working class, and similar broad policies calculated to enable their central business of money-making to go forward without too much interference. And all of this is done by men like the X's with a strong sense of their actions being 'in the public interest.' " [20]

The inner business control group's notion of the public interest did not prevent them, the Lynds suggest, from "using relief expenditures to pull certain of their business chestnuts out of the fire," [21] or from making "interested 'deals' whereby the controls of the local *Realpolitik* are made to work in the interest of private interests or private interpretations of the public interest." [22]

One prominent example of such a "deal" was the sudden, unexpected increase by 50 per cent in the Middletown police force, following a decision by General Motors to quit Toledo, where their workers were on strike, and locate in Middletown *after*, it is alleged, the city administration pledged, "There will be no labor trouble in Middletown." The Lynds speculate on the effect of the request to increase the police de-

17. *MIT*, passim.                18. *MIT*, p. 74
19. *MIT*, p. 99.                 20. *MIT*, p. 89.
21. *MIT*, p. 117.               22. *MIT*, p. 321.

partment's budget from $83,255 to $124,182 on Middletown's taxpayers
—"particularly . . . the working class."[23]

It puzzles the Lynds that conflict between the classes did not take
place more often in Middletown. They report "a common sense of direction"[24] among members of Middletown's top ruling elite, which they
contrast with the diffuse, disorganized, haphazard political stance of the
working class.

> Middletown labor . . . has no dynamic symbols for itself as *over
> against* the business class; but it has been taught by press, by school,
> by church, and by tradition to accept, as its own, watered versions
> of the official business-class symbols. . . . Unless there is a sharp
> rise in working-class solidarity in the interim, this Middletown
> working class, nurtured on business-class symbols, and despite its
> rebellious Roosevelt vote in 1936, may be expected to follow patiently
> and even optimistically any bright flag a middle-class strong man
> waves.[25]

The major arena in which the interests of the classes clashed in peace-
ful Middletown was in labor-management relations.[26] The Lynds describe
the lengths to which "business controlled local agencies" went to discourage an AFL organizer from attempting to unionize Middletown's
auto workers.[27]

> Middletown's controlling businessmen have always realized that
> such competitive advantage as their city possesses in the national
> market is traceable to its lower living costs and to its ability to mop
> up an "easy labor market" of corn-fed, unorganized American
> workers, willing to work for relatively low wages.[28]

Consequently, the "will of the business-class control mechanisms"[29]
was set against unionization. The Lynds indicate that these mechanisms
acted in two ways—to keep the city open shop and to coopt the working class. "Working in an open-shop city with its public opinion set
by the business class . . . workers do not readily segregate themselves
from the rest of the city."[30]

Nonetheless, the Lynds detect some indications of class cleavage, as
for example in local attitudes toward national politics[31] and in con-

23. *MIT*, p. 351.                    24. *MIT*, pp. 91, 93.
25. *MIT*, pp. 454–55 (emphasis in original). See also pp. 367, 509.
26. *MIT*, pp. 25–44.                 27. *MIT*, p. 37.
28. *MIT*, p. 36.                     29. *MIT*, p. 28.
30. *MIT*, p. 26.                     31. *MIT*, pp. 22, 360.

troversies over public sanitation[32] and shopping and school facilities.[33] They point also to obstacles on "the American ladder of opportunity." Workers in industries may no longer hope realistically to climb to the top, yet "in the past reality and the alleged permanent continuance of this universally accessible ladder lies the popular justification of the reigning *laissez faire* philosophy . . . As symbol and reality draw thus apart, the scene would seem to be set for the emergence of class consciousness and possible eventual conflict." [34]

The Lynds note one prominent exception to their claim that power in Middletown was in the hands of the economic elite. They observe that the Y family, almost as numerous and wealthy as the dominant X's, chose to withdraw from civic life and thus forfeit what one presumes would have been a position of power.[35] This immediately suggests that the Lynds recognize criteria other than the availability of financial resources as important in determining one's power position in the community. Civic participation appears also to be a criterion. However, as soon as a certain threshold of participation is reached, this criterion is ignored. The X family, for example, is represented as having diverse interests, most of them apolitical, but members of the family were active in both political parties.[36] The contents of these diverse participations are held to be unimportant, however. By asserting, though without supporting evidence, that the X's were guided by a "common sense of direction," the Lynds divest the criterion of participation of most of its utility.[37]

Other, more striking examples contradict propositions 1 and 2, which are, respectively, that the upper class rules, and political and civic leaders are subordinate to them. In these examples, the Lynds suggest the importance of Middletown's political organizations in determining policy outcomes even over the objections of the business class.

The first of these is the rejection of the sewage disposal plan.[38] A problem which literally pervaded the atmosphere throughout both Middletown studies was the dumping of factory wastes and other sewage into the White River. This river wound through the "nice" northern part of town, giving incongruous air to the pleasant upper- and middleclass homes situated there. On numerous occasions the North Side, represented by homeowners, leading business and professional people,

32. *MIT*, pp. 329, 340.
34. *MIT*, p. 72.
36. *MIT*, pp. 87, 91–93.
38. *MIT*, pp. 93, 121–22, 340 f.

33. *MIT*, pp. 451, 454.
35. *MIT*, p. 91.
37. *MIT*, pp. 91, 93.

the newspapers, and the Isaac Walton League, agitated to "keep White River white," but nothing was ever done about the problem because representatives on the City Council from the working-class section of town on the South Side saw no advantage to themselves and refused to authorize the expenditure of the necessary money. The issue arose again in 1935, when civic leaders succeeded in promoting a federal grant to help improve the sewage system, but even then the South Side refused to allow the bond issue which would have brought the city this improvement at bargain-basement prices.

Periodically members of the business class attempted to institute various kinds of political reform. Once they ran an able and attractive young businessman for mayor on a reform ticket. At other times they agitated for the city manager form of government. On every occasion, professional politicians succeeded in squashing this opposition, either by turning out large votes against the business-class proposals or by preventing them from appearing on the ballot.[39]

There are contradictions, too, of the third proposition, which implies that no difference can be discerned from issue to issue in the composition of the ruling elite. The Lynds mention numerous instances where small "special-purpose" minorities controlled certain areas of decision-making that were especially important to them, such as the "small minority" that cut the heart out of the Middletown library appropriation,[40] or the "small group" of businessmen who successfully opposed the elimination of dangerous railroad grade crossings.[41] Another example involved the Ku Klux Klan, which was originally brought to the city "by leading businessmen" as an anti-Democratic party organization. With the help of an outside professional organizer, the lower classes took the Klan over.[42] And there are the myriad instances recounted by the Lynds where administrators and functionaries of various of Middletown's public services—public health doctors, the township trustee, the Board of Safety, sanitation inspectors—refused to accept "overall coordination" in place of their accustomed autonomy.[43]

It can easily be seen that these examples also tend to disprove the fourth proposition, that the power elite rules in its own interests, since they indicate that at various times values were distributed in different

39. *M*, p. 427; *MIT*, p. 320.          40. *M*, p. 425.
41. *M*, p. 488; *MIT*, p. 320.          42. *M*, p. 481–82.
43. *M*, pp. 452, 455–56, 457, 466; *MIT*, p. 104. For other examples of "special-purpose" minorities, see *M*, pp. 423–25, 492; *MIT*, pp. 108, 113–14, 116, 130, 133, 395, 396, 461, 464.

ways to groups within classes, to lower rather than higher classes, and to groups cutting across class boundaries. A conspicuous example of the sharing of values across class lines was the situation at Middletown's community college. This school, say the Lynds, was run as a private satrapy by certain members of the X family, who gave the money to set it up. The X family retained an interest in the college through its memberships on the board of trustees, and they allegedly removed books from the library shelves and screened speakers who visited the campus.[44] But the presidency of this institution was apparently given to a nonelite politician as a payoff, in order to dissuade him from running for Congress.[45]

The notion that an upper-class power elite rules in its own interests rests on the presumption that the upper-class power elite in fact rules. We have seen that this describes only a part of the situation as reported by the Lynds. It may very well be that *when* the upper classes rule they do so in their own interests, although this is by no means a certainty. The Lynds assert, for example, that one of the areas in which the business class unequivocally held sway was in decisions pertaining to Middletown's Community Chest.[46] Most decisions taken by directors of the Community Chest were likely, however, to distribute some values disproportionately to members of the lower classes.

Another kind of decision remains to be considered in this connection: instances where nonelite members have a hand in distributing values to the upper classes. One can say that something like this took place when mass-scale unionization failed in Middletown. In spite of the fact that the business class intensely desired the defeat of the unions and actively mobilized to further this end, the Lynds report that three *other* factors defeated unionization in Middletown: the apathy of the workers, labor racketeering, and a hopelessly bungled effort at collective bargaining by incompetent union leaders.[47] In general, the business class is supposed to have reaped the benefit from the failure to organize open-shop Middletown, although the Lynds are at pains to point out both that the workers were not eager for unions and that unionization made headway in several small instances anyway.[48]

The evidence we have been considering also disproves the fifth proposition, which says that significant social conflict takes place exclusively

44. *MIT*, pp. 83–84.                     45. *MIT*, pp. 216–17.
46. *MIT*, pp. 79, 139, 140. But see p. 142 where members of lower classes apparently distributed some forms of charity themselves.
47. *MIT*, pp. 28–33.                     48. *MIT*, p. 33.

between the upper and lower classes. The Lynds describe conflicts within as well as between classes—for example, in their discussions of the "special-purpose" minorities, and in their description of the conflict between Middletown's real estate men and businessmen over a boost in taxes.[49] In contrast, it seems clear that class conflict in Middletown was anything but sharp.[50] This shows up particularly in Middletown's attitude toward national elections, where "local factories tried to exert a lot of pressure on their employees to vote Republican . . . The X glass plant practically forced employees to wear Landon buttons." [51] This might seem to indicate a business class united against the Democrats, but the Lynds document the fact that fully 46.8 per cent of the two-party vote in Middletown's *business-class* precincts went to Roosevelt in 1936, while working-class districts were giving Roosevelt a two-to-one majority.[52] The fact that Middletown went for Roosevelt in 1936 is to the Lynds an indication of a "rebellious" working-class vote,[53] but their own figures show that almost half the business class contributed to the rebellion.

For evidence of political rebelliousness, we would perhaps do better to inspect the extent of third-party Presidential voting, for the Socialists of Norman Thomas, William Lemke's right-wing Union party, and the Communist party. The number of Middletowners voting for any third-party candidate in 1936 was too small to provide more than a general suggestion of the distribution of rebels in the population. However, according to the Lynds' figures, a third-party vote for President was cast by one per cent of the voters in the business-class precincts, but only .7 per cent of the voters in working-class precincts.[54] While this should not be overinterpreted, it at least suggests that interclass cleavages and conflicts were relatively muted in the community.

It has already been noted that the Lynds grant that Middletown's workers seemed (to them abnormally) prone to avoid expressions of class antagonism. However, "real" conflicts apparently can take place, in the view of stratification analysts, without overt disagreement between alleged adversaries. Likewise "real" agreement is assumed to exist between Democratic and Republican members of the X family. For the moment, rejecting this presumption of "objectivity of interests," we may view instances of intraclass disagreement as intraclass conflict of in-

49. *MIT*, pp. 38–39.

50. The Lynds indicate this many times. For examples, see *MIT*, pp. 41, 448–49, 451, 453, 454, 503.

51. *MIT*, p. 361.          53. *MIT*, p. 509.

52. *MIT*, p. 359.          54. *MIT*, p. 359.

terests, and interclass agreement as interclass harmony of interests. To maintain the opposite seems perverse. If information about the actual behavior of groups in the community is not considered relevant when it is different from the researcher's expectations, then it is impossible ever to disprove the empirical propositions of the stratification theory, and they will then have to be regarded as metaphysical rather than empirical statements. The presumption that the "real" interests of a class can be assigned to them by an analyst allows the analyst to charge "false class consciousness" when the class in question disagrees with the analyst.[55] If we presume that the class is always wrong and the analyst invariably right when the two disagree, then there seems to be no way to disprove the analyst's empirical propositions by referring to the data his propositions are supposed to encompass. Alternatively, if a decision to regard an action as "for" or "against" one's "real" class interests is not purely captious and personal, the researcher must provide us with some reasonably objective way of deciding the matter.

The most important observation to be made about the Lynds' presentation, then, is that their data never confront their working propositions. The presumption of objectivity of interests is one device by which this confrontation is avoided. Perhaps because the Lynds never state this presumption directly, they fail to appreciate its methodological consequences. But, more explicitly, the Lynds resort to an explanation of

55. As, for example, in *MIT*, p. 41. See also C. Wright Mills, "The Middle Classes in the Middle-sized Cities," *Am. Soc. Rev., 11* (Oct. 1946), pp. 520–29. Mills says:

"The general problem of stratification and political mentality has to do with the extent to which the members of an objectively defined stratum are homogeneous in their political alertness, outlook, and allegiances, and with the degree to which their political mentalities and actions are in line with the interests demanded by the juxtaposition of their objective position and their accepted values.

"Irrational discrepancies between the objectively defined bases of a stratum, the subjectively held policies of its members and their commonly accepted values do not necessarily point to problems of method. They may indicate the 'false consciousness' of the stratum we are examining."

In a footnote, he continues: " 'False consciousness,' the lack of awareness of and identification with one's objective interests, may be statistically defined as the deviant cases . . . for example, the rich who vote socialist, the poor who vote Republican. 'Objective interests' refers to those *allegiances and actions* which would have to be followed if the accepted values and desires of the people *involved in given strata situations* are to be realized." (Emphasis in the original.)

Note the presumption that "objective interests" exist; that there is a set of allegiances and actions which is appropriate for *all* members of a class. This presupposes a homogeneous set of "accepted values" for all class members. Secondly, Mills presumes that these particular allegiances and actions "have to be followed." This means in effect that a "best strategy" also exists. But are not these "objective" circumstances actually constructs of the analyst?

their data which may be identified as a variant of what Robert Merton calls the "and-also fallacy." [56] It will be remembered that the Lynds say of the "inner business control group" that they "bother to inject *just enough control* over the confusion of local politics to insure a tolerable tax rate, support for 'sound' municipal cooperation in maintaining an open-shop town, control over the numerically dominant working class, and similar broad policies calculated to enable their central business of money-making to go forward without too much interference." [57]

This formulation presents great difficulties to the outside observer. Any amount of evidence unfavorable to the view that the inner business control group rules can be discarded on the ground that the issues at stake were not essential for the maintenance of the power elite's position. The inner business control group only prevails on "important" issues, which are likely to be (by definition) those issues on which the inner business control group prevails. The only way out of this circle would be to apply criteria presented by the writers to distinguish important issues. But as long as this sort of explanation is resorted to, the Lynds' conclusions with respect to who rules Middletown cannot meet the standards of veracity previously proposed.

## YANKEE CITY (NEWBURYPORT, MASSACHUSETTS)

William Lloyd Warner, in his monumental five-volume study of Yankee City, has little to say explicitly about power in the community.[58] However, his contribution to the study of communities cannot be ignored here because of its occasional use by other sociologists as corroborative evidence for the correctness of one or another of the five propositions. As Milton Gordon says, "a careful examination of his work will show that many aspects of the operation of community power controls appear in the studies and are related to position in the status structure." [59]

56. See Merton's comments in Paul F. Lazarsfeld and Robert K. Merton, "Friendship as a Social Process," in M. Berger, T. Abel, and C. Page, eds., *Freedom and Control in Modern Society* (New York, Van Nostrand, 1954), pp. 61–62.

57. *MIT*, p. 89. Emphasis supplied.

58. The Yankee City series includes the following titles: Vol. 1, W. Lloyd Warner and Paul S. Lunt, *The Social Life of a Modern Community* (1941); Vol. 2, Warner and Lunt, *The Status System of a Modern Community* (1942); Vol. 3, Warner and Leo Srole, *The Social Systems of American Ethnic Groups* (1945); Vol. 4, Warner and J. O. Low, *The Social System of a Modern Factory* (1947); Vol. 5, Warner, *The Living and the Dead* (1959). All were published in New Haven by the Yale University Press (see Short Titles and Abbreviations).

59. Gordon, *Social Class in American Sociology*, p. 95. See also, e.g., Bernard Barber, *Social Stratification* (New York, Harcourt, Brace, 1957), p. 67.

Warner never mobilizes data bearing directly upon the question of community power, except in a single chapter where he attempts to show (1) that the greater the importance of a city official the higher his social status, and (2) that members of the lower classes tended to be arrested by the police more often than upper-class members.[60]

Warner presents his findings on his first point in a figure (reproduced here) which he interprets in these words: "In summary, it can be said

*The Class Composition of the Officeholders and Voters*
Source: Warner, YC 1, p. 370.

that the upper classes, together with the upper middle class, dominate the high control offices. They have a proportion of these offices far out of keeping with their representation in the general population."[61]

60. Warner, YC 1, pp. 366–78. Warner's second point is discussed below (p. 32) in connection with Hollingshead's similar observation.
61. Ibid., p. 372.

This chart deserves close examination, for it clearly shows that the "dominance" of the upper classes even in high control city government posts depended entirely upon their "togetherness" with the upper middle class. Since this dominance is unequivocally asserted by Warner, we may assume that Warner wishes to indicate by the chart that a coalition existed between certain adjacent classes. Assuming that coalitions are based on an expectation of common or complementary benefits and deprivations, we may infer from Warner's statement that the lower middle and lower classes did not share in the dominant coalition and hence may be presumed to have enjoyed noncomplementary, that is, different, benefits and deprivations from policy outcomes. Thus Warner indirectly asserts the propositions of the stratification theory which hold that upper classes are politically separated from those beneath, and in competition rather than in alliance with them in decisions allocating scarce resources —such as public office—in the community.

Other indications of conflict and divergence of interest appear in the Yankee City volumes. For example, Warner discusses at length an incident illustrating "how a very small number of upper class people can control the large number from the lower ranks." [62] In this incident the candidate supported by upper-class members of a community fraternal organization, the Veterans of All Wars, was elected president of the group.[63] Upper-class members of the organization became interested in the election after upper-class ministers asked them to put a stop to the importation by the organization of burlesque dancers from Boston. Warner indicates, in his description of this election, that upper-class members, in influencing the outcome in their favor, had at stake a certain special interest in the election, namely, the protection of the status reputation of Yankee City—an indulgence which could be expected to accrue largely to their own benefit.[64]

The first proposition of the stratification theory states that the highest group in terms of social-economic standing is also the most powerful group in the community. Thus, in Yankee City, according to Warner, "The Yankees are the most powerful group in the city, but the ethnics each year increase their power and prestige while they shed their variant mores and accept those of the dominant Yankees." [65] However, Warner makes clear that not *all* Yankees were members of the Yankee City ruling elite; the "solid, highly respectable upper-middle class," which was 81.2

62. Ibid., p. 198.
63. Ibid., pp. 143–44, 168–73; YC 2, pp. 46–50.
64. Ibid., p. 172.                    65. Warner, YC 4, p. 3.

per cent Yankee,[66] is described as "the people who get things done and provide an active front for the classes above them." [67] The provision of an "active front" was, of course, anticipated in the second key proposition.

Finally, what of social conflict between the classes? Warner describes several such conflicts in Yankee City. For example, upper-class members got an injunction to prevent a factory near their homes from performing night work. The owner of the factory, miffed, moved his operation out of the community, throwing 120 lower-class workers out of jobs. This occasioned much interclass resentment, it is alleged.[68] Warner also reminds us frequently of the latent struggle between the classes inherent in the Veterans of All Wars election.

These were of relatively small magnitude, compared to the major strike in which all the workers in Yankee City's principal industry walked off their jobs.[69] This Warner sees as a conflict between the classes exacerbated (if not precipitated) by two factors: blocked mobility for workers within the factory[70] and the acquisition of the factories by absentee owners who were removed from social constraints which the community might have employed on hometown owners.[71]

Warner says: "Manufacturers associations have been formed without public resistance, but labor unions have been resisted both by management and by some sectors of the general public. This dual development reflects the increasing seriousness of the conflict of interests between the different grades which has accompanied the increasing social distance between them." [72]

Data contrary to the five key propositions, which Warner clearly supports, may be found throughout the Yankee City studies, though they are never recognized as such. For example, Warner gives tacit recognition to the vote as a base of power in Yankee City when he discusses

a Yankee City mayoralty election when the only candidates were two Irishmen—Kelly [Upper-Lower] and McCormack [Upper-Middle]. The former conducted his campaign largely by castigation of Hill Street [rich people] for its iniquities to the poor of River Street and to the small taxpayers. He won the election easily, apparently

66. Warner, YC 2, p. 74. In this class are included 7,787 Yankees, while 3,813 Yankees are assigned to the classes above the upper middle.
67. W. Lloyd Warner, Marchia Meeker, and Kenneth Eels, *Social Class in America* (Gloucester, Peter Smith, 1954), p. 13.    68. Warner, YC 4, p. 10.
69. Ibid., passim.    70. Ibid., pp. 66–89.
71. Ibid., pp. 108–33.    72. Ibid., p. 122.

carrying the entire vote of the two lowest classes, both native and Irish, and at least half the votes of the lower-middle class. Even the lower-lower class native descendants of the old fisherman group, who traditionally "hate" the Irish, lined up the two candidates and decided that Kelly looked less Irish than did McCormack and so they voted for him (Kelly). Actually, Kelly conformed far more to the conventional conception of the Irish physical type than did McCormack . . .

McCormack, on the other hand, was strongly supported by members of the three highest classes, native as well as Irish, and had this to say to the interviewer; "When I ran for mayor the last time I don't think that more than two out of every ten Catholics voted for me. I think the other eight voted for Kelly, and most of the votes I got were from the Protestants." [73]

In an indication that groups other than classes may have had significance in community politics, Warner also mentions that the Negroes, Poles, and Greeks of Yankee City were socially homogeneous and politically active.[74]

Warner does not assert that Yankee City politicians subordinated themselves to economic and status leaders: he claims, after all, that they tended to have power commensurate with their status. But in the election campaign just described, the higher-status people were unable to achieve the election of the less obnoxious of two Irishmen running for mayor. This defeat of the relatively united upper classes is one aspect of Yankee City life not accounted for in the five propositions. And what happens when the upper classes are split? Such a division actually occurred in the single most significant social conflict to take place in Yankee City during Warner's research project. When the workers in Yankee City's shoe mills struck, Yankee City merchants backed the laborers against management.[75] So did the mayor and the police.[76] The workers won the right to bargain collectively and achieved the establishment of new wage and work standards.

73. Warner, YC 3, p. 94.
74. Ibid., pp. 263–64, 268–69, 276–78; Warner, YC 2, p. 82. It is well to remember in this connection that one of the criteria which originally led Warner to pick Yankee City was the apparent dominance of Yankees in the life of the town, Warner, YC 1, pp. 5, 38. And, indeed, "natives" made up over half of Yankee City's population of 17,000, leading every other ethnic group in five of Warner's six "classes." They were outnumbered only in Warner's upper-lower class, where the Irish were found to predominate, Warner, YC 2, p. 74.
75. Warner, YC 4, p. 44.          76. Ibid., pp. 34, 43, 146.

The outcomes of these conflicts directly contradict the notion that the upper classes invariably prevail; and the split in upper-class sympathies also casts doubt on the homogeneity of class positions and on the allegation that conflicts customarily pit the classes against one another.

The Yankee City books do not take up the question whether or not there was a single power elite. Warner discusses only two conflicts at length; the relatively trivial Veterans of All Wars election and the very significant city-wide strike. Certainly different people participated and prevailed in each instance, thus justifying a suspicion that decision-making in Yankee City was more fragmented than stratification theory normally allows.

Warner insists, in interpretive remarks, that the lower classes did not "really" win the great strike. He conceives of the advent of unions as an admission by workers that they no longer may rise to the top occupationally in the American tradition. While Warner grants that there may be certain mitigating changes in the American economic structure, he believes that "essentially the same basic relations of power and prestige will continue and, from all present indications, increase in strength; and the social distance between the top and bottom will be extended." [77]

One cardinal assumption is at the base of this prognosis, namely, that all men strive (or should strive) to reach "the top." [78] The top is described as a windswept plateau attained by only a few men, and then only at the expense of others; a place where community status and power are concentrated. This conception has been called the "lump of power" fallacy and criticized on the ground that power should not be conceived of as a "thing," limited in amount and located by definition in any particular place in the social structure.[79] Once power is defined as Warner proposes, there is no possible appeal to facts and no way to discover that power is exercised by those originally excluded in the terms of the definition.

Yankee City's workers, among others, were so excluded. Not being on "the top," nor even, in general, upwardly mobile in their social status, how could they possibly constitute a powerful social group? Warner's own account of the strike leaves us with the inescapable impression that they were indeed very powerful in Yankee City, but his analysis

77. Ibid., p. 189.
78. Ibid., p. 194. This theme runs through many of Warner's books; cf. his *American Life: Dream and Reality* (Chicago, Univ. of Chicago Press, 1953), pp. 103–23.
79. Cf. Charles E. Lindblom, "In Praise of Political Science," *World Politics*, 9 (Jan. 1957), 240–53, esp. 251.

takes no inventory of the range and bases of this power, the techniques through which it was exercised, or the prerequisites and consequences of its exercise in the community.

## ELMTOWN-JONESVILLE (MORRIS, ILLINOIS)

Two separate studies were concurrently made of Morris, a small town in northern Illinois, in the late 1930s and early 1940s. W. Lloyd Warner called the community Jonesville, and August B. Hollingshead called it Elmtown.[80] The major purpose of both studies was to establish empirically the connection between ascribed social status and various kinds of social participation.

Hollingshead's research centered around the high school. He discovered that the social status of students' families made significant differences in the school attendance records of children, in their nonathletic participation, their marks, and the ways in which discipline was applied to them.[81] The comments I shall make, however, deal only with the question of who "controlled" the community, which Hollingshead also discusses.

Hollingshead quotes at length an informant who describes power in Elmtown in these words:

> It's an aristocracy of wealth, nothing else . . .
>
> The inner circle of top aristocrats is made up of people who have a close community of interest. They all have property and a good income. They run around in pretty closely knit groups, and it's mighty hard for a stranger to break into one . . . Most of the husbands are dead now, but the women still play Whist and 500. That's the most powerful group in town . . . This is the group that can really put on the pressure. They own a lot of interests, land, town property, the banks and other things, and they have great prestige and power.[82]

The issues on which the "inner circle of top aristocrats" were powerful are not specified in detail, but apparently ranged over a wide array of matters. Hollingshead's informant says of this group:

> When they want something done, they bear down on their children, in-laws, relatives and grandchildren. If voting's involved, they let their tenants and employees know how they feel. When an issue

80. Warner, *Jonesville*; Hollingshead, *Elmtown*. See Short Titles and Abbreviations.
81. Hollingshead, *Elmtown*, pp. 129, 169–70, 180–92.
82. Ibid., p. 72.

comes up, I can see this crowd pull together. I've seen them take sides on so many issues. I can just about tell ahead of time how they'll line up . . . When I want something, I always go to this group . . . If I can't get them on my side I drop the idea.[83]

In discussing the relationship between "Class I" families—those of "wealth and lineage"—and political leaders, Hollingshead says:

Large tax bills accompany extensive ownership: consequently these Class I families have a direct interest in keeping assessments and tax rates low. They accomplish this effectively, within the community and the county, through the control of the two major political party organizations on the township and county levels.[84]

The Elmtown school board is described as consisting of:

Middle aged business and professional men from the top two classes who possess a highly developed sense of responsibility to these classes especially with respect to the preservation of economic interests, power and prestige. The policies they have followed in the administration of the school system have reflected the community interests of their own social classes, and, to a less extent, those of the little business and professional people in the lower middle class.[85]

The school board believed that only those high school children who could "profit from a high school education" should use the public facilities. "In general, they mean the sons and daughters of the three higher classes, and those in Class IV, if they 'behave themselves.' Adolescents in Class V are not considered to have enough ability to 'profit from a high school education.' " [86]

Hollingshead says that local school board elections were "carefully controlled" so as to elect "conservative men who have represented through the years the political, economic, social and educational interests of classes I and II *rather than* the other four-fifths to seven-eighths of the population." [87] The only instance in recent history where the school plant was materially improved came, says Hollingshead, in the "early 1920's, after a terrific struggle between the 'better families' and the 'laboring class.' " [88]

83. Ibid., pp. 72–73.          84. Ibid., p. 86.
85. Warner, *Jonesville*, p. 195 (in a chapter by Hollingshead).
86. Ibid., p. 196.
87. Hollingshead, *Elmtown*, pp. 123–24. Emphasis supplied.
88. Ibid., p. 135.

However, Hollingshead indicates that conflicts were rare. Most Elm-towners, he says, took the "control of community institutions by the upper classes" as "natural." This upper-class control, says Hollingshead, "tends to result in the manipulation of institutional functions in the interests of individuals and families who have wealth, prestige, and power," and this in turn "guarantees the continuation, into the indefinable future, of the class system and its inequalities." [89]

Four kinds of evidence are proposed to substantiate the claim that Elmtown's social "Class I" constituted the community's power elite. First, Hollingshead makes a series of compelling observations on the relationship between class and law enforcement. Hollingshead says of Class I people: "Some of them may not observe the laws of the community with care, yet there are no arrests." [90] Lower down on the scale, arrests and convictions were more frequent. Four per cent of Class III and 14 per cent of Class IV fathers were convicted in local courts of offenses between 1934 and 1941, and, for Class V, the comparable figure rose to 46 per cent.[91] It will be remembered that Warner made the same point in his study of Yankee City.

How does this relate to power in Elmtown? Hollingshead seems to be saying that the law was enforced differently on different classes. It is implied that crime occurred randomly throughout the population, but immunity from arrest was a peculiar perquisite of high status and, therefore, an indication of power.[92] The question is conceivably more complicated than Hollingshead's presentation reveals. In weighing the significance of the statistics, we should perhaps take account of (1) the possibility that owing to the unfavorable conditions of life generally present among the lower classes—conditions vividly described by Hollingshead—the lower classes would actually commit most of Elmtown's crimes; (2) the possibility that the two highest classes, comprising a few, very small, intensively interacting, "respectable" cliques, were in fact severely constrained by the circumstances of their lives from committing crime. In one sense, perhaps Hollingshead's findings on this point argue that communities produce characteristic "rational" patterns of deviance from legality as surely as they produce patterns of acquiescence.[93]

89. Ibid., pp. 451–52.

90. Ibid., p. 89.

91. Ibid., pp. 110, 119–20. The reference presumably is to fathers of the high school students whom Hollingshead studied closely.

92. Hollingshead says this explicitly on p. 79.

93. Cf. Robert A. Dentler and Kai T. Erikson, "The Functions of Deviance in Groups," Social Problems, 7 (Fall 1959), 98–107.

Both the social meanings of arrest and opportunities to commit offenses differ greatly between the top and bottom of the status pyramid. Immunity from arrest no doubt means a great deal more to members of the upper class than to those at the bottom—except possibly those lower-class members engaged for their livelihoods in illicit occupations. In this connection it is important to note that Elmtown's most illustrious bawdy house, Polish Paula's, catering to a lower-class clientele had "not been raided for a quarter of a century." [94]

Although respectability is perhaps a necessary condition of high community-wide prestige, no one, I think, will argue that it is a necessary condition of power[95]—and Hollingshead does not actually say this though he implies it. By demonstrating, then, the relative proneness to arrest of the lower classes, Hollingshead has not demonstrated that they were powerless.

The second point made by Hollingshead to substantiate his claim that the upper classes controlled community policies is that they controlled the two major party organizations.

> The candidates for public office, except the district attorney and the judge, are generally not members of Class I, but this does not mean that they are free of controls exerted by Class I interests. Money, legal talent, and political office are instruments used to translate interests into effective power. They are relied upon to implement decisions in contests which involve raising tax bills through public improvements, such as new public buildings, schools, roads or welfare programs. This behind-the-scenes control results in the formulation of conservative policies and the election of officials who act in the capacity of agents for Class I interests.[96]

This argument from evidence bears a resemblance to Hollingshead's argument that the law was enforced unequally upon the classes in that in both cases "real" power was held "behind the scenes," and was ex-

94. Hollingshead, *Elmtown*, p. 79. At this point in his book, Hollingshead seems to suggest that power is *not* an epiphenomenon of status. He never reiterates this opinion, however, and I take the very much more numerous statements such as those quoted previously in this chapter as more representative of his position.

95. For discussion and examples bearing on this point, see Robert K. Merton, "Social Structure and Anomie," in Merton, *Social Theory and Social Structure* (Glencoe, Free Press, 1957), pp. 131–60; William F. Whyte, *Street Corner Society* (Chicago, Univ. of Chicago Press, 1955), pp. 194–252. See also the Lynds' description of George R. Dale, the mayor of Middletown, who was elected to office after serving a term in jail, *MIT*, pp. 322–27.

96. Hollingshead, *Elmtown*, p. 86.

ercised covertly through "agents." The general argument of covertness in power exercise is often met with in stratification studies of community power and may be said to take two characteristic forms. The first maintains simply that there is a power-holding group behind the scenes though the characteristics of the group are not specified in detail. Researchers who are led to reject on empirical grounds the notion that a *specific* group is in fact the covert power elite can be said to have failed to disprove the proposition because there may be some *other* group which performs this function. This is the "principle of infinite regress" described by Dahl.[97] It effectively bars empirical research from contributing to the discussion of community power.

A variant of this principle appears quite frequently in stratification studies, including Hollingshead's work, as we have seen. In the case of *Elmtown's Youth*, it is not the identity of the ruling group which is left to the imagination, but rather the *means* by which the group controlled. The argument that the social-economic elite ruled Elmtown covertly means, in effect, that all overt manifestations (i.e., those observable by the researcher) of powerlessness or indifference on the part of this group are to be ignored in favor of the presumption that they were in fact secretly in control of community affairs. Once again, the findings of research are prevented from interfering with the description of social reality proffered by the author.

In the case of Hollingshead's second argument, as with the first, the evidence is by no means clear in support of the five key propositions. Warner's *Democracy in Jonesville* provides us with more detailed information about the political organization of the community, greatly supplementing Hollingshead's presentation. Little information is given about government office-holders, but the party organizations responsible for nominations and elections are described in some detail. Five of Elmtown's six Republican precinct committeemen were members of Class IV. The sixth, representing the "silk stocking" district, was a member of Class II.[98] The Republican party normally dominated Elmtown politics. Its "behind-the-scenes" leaders were three in number: an elderly Irish, Roman Catholic judge; the young editor of the newspaper; and a rich attorney with good connections in state-house Republican circles.[99] Joseph Rosenstein, the author of the political chapter in the Warner volume, makes it clear that these three men had practically no policy preferences and that they competed with one another for private power

97. Dahl, "Critique," 463–69.      98. Warner, *Jonesville*, p. 231.
99. Ibid., pp. 226–31.

within the party organization.[100] The Republican party organization, owing to long-standing lack of unity among its "big shots," was held to be a relatively unorganized machine.[101] The main beneficiaries of the organization were said to be the precinct committeemen, who were rewarded with state patronage when Republicans were in control in state politics.[102]

The Democratic party, too, had been "beset by personal rivalries and factional difficulties." [103] The Democrats subsisted almost entirely on federal and state patronage during the years studied.

> Locally, the Democratic party is poor in resources—poor in terms of friends of the party who have money to contribute, and poor in terms of voters with Democratic traditions.[104]

The Republicans, in spite of their own factional wárfare, had succeeded in gaining a strong majority position in the community.

> Financial strength at the top is complemented by the skill with which the Republican party has cultivated the voters of all classes and religious groups over a period of years . . . Today . . . large numbers of Catholics participate in the party as voters, and ambitious Catholic politicians find that the party is open to them. Among the various classes, too, the Republican party has been successful in establishing itself. The top positions of leadership go to men of the upper and upper middle classes—men who have the social skills and contacts to establish the proper "outward" relations in the party, and to maintain the local relationships demanded of leaders in the party [i.e. (apparently) in order to get financial backing from the upper classes]. But, as the statistical materials show, staunch friends of the Republican party are found in all classes. People farther down in the class system vote Republican, not only because of family tradition and social and economic pressures in the community, but also because their participation is actively solicited by the "wheel horses" of the party—men who generally come from lower classes . . . The efficient activities of these wheel horses can be traced partly to their own zeal for the party, but that zeal is reinforced by more tangible rewards—jobs and campaign money which, in turn, it is the function of the local "big shots" to ensure.[105]

100. Ibid., pp. 230–31.
102. Ibid., p. 225.
104. Ibid., p. 234.

101. Ibid., p. 228.
103. Ibid., p. 233.
105. Ibid., pp. 234–35.

A careful reading of these words suggests that in claiming upper-class control of the parties Hollingshead has mistakenly assumed that the members of a status layer have the same political interests, that they effectively unify themselves in pursuit of these interests, and that this takes place at the expense of other status groups. According to the account in the Warner book, party leaders were in general apathetic about policy, were not united, and their activities generated benefits for members of many status groups.

The third bit of concrete evidence Hollingshead advances in favor of Class I domination has to do with the selection of the Board of Education. He describes in detail the process by which prosperous, male, Protestant Republicans were selected for the board by the predominantly upper-class leaders of the Rotary Club. Hollingshead says:

> When a vacancy is to occur, the selection of a man for the Board of Education is left to the President of the Board. He discusses possible candidates with his friends on the Board and in the Rotary Club. Generally, he invites a fellow Rotarian with whom he believes he can work to become a candidate. The President then files this man's name with the election clerk; nothing is said publicly about the impending vacancy or the forthcoming election until after the last date for filing has passed. Then *The Bugle* runs a news item stating that the date for filing names for the school election has passed, that such-and-such men have filed as candidates for the Board of Education, and that Mr. X has filed again for President of the Board. Little additional publicity is given to the election until *The Bugle* carries the necessary legal notices of the polling places and names of the candidates. On election day, only a handful of voters go to the polls to elect the hand-picked candidates. In 1940, 132 votes were cast; in 1941, 114, and in 1942, 84.[106]

How can we account for the success of these maneuvers? How, for example, could a board member's intention to resign be kept a secret in Elmtown? As Hollingshead says:

> In a town of 6,000 people, everything that is done, or not done, and then talked about, tends to be personalized. One person does something at some time; other persons know about it, find out about it, and above all gossip about it, and then pass judgment on it.[107]

106. Hollingshead, *Elmtown*, p. 123.    107. Ibid., p. 44.

The Elmtown school board's term of office was set by statute, and all seven members of the board stood for election at the same time. Anyone could be placed on the ballot for election to one of the seven nonpaid, nonpolitical positions on the board by filing a petition signed by 50 voters, or by 10 per cent of the voters in the last school election, whichever was less. These basic facts were at the disposal of the public, if the public wanted to take notice of them.[108]

But, apparently, interest in elections to the Board of Education was exceedingly low, judging from Hollingshead's figures on turnout. The machinations depicted above seem likely to have assured control over the board by a small group in a situation where no other group cared to contest the matter, but we should not assume that some seriously competing group could easily have been prevented from trying to fill vacancies—or nonvacancies—on the board. Finally, we should be wary of concluding that this method for selecting board members necessarily predicts anything about the policies of the board in the conduct of its business.[109]

Hollingshead indicates that Class I and II dominance on the board would make such a prediction possible. But his discussion of a spectacular conflict over the physical condition of the public high school casts grave doubt on this proposition. This introduces the fourth kind of empirical evidence bearing on the propositions of the stratification theory. The important facts of the situation seem to have been the following.[110]

The high school, owing to an obsolete plant, lost its accreditation. Some members of the Board of Education were shocked and launched an investigation, which resulted in numerous minor repairs to the building. A new high school was clearly necessary, Hollingshead believes. It proved impossible, however, to raise money in Elmtown for this purpose.

Hollingshead attributes to Class I influence the failure of the Board of Education to build a new high school. The land in Elmtown's school district was largely in the hands of Class I people, and taxes on the land formed the main source of income for school purposes. The members of

108. A letter to me from the office of the principal of the Morris High School in September 1959 gives this current information about the laws pertaining to the election of the school board. This letter also states that, aside from minor changes in the election code, the basic facts given were the same when Warner and Hollingshead did their research in Morris some twenty years ago.

109. On this point see especially the excellent review of the literature contained in W. W. Charters, Jr., "Social Class Analysis and the Control of Education," *Harvard Educational Review*, 23 (Fall 1953), 268–83, esp. 271–72.

110. Hollingshead, *Elmtown*, pp. 132–40, 142–47.

Class I did not want their taxes raised; *therefore* nothing "serious" was done about the school.

However, Hollingshead mentions in passing that the last time any improvements were made in the community's educational plant, the vote of the "laboring class" made them possible.[111] The very element lacking in the more recent situation described by Hollingshead was an aroused populace. Despite repeated invitations to visit the school, no parents availed themselves of the opportunity.[112] Classes III, IV, and V, containing the vast majority of Elmtown's population, are described by Hollingshead as apathetic on the school issue. Class I opposed school improvements for personal financial reasons. Who in the community favored school improvements? Many members of Class II, says Hollingshead, most conspicuous among them leaders of the Board of Education.[113] But if this were the case, then it could not also be true that the Board of Education was a tool of Class I. That is, in the only community-wide conflict having to do with schools, the Board of Education seems to have opposed the "moneyed interests."

It is still true that the large landholders won their battle—at least temporarily—to hold the line on taxes. Hollingshead does not detail the techniques they used in securing their victory. But it does seem important to note that this victory was not won covertly but openly and by majority rule at the polls, where the voters rejected a proposed bond issue to build a new high school.[114]

Power relations in Jonesville are described by W. Lloyd Warner as a product of the community's main social cleavage, which separated management from workers in "The Mill" where better than a third of all Jonesville's urban workers had jobs. Not surprisingly, Warner says that the Mill dominated the town:

> When the citizens of the town talk about The Mill, they rarely refer to it in economic terms but speak in moral terms of its place in the life of the town. They are forever concerned with its power for good and evil in the lives of Jonesville.
>
> The economic and social force of The Mill affects every part of the life of the community. Everyone recognizes its power. Politicians, hat in hand, wait upon Mr. Waddell, manager of The Mill, to find out what he thinks on such important questions as "Shall the tax rate be increased to improve the education our young people are

111. Ibid., pp. 135–36.          112. Ibid., p. 136.
113. Ibid., pp. 139, 142–47.          114. Ibid., p. 139.

getting?"—"Shall the new minister be Mr. Jones or Mr. Smith?"—
"Should the city support various civic and moral enterprises?"—
"Should new industries enter the town and possibly compete with
The Mill for the town's available labor supply?" They want to know
what Mr. Waddell thinks. Mr. Waddell usually let them know.[115]

The Mill management is said to be opposed to other industries'
coming into town and to have taken steps to prevent new plants'
opening up and creating competition in the labor market. Several
informants reaffirmed the following statement of a person who knows
the town intimately: "The people out at The Mill are very strong
politically. I suppose you have been here long enough to know how
important The Mill is in this town. They seem to see to it that things
go along the way they want. Now I have heard of several cases, and
I know of some myself, where business tried to come into this town.
They get just so far and then nothing happens. Any kind of new
activity just can't get started in this town. There is the Johnson factory building. Several people have been interested in getting it
started, but nothing ever seems to happen. The people at The Mill
bought up the plant and started something there, but after a while
it folded up and the building just sits there. It seems an awful waste;
but The Mill group owns it so nobody else can get in there." [116]

Those who complain about Mill policies far outnumber those in
favor.[117]

Several comments should be made at this point. First, Hollingshead
flatly contradicts Warner's allegation that the Mill was unpopular.[118]
Warner, too, indicates some uncertainty about the Mill's standing in the
community, since he reports evidence both that Millworkers were under-
paid and that they were adequately paid.[119]

Warner implies that the Mill was successfully depressing the economy
of the town despite opposition. But Warner himself records the Mill's
efforts to "start something" at the old Johnson plant. The failure of this
project can hardly be attributed to the connivance of the Mill management since it would have been much cheaper to buy up the plant and
*not* try to "start something" there at all. Furthermore, Warner mentions
a substantial "leakage" of the Jonesville labor force to other nearby com-

115. Warner, *Jonesville*, p. 101.      116. Ibid., p. 103.
117. Ibid.      118. Hollingshead, *Elmtown*, p. 374.
119. Warner, *Jonesville*, pp. 106, 108, 112.

munities when war industries opened up job opportunities there.[120] This
to be sure did less than it might have for the economy of the town, but
it also suggests that hardship due to Jonesville's comparative lethargy
did not necessarily fall on the lower classes.

The concern of Elmtown's politicians for Mr. Waddell's civic views is
perhaps worth noting, but Warner presents no evidence to indicate that
the Mill manager got his way on any burning issue. Hollingshead records
one interesting situation, however; years before, Waddell apparently had
led the lower classes in the successful fight for school improvements, over
the objections of his fellow members of Class I.[121]

Perhaps the most important community conflict in which the Mill management engaged was the fight over unionization, which they lost. This
seems to refute the thesis that the upper classes prevailed. But, curiously
enough, Warner argues in effect that, win or lose, the upper classes win.
This is because Warner sees unions as symptomatic of regrettable changes
in American society,[122] changes which include (a) (once again) blocked
job mobility within the company for workers, (b) a correspondingly increased dependence on "impersonal" union and company bureaucracies
for decision-making affecting their daily lives, and (c) an increase in
class conflict. There is no doubt some truth in these observations, particularly insofar as they call attention to increases in the dependence of
people in local communities on superlocal institutions. However, Warner
fails to give consideration to the possibility that unionization benefited
workers and the community by channeling, directing, and even muting
class conflict, by providing new incentives for successful community participation by members of the lower classes, and by supplying new sources
of social status and social affiliation and new bases of local political
power.[123]

In the present context, it is important to note that unionization becomes, through Warner's ingenious interpretation, not a sign of increasing

120. Ibid., pp. 266–68.                121. Hollingshead, Elmtown, p. 135.
122. Cf. also Warner's comments in YC 4.
123. For instances where unions have performed these functions see C. W. M.
Hart, "Industrial Relations Research and Social Theory," Canadian Journal of Eco-
nomics and Political Science, 15 (Feb. 1949), 53–73; Charles R. Walker, Steeltown
(New York, Harper, 1950); Nelson N. Foote, "The Professionalization of Labor in
Detroit," Am. J. Soc., 58 (Jan. 1953), 371–80; George H. Hildebrand, "American
Unionism, Social Stratification, and Power," Am. J. Soc., 58 (Jan. 1953), 381–90;
Robert E. Lane, Political Life (Glencoe, Free Press, 1959), p. 322; James B. McKee,
"Status and Power in the Industrial Community: A Comment on Drucker's Thesis,"
Am. J. Soc., 58 (Jan. 1953), 362–70. See also Seymour Martin Lipset, Political Man
(Garden City, Doubleday, 1960), pp. 21–96.

power among lower status groups, but the opposite. Warner sees unions as imposing new hardships on workers without ameliorating their subordination to higher status groups. The breakup of community social patterns—especially status mobility patterns—is heralded by unionization, but corresponding benefits are left unmentioned.

It is not easy from the evidence about Morris given in these two studies to test the empirical propositions on power proposed by the stratification theory. The workers did unionize, but relatively little was done about the schools. Control of the political parties seems to have been quite decentralized. Aside from the composition of the school board, city and county government are not discussed. The bases of community power which can be inferred from the discussions in both books include (1) high status (e.g. membership in Rotary), (2) high economic position (e.g. managership in the Mill), (3) political office (e.g. in the case of the influential Republican judge), (4) access to organs of publicity (e.g. in the case of the politically important newspaper editor), (5) outside political connections (e.g. in the cases of the politically influential Republican lawyer and local Democrats who received patronage from the state organization), and (6) solidarity and numbers (e.g. in the case of the successfully unionized workers).

Aside from statements that civic leaders consulted with Waddell, the Mill manager, and acted as "agents of Class I interests," there is nothing in the two books to support the contention that civic leaders were in fact subordinate to high status persons. Indeed, in the school crisis the Board of Education seems not to have been subservient to the demands of Class I. This indicates that the composition of the power elite was not what Warner and Hollingshead say it was. In addition the diversity of bases from which members of the community could apparently exercise power seems to show that no single elite group ruled Morris.

Hollingshead and Warner are quite firm, however, in asserting that many community decisions were "rigged" in favor of the upper classes. The examples given from interviews and recounted from community folklore seem vivid enough. Yet it would be a mistake to infer from this that all community decisions followed this pattern. The assignment of "gains" and "losses" to segments of the community is at best arbitrary and difficult.

Consider the question: who gained and who lost as the result of the run-down condition of the local high school? One answer might be that, as a result of prevailing policies, high school facilities tended to be in scarce supply and lower-class children were squeezed out. But another reply, diametrically opposed, would hold that lower-class children would tend to drop out anyway, and that the real loss was sustained by the children of the upper classes, because Hollingshead's figures indicate that much higher percentages of children from these classes attended school and hence were forced to put up with an inadequate school system.[124]

A similar problem is involved when we consider the effect of the drain on Morris' working force by an out-of-town war-boom industry. These workers were forced to travel a long way to the job but were rewarded with unprecedentedly high wages, which they may or may not have spent with Morris merchants. The existence of competition for labor may or may not have forced Morris industries to raise their own pay scales, and may or may not have caused a certain number of workers to be permanently removed from the Morris labor force by out-migration. Assuming that a power elite did exist, what decisions could it have made in this real life situation to maximize its own advantage while minimizing that of others?

There are, finally, some indications that the ambiguity of class positions on a variety of issues was reflected in intraclass cleavages, as in the school controversy, and in mutually advantageous alliances between segments of several classes, as in the political party organizations.

From the data provided us about Morris, then, it is possible to construct a plausible argument which effectively denies each empirical proposition of stratification power theory.

## PHILADELPHIA

Digby Baltzell's book, *Philadelphia Gentlemen,* is perhaps unique among full-scale stratification studies. One theme Baltzell promises to explore is the question, "What is the pattern of upper class control in the city?," [125] yet he discusses this point without recourse to a single fact save the observation that businessmen predominate in the Philadelphia *Social Register.* This *tour de force* is accomplished by means of the judicious use of statements which are either proposals about the use of language (definitions) or are otherwise devoid of empirical reference. For example, Baltzell says: "An upper class may or may not be a ruling class . . . However, if it is not a ruling class, it will soon be replaced by a new upper class." [126]

The upper class, in Baltzell's terminology, refers to a group of families

124. Hollingshead, *Elmtown,* pp. 330–35.
125. Baltzell, *Philadelphia,* p. 32.        126. Ibid., p. 34.

of highest status and old wealth. "In the last analysis," Baltzell says, "power over other people is the indispensable mark of high social status, and the primary function of an upper class is the exercise of power." [127]

It seems reasonable to infer from the above that Baltzell is suggesting that high status and wealth in combination are necessary but not sufficient conditions for the exercise of power in Philadelphia. The sufficient condition, it appears, is performance of the community's "goal-integrating function," which Baltzell defines as the province of Philadelphia's business elite.[128] The men of this business elite "perform essentially similar elite functions: the exercise of power over other men in making the decisions which shape the ends of a predominantly business-oriented social structure." [129]

Baltzell provides two indications of the subordination of Philadelphia's politicians to the upper class. First, he notes that the community's aristocracy historically has had no "itch for public office." [130] Philadelphia's is a moneyed, not a public-spirited aristocracy. In any event, public office is not envisaged as a necessary condition of power because the political and opinion-making elite, according to Baltzell, "serve the ends of the business elite." [131]

It is apparently also the case in Philadelphia that a single group exercised considerable power over a wide range of activities. "Of course," Baltzell says, "economic and political power are indivisible aspects of social power." [132]

Exactly 42 Philadelphians in 1940 were, in Baltzell's judgment, in a position to exercise this power. These 42 men were listed in *Who's Who*— Baltzell's operational definition for elite membership—and were also members of either the Philadelphia or the Rittenhouse Club. They "can be said to constitute a primary group of power and influence at the top of the social structure." [133] The decisions made by these Philadelphia gentlemen, judging from their directorships, ranged from the affairs of the city's banks and financial institutions, including the Pennsylvania Railroad, to the University of Pennsylvania and the Symphony Orchestra.[134]

But the empirical basis on which these assertions rest is slim indeed. This can perhaps best be seen by recapitulating in brief and orderly form the argument in which Baltzell describes the "pattern of upper class control."

127. Ibid., p. 60.
129. Ibid., p. 35.
131. Ibid., p. 35.
133. Ibid., p. 365.

128. Ibid., pp. 34–35.
130. Ibid., e.g., pp. 170, 364.
132. Ibid., p. 364.
134. Ibid., pp. 366–71.

1.1    The Ruling Class performs society's goal-integrating functions (given by definition).

1.2    Society's goal-integrating functions are performed by businessmen (given by definition).

1.3    Hence: The Ruling Class consists of businessmen.

2.1    The Upper Class is that group appearing in the *Social Register* (given by definition).

2.2    Most Philadelphians appearing in the *Social Register* are business and financial leaders (an empirical observation).

2.3    Hence: The Upper Class = The Ruling Class.[135]

Baltzell's assertions that businessmen ruled are entirely without foundation in his data, which consists of information from the Philadelphia *Social Register, Who's Who in America, The Dictionary of American Biography*, and a large number of biographical essays, reminiscences, and memoirs. While these sources are many, they are not diverse. They provide an excellent—if somewhat accidental—report of the status aspirations and rituals of certain socially-minded Philadelphians, but nothing on *power*. No community issues are discussed within the pages of Baltzell's book. No collective decisions are reached, no conflicts over community resources take place, no activities of actors seeking values are described.[136] It is therefore surprising that Baltzell should conclude: "In the last analysis, power over other people is the indispensable mark of high social status, and the primary function of an upper class is the exercise of power." [137] *Philadelphia Gentlemen* is a stratification study which makes assertions about community power, but does not test them.

135. Ibid., pp. 34 ff.
136. See, in contrast, James Reichley, *The Art of Government: Reform and Organization Politics in Philadelphia* (New York, Fund for the Republic, 1959).
137. Baltzell, *Philadelphia*, p. 60.

# 3. Research Consequences
## of Stratification Theory (II)

REGIONAL CITY (ATLANTA, GEORGIA)

Just as the Middletown books mark both the beginning and the high point of an earlier era in the study of community power, the work of Floyd Hunter dominates the contemporary scene. Hunter is the author or co-author of three books dealing with what he calls "power structure." [1] All have been favorably reviewed, and the first, a study of power in a southern metropolis, Regional City, has had many imitators as well as admirers in the few years since its publication.[2]

As Hunter describes Regional City, it was run by a small group of powerful men who interacted socially and determined policy informally and behind the scenes. "The test for admission to this circle of decision-

1. Hunter, *CPS;* Floyd Hunter, Ruth Connor Schaffer, and Cecil B. Sheps, *Community Organization: Action and Inaction* (Chapel Hill, Univ. of North Carolina Press, 1956); Hunter, *Top Leadership, U.S.A.* (Chapel Hill, Univ. of North Carolina Press, 1959).

2. Hunter's method for studying community power, or variants thereof, can be found in Robert E. Agger, "Power Attributions in the Local Community," *Social Forces, 34* (May 1956), 322–31; Agger and Vincent Ostrom, "The Political Structure of a Small Community," *Public Opinion Quarterly, 20* (Spring 1956), 81–89; Agger and Ostrom, "Political Participation in a Small Community," in Heinz Eulau et al., eds., *Political Behavior* (Glencoe, Free Press, 1957), pp. 138–48; Agger and Daniel Goldrich, "Community Power Structures and Partisanship," *Am. Soc. Rev., 23* (August 1958), 383–92; Ernest A. T. Barth and Baha Abu-Laban, "Power Structure and the Negro Sub-community," *Am. Soc. Rev., 24* (Feb. 1959), 69–76; George M. Belknap and Ralph Smuckler, "Political Power Relations in a Mid-west City," *Public Opinion Quarterly, 20* (Spring 1956), 73–81; Miller, "Industry and CPS," 9–15; Miller, "Decision-making Cliques in Community Power Structures," *Am. J. Soc., 64* (Nov. 1958), 299–310; Robert O. Schulze and Leonard U. Blumberg, "The Determination of Local Power Elites," *Am. J. Soc., 63* (Nov. 1957), 290–96; Edwin Hoffman Rhyne, "Political Parties and Decision-making in Three Southern Counties," *Am. Pol. Sci. Rev., 52* (Dec. 1958), 1091–1107. This method is praised highly in many places, including Gordon Blackwell, "Community Analysis," in Roland Young, ed., *Approaches to the Study of Politics* (Evanston, Northwestern Univ. Press, 1958), pp. 305–17; William J. Gore and Fred S. Silander, "A Bibliographical Essay on Decision-making," *Administrative Science Quarterly, 4* (June 1959), 106–21.

makers," Hunter says, "is almost wholly a man's position in the business community in Regional City." [3]

The accompanying subordination of civic leaders and politicians to this power elite took many forms. Hunter outlines a division of labor in which the topmost leaders, comprising men with important economic connections, made basic policy decisions. "The men in the under-structure of power become the doers and are activated by the policy-makers—the initiators." [4]

> Most association presidents, however, remain in the under-structure of the power hierarchy. The organizations are not a sure route to sustained community prominence. Membership in the top brackets of one of the stable economic bureaucracies is the surest road to power, and this road is entered into by only a few. Organizational leaders are prone to get the publicity; the upper echelon economic leaders the power. [5]

Hunter speaks of Regional City's two most important politicians in these words: "Their interest may be said to be primarily business in the strict sense of the word. Both have a popular following that has kept them in office, but their close associates are businessmen." [6]

Hunter tells us that even the governor of the state was controlled by economic interests; "As the investigation proceeded, it became apparent that an economic elite member was the power behind the Governor." [7] In fact, Hunter says, on a matter of importance to Regional City the governor would seek out this businessman, who "had the responsibility for contacts with the Governor" though he himself was "subordinate to at least two other men of financial power in the community." [8]

What kind of policy resulted from this close control by Regional City's businessmen? Hunter says: "When new policy is laid down it must be consistent with the general scheme of old policy and should not radically change basic alignments of settled policy . . . so that the basic equilibrium in the social systems of the community may undergo as little disruption as possible." [9] "Any individual who comes to know the inner workings of many organizations reputedly devoted to the discussion of civic and social issues knows they are actually operated in the interests of the political and economic status quo." [10]

3. Hunter, CPS, p. 79.
5. Ibid., pp. 86–87.
7. Ibid., p. 175.
9. Ibid., p. 209.

4. Ibid., p. 100.
6. Ibid., p. 81.
8. Ibid., pp. 162–63.
10. Ibid., p. 258.

Those who are disadvantaged by the present arrangements are not an articulate group: and, while some of the professionals [Hunter apparently here refers to social service professionals] may speak for a portion of this group, they often do so only with halfhearted conviction. . . . When some of the professional and other under-structure personnel speak in behalf of the underprivileged groups they may be making an ill-defined bid for "political" support of the latter and are setting forth a veiled demand for inclusion in policy determination among the power leaders. Such disguised and scarcely conscious demands are recognized by the top leaders for what they are—a restiveness in the under-structure personnel—and they are handled accordingly. The method of handling the relatively powerless understructure is through the pressures previously described—warning, intimidations, threats and in extreme cases violence. In some cases the method may include isolation from all sources of support for the individual, including his job and therefore his income. The principle of "divide and rule" is as applicable in the community as it is in larger units of political patterning, and it is as effective.[11]

The methods Hunter used in reaching these conclusions have gained widespread acceptance as an economical, systematic, quantitative, and scientifically appropriate approach to the study of community power. It seems important, then, to undertake a critical reconstruction of this approach before considering his conclusions.

Hunter's first step was to procure four lists of leaders from the managers of civic organizations. The community council provided a list of leaders in community affairs; the chamber of commerce supplied lists of business and financial leaders; "The League of Women Voters provided lists of local political leaders who had at least major governmental committee chairmanship status"; and "newspaper editors and other civic leaders provided lists of society leaders and leaders of wealth." [12]

Hunter then asked a panel of 14 judges to cut these lists, totaling "more than 175" names, by giving "their opinions on who were the top leaders on each of the lists." All 14 judges "revealed a high degree of correlation in their choices." Hunter ended up with a roster of 40 names representing the 10 highest scoring nominees from each list.[13] This presumably means that the final 40 consists of 10 community leaders, 10 business and financial leaders, 10 local political leaders, and 10 leaders of society and wealth.

11. Ibid., pp. 247–48.                    12. Ibid., p. 269.
13. Ibid., pp. 61, 269.

Hunter provides a chart of the occupational positions of these 40 top leaders which reveals quite a different picture, however. Twenty-eight are classified as in banking, commerce, finance, or the private practice of law; two as labor leaders; one as a dentist. Five are classified as "social leaders," and four as in government—two of these in the community's school system.[14]

Some of the apparent discrepancies can be explained away. First, Hunter says that his 14 judges could not agree on the "status-society" leaders. He explains: "In a sense, therefore, names given in this area of possible leadership were arbitrarily included."[15] It is possible that Hunter supplemented his list of five "social leaders" with five high-status people who were also business and financial leaders in the community. Assuming that this is what happened, and that all 10 community leaders were also business and financial leaders, we can account for 25 of the 28 individuals on the occupational list who were classified as business and financial leaders. It is still necessary to account for the other three, and also to discover what became of the six people who were apparently subtracted from the list of 10 local political leaders, since only four of these appear in the occupational listing. And where do the latter leaders and the dentist fit into the four lists of 10?

This is not so much a criticism of Hunter's panel device as of the way he used it in Regional City. A more basic objection can be raised. Consider the question Hunter asked, first of his original list-makers, then of his panel. He wanted them to name the community's top leaders, which presupposes that a group of top leaders exists.[16] In Chapter 2 (p. 29) it was pointed out that this presumption appears elsewhere in stratification writings on community power. In a study such as the one Hunter was conducting, this presupposition creates great methodological difficulties. First, how many "top leaders" are there? Second, what differentiates

14. Ibid., p. 76.          15. Ibid., p. 269.

16. This criticism of Hunter was first made by Herbert Kaufman and Victor Jones, "The Mystery of Power," *Public Administration Review, 14* (Summer 1954), 205–12. Other critiques of Hunter include Robert A. Dahl, "Hierarchy, Democracy and Bargaining in Politics and Economics," in *Research Frontiers in Politics and Government* (Washington, Brookings, 1955), pp. 45–69; Dahl, "Critique," pp. 463–69; Norton E. Long, "The Local Community as an Ecology of Games," *Am. J. Soc., 64* (Nov. 1958), 251–61; Nelson W. Polsby, "The Sociology of Community Power: A Reassessment," *Social Forces, 37* (March 1959), 232–36; Polsby, "Three Problems in the Analysis of Community Power," *Am. Soc. Rev., 24* (Dec. 1959), 796–803; Peter H. Rossi, "Community Decision-making," *Administrative Science Quarterly, 1* (June 1957), 415–43; Raymond E. Wolfinger, "Reputation and Reality in the Study of 'Community Power,'" *Am. Soc. Rev., 25* (Oct. 1960), 636–44.

"top" from "nontop" leaders? Third, how do we know the judges are applying standards of "topness" consistent with one another and with Hunter? Fourth, how do we know the judges are correct, that in fact there *are* "top leaders" in the community, and that, if there are, they have been correctly identified?

The answer to the first question is that there is in principle no fixed number. Hunter depends on the agreement of his judges, which is at best a statistical artifact, to determine part of his answer to this question.[17] In part, he answers the question "arbitrarily" and in part, as we have seen in the case of the six missing politicians, answers were obtained which Hunter does not explain at all. Forty does not seem too large a number of top leaders for a community whose population approached half a million. But why not 41, or 39? Hunter begs this question, and in the process raises a host of others, by asserting that there were top leaders not on his list of 40 and that some on his list were not leaders. In a letter to me, Hunter says "certainly the 'social elite' [presumably the five classed as "social leaders"] were not *power* leaders." [18] In his text, Hunter gives examples of members of the top 40 who were sycophants, playboys, nonresidents of the community, and in other ways marginal or dependent on the business elite.[19] What, then, is this list of 40? "The men described," says Hunter, "come within the range of the center of power in the community." [20]

> Only a rudimentary "power pyramid" of Regional City will be presented . . . I doubt seriously that power forms a single pyramid with any nicety in a community the size of Regional City. There are *pyramids* of power in this community which seem more important to the present discussion than a pyramid . . .[21] The men being interviewed represented at least a nucleus of power grouping . . .[22] This pattern of a relatively small decision-making group working through a larger under-structure is a reality, and if data were available, the total personnel involved in a major community project might possibly form a pyramid of power, but the constituency of the

17. See Wolfinger, "Reputation and Reality."
18. Letter of May 21, 1959.
19. See, for example, the descriptions in *CPS* of the following members of the Regional City power elite: Avery Spear (pp. 33–36), Edward Stokes (p. 35), Gloria Stevens (pp. 36–39), Herman Schmidt (pp. 39–41), and Percy Latham (pp. 41–42). The names are, of course, fictitious.
20. Ibid., p. 61.               21. Ibid., p. 62.
22. Ibid., p. 65.

pyramid would change according to the project being acted upon. In other words, the personnel of the pyramid would change depending upon what needs to be done at a particular time.[23]

But at other points Hunter says:

> The relative stability of the top policy-making group is a pattern quite apparent in Regional City civic affairs . . .[24] The top leaders, the under-structure professionals, and the Negro community leaders represent community groups. They are identifiable groups . . . definitely groups.[25]

In Regional City, then, the question of how many "top" leaders there were was largely an arbitrary matter, determined either by the agreement of a panel or, in the absence of agreement, by Hunter himself.

The criteria by which top leaders were separated from lesser leaders are impossible to reconstruct, except by inference from the fact that so many business leaders landed on the final list. If it is impossible to reconstruct the standards by which the judges made their decisions, it is doubly impossible to determine the extent to which individual judges applied these standards consistently one with another.

Now we come to the question: how do we know the panel named the men who really were the top leaders of the community? This question is much more troublesome than it appears. Suppose we instruct a panel to name all those meeting criterion A as leaders. In order to determine whether the panel is correct or not, we find out which men in the community meet criterion A. However, this makes the panel superfluous, since we would then have already discovered who the top leaders are (i.e. who met criterion A). The same holds true for any additional number of criteria we wish to introduce. But it was precisely because Hunter had no clear criteria for top leadership that he enlisted his panel in the first place, and this fact makes a check on the panel's correctness impossible. This means that a panel is either superfluous or its opinions are impossible to corroborate or disprove.[26]

The panel method can be considered from still another perspective. Presumably what is being determined when judges are asked to identify influentials is who has a *reputation* for being influential. This reputation can be divided into that part which is justified by behavior and that part which is not so justified. It is clearly those in the community whose be-

23. Ibid.    24. Ibid., p. 93.
25. Ibid., p. 61.    26. See Scoble, "Yankeetown."

havior in the main justifies their reputation as leaders whom social scientists would want to call the "real" leaders in the community. In other words, asking about reputations is asking, at a remove, about behavior. It can be argued that the researcher should make it his business to study behavior directly rather than depend on the opinions of secondhand sources.

Against this criticism, as we have seen, stratification writers claim that leadership takes place behind the scenes, where only insiders in the locality can penetrate. This brings into play recourse to an infinite regression, in which the "real" leaders are always held to be "behind" those whom firsthand evidence reveals as leaders.[27] A recent research finding by Schulze and Blumberg indicates, in addition, that expertise in identifying community leaders is by no means an esoteric gift.[28] Essentially the same "leaders-by-reputation" were picked by three panels drawn from different sources—all of them of relatively high status—in the population of "Cibola," Michigan.

There are four possible alternative defenses from advocates of the panel method against this finding. First, it can be asserted that none of the panels was sufficiently expert to judge who the "real" leaders of Cibola were. This explanation can be discarded, however, on the ground that at least one and possibly more of the panels were made up of people whose outward characteristics appear to have been roughly the same as panels for whom "genuine" expertise has been claimed in sociological studies.[29] The second counter-argument would be that each panel had access to inside information likely to be denied an enterprising researcher. This would mean that each panel withheld from the researcher the grounds for its ratings of leaders, and it presupposes the existence of

27. Dahl, "Critique."

28. "The Determination of Local Power Elites."

29. Miller, "Industry and CPS," Barth and Abu-Laban, "Power Structure," and Hunter, CPS, p. 269, do not describe their panels in very much detail, but apparently panel members in these studies were of relatively high status. In Regional City, for example, Hunter's 14 panel members were "business executives and professional people." Schulze and Blumberg's three panels consisted of (1) the heads of voluntary organizations, (2) political and civic leaders, and (3) the "economic dominants." None of the earlier criticisms of Warner's use of an essentially upper-class panel for stratifying communities by status reputation seems to have had much effect on the use of this method for studying power relations, despite very clear signs that similar weaknesses prevail. See Ruth R. Kornhauser, "The Warner Approach to Social Stratification," in R. Bendix and S. M. Lipset, eds., Class, Status and Power (Glencoe, Free Press, 1953), pp. 224–55, esp. p. 253; also S. M. Lipset and R. Bendix, "Social Status and Social Structure," British Journal of Sociology, 2 (June, Sept. 1951), 150–68, 230–54.

secrets about leadership activity widely known in the community itself. Obviously facts widely enough known to be available to all three panels can hardly be considered secret. A third possibility is that the panels were sufficiently expert but based their ratings on the common stock of information available to everybody, rather than on inside knowledge. Or, fourth, they reported firsthand observations any reasonably diligent researcher could have made.

The defenses against the Schulze and Blumberg finding are clearly unsatisfactory. Their finding therefore effectively denies the panel's special knowledge, and renders the test for expertise—assuming the unlikely possibility that one could be devised—moot.

Since Hunter chose to allow his panel of judges to play such a critical part in finding facts about power, it is important to note that he gives several indications that he either mistrusted or disregarded the findings of the panel. One example is the treatment of the status elite list, mentioned above. Another is his decision to conduct a separate analysis of Regional City's Negro subcommunity:

> The need to study the Negro subcommunity in Regional City grew out of field experience. This community was found to represent a sub-power grouping of considerable significance which could not be overlooked, particularly since many of the issues suggested to the field investigator by white power personnel revolved around Negro-white relations.[30]

We have already noted that Hunter insists that some of the top 40 named by his panel were not leaders at all.

It must be concluded that Hunter does not make a very strong case for the use of the panel in community power analysis. As we have seen, he provides no standard by which the panel's work can be judged and no reliable guidelines which his panel can follow in its work. He gives no defense of the special qualifications or expertise of the panel, and indeed on certain occasions replaces its judgment with his own. Finally, he gives positive indications that he disbelieves or mistrusts many of the panel's findings.

We move now to the third step in his method, which entailed interviewing 27 of the 40 top leaders. These 27 were asked many questions, among them: (1) Have any top leaders been left off the list of 40? (2) How many men would need to be involved in a major community project

30. Hunter, *CPS*, p. 270.

in Regional City to put it over? (3) If a project were before the community that required *decision* by a group of leaders—leaders that nearly everyone would accept—which 10 on the list of 40 would you choose? (4) Who is the biggest man in town? [31]

The answers reveal a great deal about Hunter's method. First, Hunter reports that some 64 people not on his list were spontaneously nominated as top leaders. One man was named five times and five men were nominated four times. Hunter never changed his list of top leaders to include these nominees, however.[32]

No coherent pattern of responses seem to have been received to the second question. "The answers to this question," Hunter reports, "varied from: 'you've got the men right here on this list—maybe ten of them,' to 'fifty to a hundred.'" [33] In response to the third question, one man, George Delbert, received the most mentions but, in question four, the "biggest man in town" was discovered to be someone entirely different, Charles Homer.[34] The first observation that should be made is that, insofar as the identification of leaders is concerned, Hunter's interviewing contributed only a little new information, and most of it tended to discredit the notion that there was a homogeneous, discrete, top leadership group in Regional City.

Hunter develops other evidence in the course of the interviews which casts doubt on the propositions of the stratification theory. For example, he reports that the lowest economic and status group in Regional City, the Negroes, were by virtue of their political solidarity very powerful in community affairs.

> Within the city limits of Regional City almost a third of the population are Negroes. Thousands of them are registered voters, and on issues which affect them directly they are prone to follow the Organized Voters' lead in their choice of candidates. Cries of "pocket voting" are always raised by the unfavored candidate, but this only tends to weld the Negro vote into a more solid expression of political strength. Everyone politically inclined is aware of the power of the Negro vote to swing elections within the city, and Smith [a Negro political leader] gets unfeigned deference from the city's elected officials, as well as from many of the state politicians.[35]

31. Ibid., pp. 61 ff., 268–71. Emphasis Hunter's.
32. Ibid., pp. 64–65.
33. Ibid., p. 65.
34. Ibid., pp. 62, 64.
35. Ibid., p. 50.

In spite of the alleged subordination of politicians to the power elite, Hunter describes the following situation:

> After the policy line had been set and before the project could be activated, it was necessary to go to the state legislature for enabling legislation. In this process the legislators bargained with the [upper-class] policy group concerning the membership of the proposed official committee. During the horse-trading, some of the names proposed by the policy-makers were dropped in favor of local politicos agreeable to the state leaders.[36]

Contrary to the third key proposition of stratification theory, it is exceedingly important to specify issues in discussing power in Regional City. In the course of his interviews with what turned out to be an unexplained preponderance of community businessmen, Hunter asked how they went about influencing concrete policy decisions. The issues Hunter ended up treating at greatest length in his book included (1) getting an international trade association to locate in Regional City, (2) the fate of the Progressive party in Old State, (3) the decision of members of the power elite to testify in Washington before Congress on a pending tax bill, (4) getting a new industry in Regional City, (5) the political views of a columnist in a community trade publication.[37] All of these issues were either trivial or clearly of predominant concern to businessmen, or both. Furthermore, they seem to have been issues on which Hunter's "power elite" met with relative success, in contrast to other issues Hunter lists, of much wider concern in the community, where the "power elite" was either split wide open or united but ineffective. These issues included: (1) the plan of development, (2) the sales tax, (3) traffic control, and (4) race relations. In further contradiction of the notion that there is a single power elite, it is obvious that many other actors were involved in decision-making on these issues, although Hunter tells us nothing of their goals and activities.[38]

One informant, James Treat, explained the system of policy-formation in the Regional City business community as a process of negotiation among at least five independent "crowds" of leaders. These crowds sometimes competed and sometimes entered into alliances with one another on specific community programs.[39]

This description of occasional social conflict among elite groups does not exclude the possibility of interclass rivalry, of course. Hunter de-

36. Ibid., p. 98.                    37. Ibid., pp. 160, 164 ff., 175 ff.
38. Ibid., pp. 207–27.              39. Ibid., pp. 75 ff.

scribes the position of the lower strata as hierarchically subordinate rather than opposed to the power elite. He sees the "under-structure," as he calls it, as primarily involved in executing policies set by the power elite. He does not view these policies as always detrimental to the lower classes. Hunter intimates that dire things *would* happen to the lower classes if they stepped out of line, but only the case of the trade paper columnist is offered in point.[40] On the other hand, members of the lower-class Negro minority apparently exercised a considerable influence over many community policies.

It is most extraordinary to observe that Hunter limits the role of the alleged decision-makers to the relatively innocuous task of "getting consent." He specifically denies that the top members of the pyramid had special opportunities either to *innovate* or to *execute* policies. It has already been noted that one of Hunter's major points is that the "top leaders" of Regional City rarely appeared as leaders of community organizations or as executors of community policy.[41] This indicates, says Hunter, that the top leadership "delegated" the detail work downward after basic policies were set. One would expect, then, that the effectiveness of the power elite rested on its ability to initiate action and to innovate in community policy. But in this area of activity, Hunter reports, "The power leaders have action initiated for them more often than they initiate action." [42] "Of all the men talked to in Regional City, only one [the Mayor] indicated that he was aggressive in 'raising issues' for a realignment of policy." [43]

Apparently members of the power elite felt greatly constrained with respect to their ability to operate in the community. Hunter says, "a careful watch is kept for what 'will go' and what 'will not go.'" [44] This may be taken as an indication of lack of conflict among the classes and of the importance that Regional City decision-makers placed upon a widespread distribution of benefits.

How have the five key propositions of stratification theory fared in our re-examination of Hunter's discussion of Regional City? We cannot, on the evidence, conclude that the upper class ruled, that political and civic leaders were subordinate to them, that there was a power elite, that the interests of a single class were served by community policies, or that social conflicts sharply divided the classes. While Hunter claims that every one of these propositions held true in Regional City, his methods for

40. Ibid., pp. 247–48.
42. Ibid., p. 226.
44. Ibid., p. 111.

41. Ibid., passim, esp. pp. 92 ff.
43. Ibid., p. 209.

collecting the facts on these points are suspect, and much unexplained contrary evidence appears in his book. Hunter does not present enough evidence to justify an attempt at formulating an alternative description of power in Regional City, but there is more than enough to cast doubt on his own description.

## BIGTOWN (BATON ROUGE, LOUISIANA)

While an over-representation of businessmen in the interview sample may be regarded as an unhappy accident in Hunter's case, Roland Pellegrin and Charles Coates develop their discussion of power in Bigtown from an apparently purposely restricted group of "intensive interviews with 50 leading executives of the community and other persons who have worked with and observed corporation executives." [45]

In spite of the limitations within which they operated in collecting data, Pellegrin and Coates turn up a good many contradictions of stratification theory, which they analyze in an especially ingenious manner. They begin by asserting:

> The stratification system of a given community attains stability and remains basically unaltered over relatively long periods of time because . . . the control of community affairs and policies resides in dominant interest groups which feel little incentive to disrupt the existing pattern of superordination and subordination. These groups exercise power which is infinitely out of proportion to their number.[46]

But, in a footnote, Pellegrin and Coates admit that politicians were not especially cooperative with the allegedly "dominant [economic] interest groups" nor were they subservient to them.

> The typical interviewee in this study described local governmental officials as relatively powerless figures who do not have the backing of influential groups but secured their positions through the support of working-class voters. Indeed, these officials were more often than not targets of ridicule for those who evaluated their positions in the power structure.

But,

> The relative lack of integration of Bigtown's interest groups makes it possible for governmental officials to sponsor civic projects which

45. Roland J. Pellegrin and Charles H. Coates, "Absentee-owned Corporations and Community Power Structure," *Am. J. Soc., 61* (March 1956), 413–19.
46. Ibid., 413.

are sometimes successful, in spite of opposition from one or another of the "crowds" [of economic leaders]. Interest groups find it difficult to express publicly opposition to projects which attract widespread public support. To do so would be "bad public relations," perhaps unprofitable in the long run.[47]

Once again, then, the vote is mentioned as an important base of community power. Social conflict is described as occurring between competing interest groups, not classes. Pellegrin and Coates also assert that "as in Regional City, community projects can be carried out successfully only if the small group of policy-makers can marshal the cooperation of large numbers of lower-level workers who will perform the labor required to transform the policies and decisions into reality." [48]

On the other hand, Pellegrin and Coates devote most of their attention to the tactics and ideology of businessmen in community life. Their interviews turned up numerous instances in which a big-business official was expected to represent his company on citizens' committees, in part because of "an almost incredible preoccupation with 'public relations'" by the corporation and in part to "protect and foster its own interest and to promote a conservative, business-class ideology."

> Executives are constantly on guard lest fellow committee members divert funds to new projects suggestive of the "welfare state." Advocates of such measures are speedily labeled "controversial" and, if they persist, are referred to as "cranks" or "subversives"—a term once used only for political traitors. Deviants of this nature are, in the long run, however, weeded out; they are not able to obtain appointments to other committees. An old-timer, involved in such measures scores of times during the previous thirty years, observed:

>> "We freeze out these New Dealers and other Reds. When we appoint people to important committee posts, we look at their record. If an individual has gone all out on some crazy idea, his goose is cooked. If I am chairman of a group that is making appointments, I go stone deaf whenever someone suggests the name of one of these radicals. My hearing improves when a good, reliable person is mentioned as a possibility." [49]

Despite their preoccupation with the tactics and ideology of businessmen, Pellegrin and Coates give evidence that economic leaders were

47. Ibid., 414.
48. Ibid., 418.
49. Ibid., 417.

aware that they were not as powerful as the quotations above might indicate.

They dwell at great length upon the power structure of other cities in which they have resided, where an informal "Committee of 50," "Citizens' Council," or like group controls civic affairs with a firm hand. These glowing accounts are typically accompanied by a pessimistic description of the situation in Bigtown. This community, as analyzed by some of its outstanding men, has a number of powerful interest groups but lacks effective liaison among them and leadership to unite them. Under these circumstances, a given "crowd" is unlikely to participate in a proposed project unless it foresees tangible gain.[50]

Pellegrin and Coates reconcile evidence of fragmented policy-making with stratification theory in an original manner. While they assert that the managers of the large corporations did not constitute a dominant interest group in Bigtown, because (1) they were seldom united on community issues; (2) other groups, notably politicians with mass-based support, were more effectively mobilized; (3) executives were preoccupied with their own careers, which gave them a more cosmopolitan frame of reference; and (4) the policies of the large corporations were obsessively concerned with public relations, Pellegrin and Coates do insist that:

Corporation support probably assures the success of a proposed project, while disapproval spells doom for it. Thus absentee-owned corporations are a decisive force in the power structure of Bigtown, since they constitute a balance of power among the competing interest groups of the community.[51]

This "decisive force" could operate only (1) when other groups in the community were about equally distributed for and against a proposal, (2) when the big-corporation executives were all more or less united on the question, and (3) when they did something about it. No doubt all three of these conditions have been met on occasion. But similar conditions can operate so as to make many groups in the community important in the "balance of power." In fact, there may have been groups in the community much more united and more effectively mobilized than businessmen, and, consequently, these groups may have tipped the "balance" much more often. By interviewing only businessmen, Pellegrin and Coates

50. Ibid., 414.                    51. Ibid.

entirely ignored this possibility. Since Pellegrin and Coates contradict themselves in almost every paragraph on the five key propositions of the stratification theory, it is impossible to judge from their presentation who ruled in Bigtown.

## CIBOLA (YPSILANTI, MICHIGAN)

In Robert O. Schulze's study of Cibola, a midwestern "satellite" community, the major finding was that economic domination of the community had shifted from long-time local residents and local industry into the hands of local managers of large, bureaucratized, absentee-owned corporations. A concomitant of this historical trend was the tendency for economic dominants to play a smaller and smaller part in community decision-making. This finding demonstrates that something other than economic dominance (Schulze does not make entirely clear what) had come to be important as a base of community power in Cibola.

Schulze does not elaborate on this point, however. He refers to the power structure as "bifurcated," that is, as shared between the economic dominants who monopolized "potential for determinative action," and a new power elite—"a group of middle-class business and professional men" whom he calls "public leaders"—who monopolized the "*overt* direction of the political and civic life of Cibola." [52]

Schulze is using here a combination of explanatory devices already discussed: in particular, the covertness argument, with its possibility of infinite regress in case of a direct challenge, and the and-also fallacy, which recognizes direct disproof of a proposition not by modifying or discarding the proposition but by pleading "special circumstances." As we shall see shortly, even the "public leaders" of Cibola are reported by Schulze to have been far from a united, omnipotent elite group. At any rate, the economic elite did not rule Cibola.

Schulze reports that community decisions were not especially important to present-day economic dominants for numerous reasons: because the executives themselves were geographically mobile within the company bureaucracy and had no long-term attachments to the community; because most large companies had an explicit hands-off policy vis-à-vis the community, for the sake of good public relations; and, finally, because no decisions made in Cibola seemed likely materially to affect a mam-

52. Emphasis supplied. This discussion is drawn from two sources: Robert O. Schulze, "The Role of Economic Dominants in Community Power Structure," *Am. Soc. Rev.*, 23 (Feb. 1958), 3–9; and Schulze, "Bifurcation." The quotations are from "The Role of Economic Dominants," 6, 8, 9.

moth, worldwide business, one of whose units was located there. However, Schulze believes that these large corporations *could* have determined policy had they wanted to, both in Cibola and in the larger
arenas more salient to them.[53]

The assertion that any group "potentially" could exercise significant,
or decisive, or any influence in community affairs is not easy to discuss
in a scientific manner. How can one tell, after all, whether or not an
actor is powerful unless some sequence of events, competently observed,
attests to his power? If these events take place, then the power of the
actor is not "potential" but actual. If these events do not occur, then
what grounds have we to suppose that the actor is powerful? There appear to be no scientific grounds for such a supposition; therefore, by
assigning a high "power potential" to economic dominants, and referring to this potential as one-half of a bifurcated system, Schulze is indulging in empirically unjustified speculation.

Another of Schulze's major points is that, in Cibola, the "potential"
of the large companies would probably never be put to the test. He
mentions two factors operating in contradictory directions with respect
to the possible exploitation of the power potential of absentee-owned
corporations. The first was a pronounced sensitivity on the part of many
Cibola decision-makers to *any* sentiments expressed by minions of the
large corporations.[54] Schulze pictures the leaders of Cibola's civic life
as extremely eager to anticipate the reactions of the economic dominants;
this, he believes, acted as an important constraint on community policy-
making. The economic dominants reacted to the jumpiness of the city
fathers by withdrawing even further from community participation, to
the extent that they felt inhibited from expressing even idle or personal
opinions for fear of causing inappropriately servile responses.[55]

The second, contradictory, factor was that with the economic dominants largely silent and apathetic on community issues, their roles and
images in the community became subject to possible manipulation by
noneconomic dominants who wished to use the large corporations'
power potential to further their own ends.[56] This reverses the usual
formula, which has the economic leaders doing the manipulating. Schulze
does not say, incidentally, that economic dominants *were* so victimized;
only that their position made them increasingly vulnerable to this kind
of control by civic leaders.

53. Schulze, "Bifurcation," 49, 68–72.        54. Ibid., 68–71.
55. Ibid., and 58–60.
56. Schulze, "The Role of Economic Dominants," 8.

One lone instance was recorded by Schulze in which an economic dominant attempted to "cash in" on his "potential." The dominant in question ran for a seat on the board of directors of the Cibola Chamber of Commerce and was badly beaten.[57] With respect to larger arenas, the decay in recent years of the influence of economically dominant corporations in the politics of Michigan, where Cibola is located, is a well-known phenomenon which Schulze neither mentions nor studies.[58]

Schulze finds that economic dominants played essentially unimportant roles in Cibola's civic life. This hardly constitutes a significant contribution to an understanding of how decision-making processes in Cibola *did* work. Another aspect of Schulze's research is more clearly to the point. He reconstructs from interviews and documentary sources the circumstances and events of two community controversies. These case studies provide better information about the distribution of influence among the people Schulze identifies as "public leaders," as well as among other members of the community.

Both of these case studies involve attempts at planned community change. The attempt to institute a city manager form of government, by changing the city charter, failed at first but succeeded later, after proponents of the change made concessions to "hold-out" groups.[59] The attempt by the city to annex land in Pottawatomie township failed because, as one public leader said,

> Our real problem was that we had nothing to offer the people who carried weight in the township. The officials there are an entrenched bunch, and they know perfectly well that for every acre of land they might let us have, they'd lose money on the state sales tax diversions.[60]

Of the two case studies, the annexation battle is the less informative because it involves negotiations between a relatively united set of community leaders on the one hand and an intransigent group of politicians outside the community on the other.

The charter battle, which was carried on entirely within the community, is more relevant. Schulze points out that the major difference between the first round of the charter fight, which proponents of

57. Ibid., 4; "Bifurcation," 20, 48–49.
58. See Duncan Norton-Taylor, "What's Wrong with Michigan?" *Fortune* (Dec. 1955), 142 ff. The election by a narrow margin of a Republican businessman to the governorship of the state in 1962 after a 16-year famine does not materially alter the force of this point, I think.
59. Schulze, "Bifurcation," 60.          60. Ibid., 63.

change lost, and the second round, which they won, was a broadening of the base of decision-making, to include, for example, "younger business and professional men in the community." [61]

> Likewise [Schulze says], the public leaders, following the charter's defeat in March, had been obliged to try to "win over" certain key leaders in the Negro and working class sub-communities.[62]

The second charter vote indicated that they succeeded in these efforts. But in the process, promises and commitments had been made—as evidenced by the fact that since 1946 one prominent Negro leader and one pivotal labor union official almost invariably have been named to "represent" their elements in the community on important citizen committees appointed by the Chamber of Commerce and the city council. In all of these instances, a somewhat wider sharing in the decision-making processes resulted.[63]

Others to whom concessions had to be made were the professional politicians—themselves public leaders—who were put out of work as a result of the adoption of the new charter. As Schulze points out:

> The men intimately involved in the informal leadership structure of a small community could afford neither to flaunt nor to be vindictive—for they realized that if the effort to renovate the local government was to result in the lasting alienation of significant segments of community opinion, theirs would have been a Pyrrhic victory indeed.[64]

The charter episode divided the city along the lines of political interests, which coincided only adventitiously with economic and status groupings. The economic dominants gave token approval to the charter change. When leadership was concentrated in the hands of many of Schulze's "public leaders," it was unsuccessful. Later, a coalition of "public leaders" and "sub-community" leaders was successful despite the opposition of some public leaders, namely the professional politicians.

61. Ibid., 59.

62. Ibid., 60. Schulze's use of the category "sub-community" (in which he follows Hunter) has interesting methodological consequences. We could say, for example, that a Negro powerful in community decision-making is a community leader. Instead, Schulze classifies this leader according to the limits of his presumed power base and calls him a "leader of the Negro sub-community." Only businessmen fail to receive this treatment, thus preserving an illusion of general pervasiveness about the influence and activities of the leaders of the business subcommunity, which may not accord at all with the facts.

63. Schulze "Bifurcation," 60.                    64. Ibid.

There was concerted effort, as we have seen, to distribute values broadly among Cibola's economic and status groups. Indeed, Schulze indicates that this was the price of success.

To summarize: the only concrete community decision discussed at any length by Schulze calls into question all of the propositions of the stratification analysis. Whether or not the coalition that won on the charter issue held together on a variety of other issues is a question that can be answered only by examining other issues. Certainly we would not want to call the broad alliance that prevailed in the charter battle a "power elite" in the usual sense of the term, according to which the ruling or prevailing group must constitute less than a majority of the population and should also not be an artifact of the application of majoritarian principles (as in the case of a representative assembly).[65] Since the new charter was adopted in a referendum, after the leaders of a majority of the population became convinced of its desirability, it could be argued that the group that prevailed in this case was not an elite.

## Pacific City (Seattle, Washington)

In Pacific City, an attempt was made to copy and improve upon Hunter's research in Regional City. Delbert C. Miller has written two articles on power in Pacific City, and Ernest Barth and Baha Abu-Laban have contributed an article on the power structure of Pacific City's Negro subcommunity.

Miller compares his Pacific City findings with data gathered in an English city. Among the hypotheses he seeks to test are the following: (1) Do business leaders predominate in the community's power structure?[66] (2) Is community power exercised through "cliques" of leaders?[67] Miller claims to have found evidence supporting an affirmative conclusion to the first question and a somewhat more limited affirmative to the second. But a close reading of his presentation reveals that the facts support the opposite conclusions equally well.

Miller's method of data collection is an elaboration of the Hunter technique criticized above. Community organizations and informants were asked to nominate leaders in nine (rather than four) sectors of community life. Ten judges were asked to rate the 312 resulting names as "most influential," "influential," and "less influential" according to the

65. See the discussion in Chapter 1 and in Dahl, "Critique."
66. Miller, "Industry and CPS," 9.
67. Miller, "Decision-making Cliques," 299.

specific criterion: "person participates actively either in supporting or initiating policy decisions which have the most effect on the community." [68]

Forty-four persons were nominated in this way as "most influential" in the community—a group Miller calls "Top Influentials." The next step was to interview half of these Top Influentials, who were asked, among other things, "If you were responsible for a major project which was before the community that required decision by a group of leaders —leaders that nearly everybody would accept—which ten on this list would you choose?" Those nominated most often in this manner by Top Influentials were designated "Key Influentials." [69] The top dozen Key Influentials were found to be mostly businessmen (67 per cent), and on the basis of this evidence Miller concludes: "Businessmen do exert a predominant influence in community decision-making in Pacific City." [70] "Key Influentials," Miller asserts, "are a significant feature of any community power structure for they are the sociometric leaders. The initiation and sanction of policy tends to be centered about them so that they may greatly influence the values which dominate in decision-making." [71]

This conclusion does not follow for several reasons. First, Miller's Key Influentials were picked from among Top Influentials for unanimous acceptability, and not because they initiated and sanctioned policies. Miller presents no evidence at all about the actual initiation and sanction of any community policy. Second, they were picked on the basis of a vague and hypothetical question, not on the basis of a concrete issue or a specific pattern of past behavior. This is very important because, as Dahl, Wolfinger, and I have pointed out, answers to Miller's question may mean many things, and their meanings are in any case irrelevant until concrete instances of policy formation are examined.[72] Also, by specifying particular issues it is possible to determine whether 12 is an appropriate number of Key Influentials. If 40 seemed too small in Regional City, 12 seems ridiculous in the hub of America's Northwest.

68. Miller, "Industry and CPS," 10.          69. Ibid.
70. Ibid., 13.          71. Ibid., 12.
72. See works previously cited. Alternative interpretations of responses to general questions which fail to enumerate specific issues, such as the ones Miller and Hunter asked, might be: Respondents (1) are naming the status elite; (2) have in mind some specific issue or issues which are (A) of recent interest, (B) especially salient to the respondent, or (C) characteristic of the community—as public power might be in the West or the race issue in the South; (3) are naming the community's old civic warhorses or primarily letterhead names; (4) are naming the community's formal leadership; (5) are naming the most vocal leaders in the community.

If these 12 Key Influentials were truly influential on an appreciable number of issues in Pacific City, then it seems unlikely that they would have had any time or energy left over to run their own businesses. If their influence was in fact restricted to only one or a few issues, then Miller should have told us what these issues were.

Miller's data are even more ambiguous with respect to his second hypothesis—that "cliques" ran Pacific City. He presents figures attesting to the following:

1. Key Influentials tend to choose one another rather than outsiders as members of the "top ten."

2. Key Influentials know more Top Influentials better, on the average, than Top Influentials know Top Influentials.

3. Key Influentials serve on more committees than Top Influentials.

4. Key Influentials tend to participate in more organizations than Top Influentials.

5. There is a slightly disproportionate tendency for Key Influentials to belong to business organizations, which, Miller believes, are the most important in the community.[73]

From this compendium of indirect evidence, Miller concludes that there is reason to believe that Key Influentials form cliques of intensively interacting people. Direct testimony on this point robs the finding of almost all meaning, however. While both Top Influentials and Key Influentials believe that "crowds" exist, Miller quotes 11 interviews—fully half the number he conducted in Pacific City—which indicate that (1) there is no "top" group of leaders, but leaders are instead specialized around specific issues (which he does not study), and (2) none of the specialized "top" groups can singlehandedly execute its policies without widespread cooperation from others in the community.[74] In spite of this testimony, Miller concludes that "The stratified pyramid, with its solidary top business elite . . . is . . . a useful guide to the power potential in Pacific City." [75] And in another place: the pyramid "applies to Pacific City for a wide range of issues and projects [unspecified] but it does not apply during many political campaigns when coalitions form and often defeat the leaders who are ranked according to the stratified model." [76]

Miller's research, in short, combines to an extraordinary degree the three symptoms of scientific inadequacy advanced at the beginning of

73. Miller, "Decision-making Cliques," 301–03.
74. Ibid., 305–10.                         75. Ibid., 309.
76. Ibid., 307.

the previous chapter. First, he ignores much data which tend to discredit his thesis: specific examples of social conflict mentioned in the course of his two papers (and in Barth and Abu-Laban's companion piece) consistently deny the utility of the elaborate model of power structure he postulates. Examples of this are the political campaigns and "The defeat of the right to work issue in Pacific City in 1956." [77] Second, Miller's methods, which include not specifying issues and developing meaningless statistical artifacts like a 12-member "Key" elite, purport to confirm hypotheses which they do not actually test. Third, by recourse to the argument of "potential" power, Miller resorts to an ad hoc explanation in order to reconcile with his thesis findings that are contrary to it.

Barth and Abu-Laban engage in something similar when they find that the Negro subcommunity "has no genuine power structure" [78]— even though on the issues most salient to them Negro leaders "have been remarkably successful." [79] The reason why Negroes are said to be without power in the community is because "Their sub-community lacked large scale business and industrial organizations and, *consequently*, no *genuine* power structure had developed." [80]

The reasoning here is crystal clear. A power structure is "genuine," to these researchers, only if they discover big businessmen in it. This explains Miller's otherwise inexplicable account indicating that the City Council of Pacific City was relatively powerless by virtue of the fact that it was made up of small businessmen. [81] The failure of Pacific City to conform to the propositions of stratification theory is attributed not to the incorrectness of the propositions but to immaturities, situations of flux, or other abnormalities in the social structure of the city.

In the latter part of his second article, Miller attempts to construct a model of community power structure applicable to Pacific City. [82] He posits a pyramid-shaped model on the one hand and a concentric ring-shaped model on the other. The second model is supposed to symbolize the accessibility of centers of power to a wider range of community leaders. Pacific City, Miller suggests, lies somewhere between these two models. Unfortunately, this conclusion suggests only

77. Ibid.
78. Barth and Abu-Laban, "Power Structure," 76.
79. Ibid., 71, 76.
80. Ibid., Abstract, p. 69. Emphasis supplied.
81. Miller, "Industry and CPS," 14–15.
82. Miller, "Decision-making Cliques," 307–10.

that the key propositions of stratification theory do not apply in Pacific City; it does not offer further information on which a corrected statement about power in Pacific City could be based.

The purpose of the second and third chapters of this book has been to examine eight stratification studies of community power, all of which are generally considered to be contributions to current knowledge about community power.[83] In all we have found reasons to mistrust the findings of their authors. In concluding this examination, it might be useful to summarize the various ways in which the authors have tried to save stratification theory despite what appears to be contradictory evidence. These have included:

1. The "false consciousness" argument, which holds that when a social group violates an analyst's expectations the group is acting "irrationally."

2. The "and-also" argument, which suggests that instances in which the analyst's expectations are not met are trivial or irrelevant.

3. The "lump of power" assumption, which denies that power can be exercised by any persons or groups not defined as being at the "top" of the status or economic structure.

4. The assumption of covertness, which allows analysts to assert that somewhere "behind the scenes" things are exactly the opposite from the way they seem.

5. The "balance of power" assumption, which holds that an apparently powerless economic elite is "really" powerful because of its (undemonstrated) strategic position among community groups.

83. Recent works citing stratification studies with approval include: Ernest A. T. Barth, "Community Influence Systems: Structure and Change," *Social Forces*, 40 (Oct. 1961), 58-63; Orrin E. Klapp and L. Vincent Padgett, "Power Structures and Decision-making in a Mexican Border City," *Am. J. Soc.*, 65 (Jan. 1960), 400–06; William H. Form and Warren L. Sauer, "Organized Labor's Image of Community Power Structure," *Social Forces*, 38 (May 1960), 332–41; Ted C. Smith, "The Structuring of Power in a Suburban Community," *Pacific Sociological Review*, 3 (Fall 1960), 83–88; Peter H. Rossi, "Power and Community Structure," *Midwest Journal of Political Science*, 4 (Nov. 1960), 390–401; Nicholas Babchuk, Ruth Marsey, and C. Wayne Gordon, "Men and Women in Community Agencies: A Note on Power and Prestige," *Am. Soc. Rev.*, 25 (June 1960), 399–403; Harry R. Dick, "A Method for Ranking Community Influentials," *Am. Soc. Rev.*, 25 (June 1960), 395–99; William V. D'Antonio, William H. Form, Charles P. Loomis, and Eugene C. Erickson, "Institutional and Occupational Representations in Eleven Community Influence Systems," *Am. Soc. Rev.*, 26 (June 1961), 440–46; Howard J. Ehrlich, "The Reputational Approach to the Study of Community Power," *Am. Soc. Rev.*, 26 (Dec. 1961), 926–27; Richard A. Schermerhorn, *Society and Power* (New York, Random House, 1961), pp. 87–105.

6. The "power potential" allegation, which holds that the economic (or social) elite could determine community decisions if it wanted to, and only refrains because of lack of interest in community affairs.

These six formulas explain away evidence indicating that the economic and status elites of communities are not as important as stratification theory insists. All of these explanations share at least one common element: all are impossible to confirm or disprove *in principle*. All depend for their "correctness" upon the definitions adopted by analysts rather than upon the evidence of the facts.

Three methodological errors leading to failure to test propositions empirically have been noted. First, there is the identification, by definition, of economic or status elites with power elites, as in the cases of Miller, Barth and Abu-Laban, and Baltzell. Second, there is the strong propensity to interview only, or primarily, businessmen, as in the cases of Hunter, Coates and Pellegrin, and Schulze. This fundamental decision of research strategy is understandable in the light of the expectations of stratification theory, but it is incomprehensible as a device for *testing* these expectations. Third, there is the habit of never specifying issues. This not only short-circuits communication between researcher and respondent and makes tests of the accuracy of responses difficult, if not impossible, but, given the disproportionate number of businessmen among respondents, it also guarantees that issues salient to businessmen will receive disproportionate attention. This in turn provides an artificially produced confirmation of the hegemony of businessmen.

Finally, factual information given in these community studies by no means unambiguously supports the five key propositions of stratification theory. Thus the conclusion of this chapter must be that the stratification studies of community power all exhibit symptoms of scientific inadequacy resembling those postulated at the beginning of Chapter 2.

# 4. Who Rules in New Haven?

## An Empirical Test
## of the Stratification Theory

The two preceding chapters point to inadequacies in a good many studies of community power, but it can be argued that none of these studies was a faithful test of the key propositions of the stratification theory. It is still possible that stratification theory gives a correct description of community power and politics in America. It appears that each of the key propositions has often been phrased so as to make it extremely difficult, if not impossible, to design empirical tests for them. The purpose of this chapter is to design and make such a test, using data from a study of New Haven, Connecticut, which was collected for the most part in the years 1957 and 1958. Perhaps the simplest way to begin would be to describe briefly the New Haven research, leaving a defense of its adequacy for later.

The major purpose of the study was to explain certain events which took place in New Haven. These events related to the making and executing of public policy in several issue-areas, of which three will be discussed here in detail: urban redevelopment, public education, and political nominations. A variety of methods were used to identify the events we wanted to study. Publicly visible participants in some events in each issue-area were identified by reading the newspapers and examining public documents. Participants in and observers of each issue-area were interviewed and asked to describe the events in which they were involved, their roles, and the roles of others. For almost a year, a member of the research group observed the course of events from a position close to the Mayor and his Development Administrator; we discovered that they were clearly the most significant actors in urban redevelopment and were quite important in other issue-areas as well. The methods used to gather data were, in other words, comparable in some ways to those of the journalist, the historian, the anthropologist, and the sociologist.[1]

In what sense were public policies in these issue-areas going to be "explained"? Since the research was organized around the question "who governs?", we wanted to frame explanations that would identify participants in policy-making and describe what they did. The intention was to arrive at some understanding of normal policy-making processes in each of three issue-areas and to compare these findings with conventional theories of policy-making—which also describe who participates and how—such as a theory of the ruling elite or a theory of majoritarian democracy. My purpose here, as distinct from the more general purposes of the New Haven study, is to present a picture of the normal policy-making processes in each of the three issue-areas and then to compare this with the picture presented in stratification theory.

URBAN REDEVELOPMENT

Urban redevelopment was the first issue-area selected for study. It was an obvious choice; the redevelopment program during the years studied was by most criteria the biggest thing in New Haven.[2] Urban redevelopment had been the focus of several campaigns for re-election by the incumbent mayor, Richard C. Lee. The program had gained nationwide publicity in popular magazines.[3] The federal government had spent, allocated, or promised more redevelopment money per capita

1. The sociologist Morris Zelditch, Jr., has written a very useful essay in which he discusses various strategies of field research, "Some Methodological Problems of Field Studies," *Am. J. Soc.*, 67 (March 1962), 566–76. Zelditch enumerates three types of information: Distributions and Frequencies, Incidents and Histories, and Generally Known Roles and Statuses. The three ways of obtaining information he mentions are Participant Observation, Interviewing Informants, and Enumerations and Samples. Each of these methods was employed in the New Haven study and all three types of information were gathered and put together in a variety of ways. For a full description of the field research methods employed in the New Haven study, see Dahl, *Who Governs?*, pp. 330–43.

2. Criteria by which policies can be ranked according to their importance are enumerated in the appendix to this chapter. No doubt other criteria will occur to the ingenious reader. But there seems, in any case, to be no doubt that each of the issue-areas studied in New Haven comfortably meets any criteria of importance likely to be proposed.

The politics of the New Haven urban redevelopment program are reported on and discussed in detail in Raymond E. Wolfinger, *The Politics of Progress, op.cit.* See also Dahl, *Who Governs?*, esp. chap. 10.

3. For example, Jeanne R. Lowe, "Lee of New Haven and His Political Jackpot," *Harper's Magazine* (Oct. 1957), and Joe Alex Morris, "He Is Saving a 'Dead' City," *The Saturday Evening Post* (April 19, 1958).

to New Haven than to any other city in the nation.[4] The program was an ambitious one, involving the razing of much of the central business district and a series of projects designed to transform the physical plant of a large portion of the city.

Who wanted urban redevelopment? By 1957, practically everyone in New Haven who had anything to say in public strongly favored the program. But a few years before, urban redevelopment was not especially salient as a community issue.

The change in the climate of opinion from indifference to strong support was largely the work of one man, Mayor Lee. As an alderman, Lee had had a mild interest in city planning, but this interest was not expressed at all strongly in two losing races for mayor which Lee ran in 1949 and 1951. During the latter campaign, however, Lee recalled certain experiences that persuaded him of the need for urban redevelopment as a method of alleviating the human misery which accompanied slum life.

> I went into the homes on Oak Street and they set up neighborhood meetings for me . . . three and four in one night. And I came out from one of those homes on Oak Street, and I sat on the curb and I was just as sick as a puppy. Why, the smell of this building; it had no electricity, it had no gas, it had kerosene lamps, light had never seen those corridors in generations . . . and there . . . right there was when I began to tie in all these ideas we'd been practicing in city planning for years in terms of the human benefits that a program like this could reap for a city.

By 1953 Lee was aware of the possibilities for federal aid contained in the Housing Act of 1949. He needed a positive issue with which to confront the voters after two narrow losses at the polls in campaigns in which he felt he had concentrated too much on the shortcomings of his opponent. It would, however, be inaccurate to suppose that in 1953 Lee envisioned a redevelopment program as vast as the one subsequently undertaken. Rather, the redevelopment program grew piecemeal, as Lee's popularity and his electoral margins grew. In the beginning, urban redevelopment was not simply a social experiment testing whether the city center could be saved from blight and commercial strangulation; it was also a political experiment in which Lee sought to discover whether sufficient political support could be rallied behind such a program.

4. See Dahl, *Who Governs?*, pp. 121–33, esp. Fig. 10.1; Wolfinger, *The Politics of Progress*, pp. 133–56.

Lee pledged in 1953 to mount a coordinated attack on the problem of urban blight. He promised that within 60 days of the time he took office he would appoint a nonpartisan committee of distinguished and representative citizens to advise him on the general problem of "doing something" about the decay in the center of New Haven.

He won the election, but found it impossible to redeem his pledge within the time he had allotted himself. Several distinguished business leaders turned him down when he asked them to head his Citizens Action Commission. At least one leader declined to serve because he felt that Lee was too inexperienced to succeed. However, Lee persevered and finally persuaded a banker, Carl Freese, to become his CAC chairman. Freese in turn assisted Lee in filling the other places on the Commission. As it was finally constituted, the Commission included what Mayor Lee called the "biggest muscles" in the community: heads of most of New Haven's largest business firms, two representatives of Yale, three high-ranking bank officers, labor leaders, manufacturers, utility officers, Yankee Protestants, Italian and Irish Catholics, Jews, the leader of the Democratic party, and prominent Republicans (though no local Republican party officials).

This group was buttressed by numerous subject-matter subcommittees which drew heavily from the bipartisan, ethnically diverse population of civic activists throughout the greater New Haven area.

The influence of this conglomeration of economic, status, ethnic, and civic leaders on the making of urban redevelopment policies was negligible. But the CAC performed several significant functions. It acted as a sounding board for proposals which the city administration wished to try out before announcing them to the general public. It helped to sell the urban redevelopment program by opinion leadership within the various groups in the community. Finally, its nonpartisan quasi-official status gave the program an aura of having been "cleared" with "the people" and of being "above politics."

The Citizens Action Commission was an invention of great usefulness in assuring the political acceptability of urban redevelopment. But the Commission itself was not the source of redevelopment planning. Concrete, specific plans for redevelopment, site acquisition, relocation of residents, pricing of parcels for resale, and so on were the responsibility of the Redevelopment Agency. Coordination of these plans with the master plan for the city, traffic, zoning, housing code enforcement, and a variety of other city services were supervised by the office of the Development Administrator.

This office was also an innovation of Mayor Lee's and matches in significance his elevation of redevelopment to political prominence and then to nonpartisan untouchability. The invention of the office of Development Administrator (at a substantial salary) was the device Mayor Lee used to focus his entire city administration upon redevelopment. The job was created for Edward Logue, an energetic, aggressive, and able lawyer-administrator, to whom Mayor Lee delegated full authority to coordinate all governmental activities bearing on maintenance of the city's physical plant *in behalf of the redevelopment program.* This last phrase is crucial, because the existence of an office such as Logue's is not uncommon in communities with much less active redevelopment programs. In New Haven, however, the Development Administrator enjoyed unique powers because of the Mayor's commitment to urban redevelopment and because of his determination to make this commitment stick throughout the entire city administration.

The major substantive decisions on urban redevelopment were made by Logue, Lee, and H. Ralph Taylor, executive director of the Redevelopment Agency. Most of these decisions were made in secret. As one official said, the redevelopment program, like a submarine, "surfaced" only when it was legally or politically necessary to receive approval from the Board of Aldermen, the Redevelopment Agency, or the CAC. Our research group was unable to find a single case where this approval was not forthcoming.

Descriptions of CAC meetings were illuminating on this point. While few CAC members were willing to concede that they were a rubber stamp for the Mayor, we were able to uncover only a very few trivial instances in which modifications were made in plans presented by city technicians. More typical behavior was described to us by a CAC member in these words:

> Well, the matter was taken up by the Mayor at a meeting of the Citizens Action Commission. It was discussed and debated around and we agreed with the Mayor. He got his information, of course, from the traffic commission, from the engineers, from the Redevelopment Agency and all the others and he passed it on to us. We represent the group through which these decisions are filtered. I've often felt that the group as a group is inadequate in the sense that we don't really initiate anything as far as I can recall. We haven't yet initiated anything that I know of. We discuss what has been developed by the Redevelopment Agency or the City

Planning Commission or one of the other groups. The Mayor or somebody from one of these groups presents it to us and we discuss it, we analyze it, we modify some of it, we change—

*Could you give me an example of some case where you modified or changed some proposal?*

Well, I don't think that I can give you an example of anything where I can say that the Commission actually changed a proposal.

*You can't?*

No. I say actually changed—I don't recall any.

This does not mean that the Mayor, Logue, and Taylor were able to proceed without any constraints. In fact, decision-making in redevelopment was governed by a rather comprehensive set of constraints imposed on decision-makers from the outside. Many could be stretched or neutralized, but only by the application of a variety of rather esoteric skills—in negotiation with redevelopers, in the filling out of federal forms, in the gerrymandering of project areas, and so on. Hence the significance of these constraints varied from project to project. It would, I think, be incorrect to conclude that because Lee, Logue, and Taylor succeeded in surmounting many of these obstacles with ease they could not easily have stymied a less able or ambitious city administration.

First, rather strict rules and regulations were prescribed by the Housing and Home Finance Agency which granted the federal share of the costs of redevelopment programs. These regulations covered such items as (1) whether the area to be redeveloped was sufficiently deteriorated to fall under the federal program, (2) how the city planned to finance its share of the program, (3) whether the parcel to be redeveloped was suitably shaped and sized for reuse according to accepted planning practices, (4) whether the reuse plan submitted by the city conformed to the city's master plan and to good planning practices and was economically promising, (5) whether the proper clearances had been received from competent local authorities.

Second, the programs had to be economically feasible. Federal grants for urban redevelopment pay for planning and subsidize the city sufficiently so that it can buy properties, knock down buildings, and sell land at a loss to redevelopers. But the city must find redevelopers willing to risk their capital while staying within the strictures of a reuse plan that can be approved by the federal government.

Other economic problems relate to the retention of industries in the community. Suppose a large industrial establishment wishes to be included in a redevelopment area but is not, or wishes to be excluded but is slated for demolition. The city may run the risk of losing the industry unless it makes an attempt to accommodate to the firm's wishes. But suppose in order to accommodate the firm the federal rules of eligibility for a project are stretched? In such a case the whole project is jeopardized. Calculations of economic feasibility thus play a substantial part in determining the content of urban redevelopment proposals.

A third set of constraints involves political questions. One general political constraint which the New Haven redevelopment decision-makers felt heavily was the dread of having to raise taxes in order to meet the city's share of the cost of redevelopment. This political problem strained the ingenuity of planners to the limit. Their problem was in part to find ways of justifying to the federal government, as contributions toward the city's share of the costs, expenditures which the city had to make sooner or later anyway, and in part to find money in other ways, such as by raising assessments on real estate on a piecemeal basis.

Another political constraint—the necessity of obtaining clearance from the Board of Aldermen—was not a serious problem during the period of our study owing to Mayor Lee's overwhelming Democratic majority on the Board.

Still another political constraint was exercised by actors in the community: owners of properties to be acquired, for example, who had resources sufficient to tie the redevelopment program up in the courts. Acquisition costs and reuse plans had to a certain extent to be accommodated to these interests.

Throughout, as a general protection against litigation, an airtight case had to be presented at public hearings for each separate project. Supporters had to be mobilized. The conservative, anti-Lee newspapers had to be watched, and if possible kept at bay. Finally, and most importantly, Mayor Lee's political popularity, as measured by his electoral majorities, could not be jeopardized. All of these political problems entered into decisions on the content and timing of plans.

On the whole, opposition to the urban redevelopment program and its component projects was slight. The community consensus favoring the program was widespread and the level of saliency on the community political agenda was high. The Mayor, his appointees in the city government, and his allies in the community were mainly responsible for this. External factors favoring the program included the availability of federal funds and a general sense among many responsible New Haven citizens that it was appropriate to "do something" about their decaying downtown area. But these conditions existed in many communities having small redevelopment programs or none. Many constraints operated on decision-makers in this area, but substantial innovations in political organization, public opinion-making, municipal administration, and in the physical landscape were effected by virtue of the ingenuity, hard work, skill, and expertise of the Mayor and his principal assistants.[5]

## PUBLIC EDUCATION

In spite of the fact that as many as one-fifth of New Haven's school children are educated in private or parochial schools, the public school system of the city is by far the largest item in the municipal budget.[6] The determination of policy in this issue-area would be important if only because of the sheer size of the city's school system in comparison with other city services. But in addition the schools have great importance in any community as the major public agency which transmits to the young salient facts about the adult society. Hence a variety of valued outcomes are routinely distributed by decisions made in the area of public education. These outcomes do not relate exclusively to the distribution of jobs and money, but also to what is often loosely and somewhat melodramatically termed "control over the minds of the young."

During the years we were studying New Haven, several significant events in public education took place, including the sale of the city's two high schools and the erection of two new high schools, the appointment of a new assistant superintendent, and the emergence on several occasions of the previously uninfluential Board of Education as an important force in the process of policy-making.

New Haven's school system has a pyramidal table of organization, not unlike that of any large bureaucratic organization. The number and diversity of decisions made within this organization must, in the aggregate, be staggering. Thousands of students are placed, scheduled, tested, graded, promoted, and graduated. Truants are identified and pursued, or not. Textbooks are adopted or rejected. Teachers are hired, trans-

5. I am not, of course, assessing the "goodness" in any sense of the New Haven urban redevelopment plan nor am I suggesting that the plan will or will not succeed in doing what its proponents have hoped it would do.

6. See Dahl, *Who Governs?*, Chap. 11.

ferred, and promoted. And so on. Most of these decisions are, needless to say, decentralized and have only limited consequences. Hence a convenient way to begin a description of the "normal political process" in this issue-area would be to indicate that, as far as we know, the vast preponderance of decisions in the school system were made more or less according to the prescriptions implied in its organization chart. The most significant actor in most public education issues was therefore the superintendent of schools.[7]

In what ways did major decisions in public education reflect significant deviations from this pattern? Perhaps the most conspicuous deviations had to do with the sale and rebuilding of high schools, since these decisions were made primarily outside the organizational hierarchy of the school system.

New Haven's two high schools and a vocational school, all badly run down, were located in a downtown enclave completely surrounded by Yale University. Yale authorities were finding it quite difficult to acquire land for expansion, and the land the high schools occupied was from their point of view an especially desirable parcel. They were also concerned about the ever-present threat to precarious town-gown relations posed by the daily movement of high school students through Yale precincts on their way to and from school. Thus Yale's needs complemented the city's rather well. From either standpoint, the sale of this land was logical.

The main actor in this series of decisions was the Mayor. He proposed to the president of Yale that the university buy the old high schools. He conducted the major share of the negotiations on the price

7. Students of bureaucratic decision-making have repeatedly shown that workers in bureaucratic organizations quite often behave in ways which are not formally prescribed and which change significantly the goals their agencies actually seek. See, for example, Peter Blau, *The Dynamics of Bureaucracy* (Chicago, Univ. of Chicago Press, 1955); Blau, *Bureaucracy in Modern Society* (New York, Random House, 1956); James G. March and Herbert A. Simon, *Organizations* (New York, Wiley, 1958); Alvin Gouldner, *Patterns of Industrial Bureaucracy* (Glencoe, Free Press, 1954); Robert K. Merton et al., *Reader in Bureaucracy* (Glencoe, Free Press, 1952).

We did not conduct our research in New Haven in such a way that we could ascertain the extent to which people below the top levels of the school system had modified the outcomes of the system by emphasizing some aspects of their jobs and ignoring others. Evidence gathered in other bureaucracies suggests that some of this was going on in the New Haven school system but how much change or what kinds of changes were being introduced, I cannot say. In the appendix to this chapter I discuss how this gap in our research (i.e. the fact that we failed to study all but "major" decisions) bears on the question of the confidence that can be placed in the conclusions our study reached.

of the property. He participated actively in negotiations with the semi-autonomous Park Board on the location of the new schools, and, with his Development Administrator, made several significant decisions about the plans for the new buildings themselves.

The Mayor has, formally, only one vote out of eight on the Board of Education, although he appoints the other members to fixed terms of office (whose duration exceeds his own). In the protracted and arduous negotiations over the schools, the Mayor had the acquiescence of the entire Board, and the especially strong support of two members whom he had himself originally appointed.

These members—a Yale professor and a labor union leader (later joined by a headquarters official of a national educational organization) —formed a coalition within the Board; on a variety of issues they attempted to take certain initiatives they felt would improve the operation of the school system. There was a general feeling among them that the superintendent of schools had not surrounded himself with the ablest top assistants available; that, rather, in his promotions policy, he placed more emphasis on loyalty to him than on general competence. On the initiative of the new coalition, the Board took several steps which brought it into conflict with the superintendent.

The most important of these from the standpoint of the Board was the appointment of an assistant superintendent who was quite independent of the superintendent in her attitudes and professional commitments and who enjoyed high standing in her own right professionally and in the community. On the next most important issue, an attempt by the Board activists to change and to regularize promotions policy to a greater degree, the proposed plan failed to receive the support of the leading teachers' union and was not adopted.

The existence of two teachers' unions, a custodians' union, and a principals' association, and the close involvement of the leaders of these groups in both educational policy recommendations and election-year bargaining with public officials, suggests the possibility of other deviations from strict hierarchy in decision-making through the activity of interest groups. The appointment of a high official of one of the unions to an important post in one of the high schools occasioned unfavorable comment in the community during the course of our research. A more significant indication of the role of the unions in educational policy-making was the rejection of the personnel scheme proposed by the Mayor's close allies on the Board of Education. The activities of the teachers' unions are also alleged by many close observers of the city's politics to have been decisive in electing Mayor Lee's predecessor, William Celentano, in 1945.

One kind of decision in the school system seems especially vulnerable to interest-group activity. This is the hiring, transfer, and promotion of personnel. Factional alignments within the school hierarchy, the unions, and (for top-level vacancies) the Board of Education play a part in the determination of personnel policy. In addition, the leaders of New Haven's political parties have been known to take a rather persistent interest in the outcomes of personnel decisions, with varying degrees of success. The intervention of political leaders in personnel policy is no doubt related to a desire to do favors for political allies in order to build and maintain their political strength, and so it may be that party leaders are themselves, to a certain extent, transmitting pressures they are receiving from the leaders of ethnic voting groups in the community for "proper" representation in the upper echelons of the school system.

While the ethnic groups seem to be more interested in personnel than other kinds of policy, other interest groups also focus their attention on different aspects of school policy. At least one local PTA was able to force improvements of its school, and the unions have concerned themselves with general levels of compensation and work rules. The activities of these organizations have not been confined to formalities such as collective bargaining, but have also extended explicitly into attempts to mobilize public opinion and to influence the outcomes of elections. City administrations have, at least since 1945, found it expedient to attend to the preferences expressed by these groups, for fear of consequences at the next election.

Most decisions in public education, then, were made by educational administrators, more or less hierarchically. A set of particularly significant decisions was made in a process of negotiation in which the Mayor was the central figure. Other sets of significant decisions were made by means of negotiations within the Board of Education, among a cohesive group on the Board, the superintendent and miscellaneous interest groups, and between the Board and the superintendent, and still other decisions were made by negotiation between party leaders and educational administrators.

## POLITICAL NOMINATIONS

Public officials, as we have seen, played significant roles in community decision-making in New Haven. But how did these public officials come to occupy the positions which made it possible for them to have an impact on outcomes? Most of the public officials mentioned thus far were appointed to office, and most of the appointments were made by the mayor, who is elected every two years.

New Haven's charter provides for a "weak mayor" form of government in which the chief executive is constitutionally constrained in three ways. First, legislation and the budget must be approved by the Board of Aldermen, a body of elective officials who represent each of the thirty-three wards of New Haven. Second, many executive prerogatives are vested in semi-autonomous boards and commissions whose members are appointed by the mayor for fixed terms, usually longer than his own. The mayor is normally an *ex officio* member of each of these boards, but he is not a member of the Board of Aldermen. Third, some executive responsibilities devolve upon lesser city officials who are also elected bi-annually: the city treasurer, the city clerk, the registrar of vital statistics, and so on.

In practice, the office of the mayor provides great opportunities for an ambitious and popular incumbent to be as strong as he likes. The many boards and commissions provide the mayor with numerous opportunities to make appointments with a variety of ends in view. He can use his powers of appointment to make friends and mend fences, to further policies he favors, or to confer honors. In addition, the mayor has many other indulgences and deprivations at his command. Many millions of dollars in contracts for insurance, for snow removal and garbage collection, for printing, and so on move through various agencies under the mayor's aegis. The laws may be enforced rigidly or leniently. City agencies may hire, transfer, and discharge personnel.

Obviously the manipulability of outcomes from the mayor's office varies from case to case, and a variety of informal constraints reduces the likelihood that all conceivable opportunities will be grasped by any one mayor; nonetheless the opportunities are there. No other city official enjoys comparable opportunities, although the city courts, whose judges are appointed by the governor, also distribute indulgences. These were allocated in New Haven mostly in accordance with the wishes of the local political leader, John Golden.

The extent to which public officials distribute the indulgences of their offices autonomously has for years been a matter of some interest to students of politics.[8] In New Haven, it appears that most elected

8. The literature on presidential appointments to high-level office is most intriguing on this point. Dean Mann and Jameson Doig of the Brookings Institution are currently conducting a large-scale historical study of presidential appointments in order to

officials are granted nomination on the condition that the patronage of their office will be placed at the disposal of the party leaders instrumental in nominating them. This was not the case with Mayor Lee, who cooperated on equal terms with his party leader, John Golden, but his autonomy has been a temporary phenomenon earned by smashing successes at the polls in 1957 and 1959. A public official said in 1962, after an election in which Lee's majority was sharply reduced, "This patronage thing ebbs and flows. Now they don't go to [Mayor Lee] so much, but they're more likely to go to John Golden for favors."

If public office is a base of influence of major significance in determining the outcomes of public policy, then the process of nominating public officials is likewise of major significance. Both major parties in New Haven are well organized and normally have a fighting chance in every election. That is, a popular candidate running on either ticket has a good chance of winning—a circumstance which is not typical of American cities.

New Haven is an ethnically diverse community. The largest minority groups are composed of the children and grandchildren of Irish and Italian immigrants. The Irish appear to predominate in the Democratic party, and the Italians in the Republican. Both parties, however, take pains to appeal to both groups.[9] A typical city ticket for either party will have Irish, Italian, Jewish, Polish, Yankee, and Negro "names" on it. There appears to be a slight tendency for the smaller ethnic groups to pre-empt minor places on the ticket. For example, someone of Polish descent is customarily nominated for sheriff.

Although ethnic segregation is declining, New Haven's population is still clustered residentially more or less according to ethnic groups, and the ward political organizations and nominees for aldermen reflect these clusters. Temporary variations from this pattern occasionally occur, as, for example, when Negroes move into previously white areas but the ward committee continues to nominate white aldermen.

---

answer some of the questions about the actual extent of presidential autonomy raised by Hoover Commission proposals for a senior civil service and strong academic objections that this would harm the political position of the President. For highlights of this debate see George A. Graham, "The Presidency and the Executive Office of the President," *Journal of Politics, 12* (Nov. 1950), 599–621; Stephen K. Bailey, "The President and His Political Executives," *The Annals, 307* (Sept. 1956), 24–36; Wallace S. Sayre, "The Presidency and the Political Executives" (mimeo.) delivered at the Conference on the Political Executive, Woodrow Wilson School, Princeton, N.J., March 1956; James W. Fesler, "Administrative Literature and the Second Hoover Commission Reports," *Am. Pol. Sci. Rev., 51* (March 1957), 135–57.

9. Dahl, *Who Governs?*, pp. 38–39, 45–46, 110, 216–17.

The first general point that can be made is that most political nominations are determined by the logic of the situation described above.
Prospective candidates must display an ethnic membership appropriate
for the office they aspire to. Which ethnic group gets which office
depends on the competitive situation between the parties and the probable distribution of offices among prospects on the rest of the party slate.
Second, the prospective candidate must be "deserving," that is, un-
usually well qualified for the office, or especially well liked, or, no doubt
most important, a party worker. Some combination of all of these
factors enters into party slate-making. Mayor Lee's own nomination reflected this process. He had worked his way up through the ranks,
joining the party at an early age and participating in party work over
many years. Although he came from mixed Irish, Scottish, and English
ancestry, for public and party purposes he referred to himself as Irish,
the predominant ethnic strain in the New Haven Democratic party.
Some years ago, Lee sided with party leader John Golden in a particularly serious intraparty fight, and thereafter Golden assisted Lee's ad-
vancement to a position of leadership on the Board of Aldermen and
subsequently to candidacy for mayor.

How are the varying claims of competing aspirants for public office
adjudicated? Who determines the actual party slate and selects the
strategy of appeal to the voters which the slate implies? For the Democratic party, during the years of our study, this process rested almost
wholly with three men; John Golden (Democratic national committee-
man), Mayor Lee, and Arthur T. Barbieri (Democratic town chairman).

Each of these men had somewhat independent, though overlapping,
bases of power: Golden had old and close connections throughout the
party organization, including ties with the courts and statewide and
up-county party leaders; Lee had great popularity with the electorate,
which he nourished by exercising his considerable skills in public relations, and he controlled the city administration, with its several hundred patronage appointments annually and millions of dollars in contracts
of various kinds; and Barbieri, the weakest of the three, dispensed a
great deal of patronage directly as managing head of the party organization, a position he attained through Lee and Golden. Differences in
temperament, age, background, and political support among these three
men made policy disagreements among them possible—indeed even
probable—on many occasions. But none of the three seems to have desired a showdown, especially over a trivial matter—and most matters

were likely to be defined as trivial by successful politicians as interdependent as these three.

They were known to have split on some policy issues; Barbieri, for example, is supposed to have been responsible for the defeat of a charter reform referendum, which Lee favored, in 1955, and Golden opposed a charter proposal backed by Lee in 1958.[10] In general, however, the three leaders worked out a pattern of consultation. Golden and Barbieri were largely indifferent to policy questions, except as they affected elections and contracts. This left a broad but vague zone of indifference within which Lee could determine the policies of the party in New Haven. Lee seldom found it worthwhile to back policies distasteful to the other two, since he could innovate in so many areas without provoking their opposition. Candidate selection is one area of great importance to the morale of the organization, but, except for the position of mayor, has limited policy consequences. The party organization treated nomination for office as a kind of patronage; election to offices other than mayor and probate judge did not confer on the office-holder any independence of the party organization in dispensing the patronage normally attached to the office. For these reasons, all three leaders could afford to allow the process of candidate selection to become a quasi-technical problem of putting together a ticket that would maximize appeals to the electorate and maintain the good will of rank-and-file party workers by following the well-known rules propounded above.

While the Democratic party leadership during 1957–59 consisted of a peaceable coalition, New Haven Republicans presented a somewhat more disorganized picture. There was definite rivalry between Frank Lynch, the "old" boss whose local power was based on his connections with past Republican governors and the state party leadership, and William Celentano, an ex-mayor who not unexpectedly enjoyed great personal popularity among New Haven's very large segment of Italian Republican voters. In 1958 Lynch controlled more wards, but Celentano, in coalition with the leader of his faction, George DiCenzo, controlled one entire senatorial district. Celentano was the strongest Republican mayoralty candidate, and this was the major base of his power. In a variety of instances, these two factions found it difficult to compose their differences. Lynch felt Celentano failed to cooperate sufficiently with him in dispensing City Hall patronage when Celentano was mayor. This was no doubt true since Lynch opposed Celentano's nomination

10. Discussed in detail in Wolfinger, *The Politics of Progress*, pp. 357–90.

as mayor in 1945, the year Celentano succeeded in overturning the Democratic regime of Mayor Murphy. Celentano felt that Lynch was equally at fault for not letting him share state patronage during John Lodge's term as governor. Celentano also felt that Lynch failed to boost him for lieutenant governor with the state leadership.

Celentano refused steadfastly to run against the extremely popular Mayor Lee, apparently preferring to wait until Lee moved on to higher office. Lynch and his ally, Republican town chairman Henry DeVita, were unable to find a candidate for mayor who could beat Lee, and the Celentano forces probably worked covertly against Republican nominees for mayor in order to enhance Celentano's intraparty position. Needless to say, Lee encouraged the DiCenzo-Celentano segment of the Republican party, which considered his success (and, they hoped, his subsequent movement out of New Haven city politics) a prerequisite to its own.

## THE STRATIFICATION THEORY REVISITED

We now return to the five key propositions of the stratification theory. Are these propositions useful in analyzing information about policy-making in New Haven? Or, alternatively, what does a description of policy-making processes in New Haven suggest about the relevance of the five propositions?

First, did an economic or status elite make significant decisions in any of the three issue-areas studied? Obviously the answer depends on the definition of the term "economic or status elite." As we have seen, no uniform criteria for inclusion in these elites are specified in the literature, nor are elites even defined as necessarily having any particular size. These are matters of some inconvenience to a student who wishes to make an independent test of the stratification theory. If we cannot be sure what the criteria for inclusion in the elite group are, then we cannot be sure whether any particular individual satisfies these criteria, and the theory can never be substantiated or disproved. I shall proceed, however, under the assumption that, as social scientists, stratification theorists value empirical validation of their theories, and so I shall suggest criteria that can be used to identify members of New Haven's economic and social "elites."

The definition of "economic elite" to be used here is an adaptation of the definition Schulze used in his stratification analysis of Cibola.[11] For

11. Schulze's criteria for determining the composition of the economic elite are the most inclusive of any stratification study that describes operations for identifying an

the purposes of studying New Haven, let us assume that the economic
leaders of the community are to be found among the following groups:
(1) the president and chairman of the board of every company having
a total assessed evaluation putting it among the city's top 50 taxpayers
during any of the five years 1953–58; (2) any individual whose total
assessed evaluation during the years 1957 or 1958 was greater than
$250,000; (3) the presidents and chairmen of the board of all banks and
utilities; (4) any individual who was a director of a New Haven bank
or of three or more local corporations having an assessment of $250,000
or more or employing more than 50 if a manufacturer, or employing
more than 25 if a retailer.[12] These four criteria yield a list of 239
names, which we may take as a suitable "economic elite" for the purposes of our study.

Who are the status elite? The New Haven *Blue Book*, a privately published social register last issued in 1951, identifies some 2,000 families.[13]
In this book special mention is made of the names of the "Cotillion
Set," the group of families which subscribed to the Assembly of the
New Haven Lawn Club in that year. This Cotillion list is published annually in the New Haven *Register*. All families subscribing in 1951,
1958, or 1959 may be considered members of the social status elite, a
list of 231 names after duplicates are stricken.[14]

We may now inquire: can any of the major participants in the issue-
areas just described be found on either of these lists? The answer is yes.

In the field of public education, A. Whitney Griswold, president of
Yale and a member of both economic and status elites, agreed in behalf
of Yale to purchase the old high schools. The detailed negotiations
were carried forward by others, however. The purchase of the high
schools afforded political opponents of Mayor Lee the opportunity to
charge that the Mayor was controlled by Yale interests. Lee, although

economic elite. The criteria used here are even more inclusive than Schulze's. See
Schulze, "The Role of Economic Dominants in Community Power Structure," *Am.
Soc. Rev.*, 23 (Feb. 1958), 3–9. This definition has previously been used in my
article, "Three Problems in the Analysis of Community Power," *Am. Soc. Rev.*, 24
(Dec. 1959), 796–803, and in Dahl, *Who Governs?*, p. 67.

12. The President of Yale University, one of the three largest employers in New
Haven, is included in the list of economic leaders, although he meets none of the
criteria for inclusion since Yale is not a manufacturer or a retailer, or as heavy a
taxpayer as it would be if its land were put to commercial uses.

13. New Haven, 1951.

14. The temptation would ordinarily be great to use all 2,000 families in the *Blue
Book* as the status elite. The decision to use the somewhat more restricted Cotillion
list is based on the availability of Cotillion lists during the years 1958 and 1959, at
which point the *Blue Book* was almost a decade out of date.

not a college man himself, had been director of the Yale News Bureau before he became mayor and was known to prize highly his social connections with members of the Yale faculty and administration.[15] However, Lee's surface vulnerability on this point seemed to inspire him to lean over backward in his dealings with the university. A substantial city tax assessment was slapped on Yale's handsome new hockey rink. Yale's attempts to purchase redevelopment land from the city for middle-income faculty apartments were balked by stringent conditions set by the Mayor. And, on the high schools, Mayor Lee asked and received an extremely high price, three million dollars. A Yale official once said, "as the university sees it . . . we paid the city more for those schools than either they were worth intrinsically or than the city could have got from any other purchaser."

Members of the social elite appear in another connection in the area of public education. When Mayor Lee decided to sell the high schools, it became necessary to locate land on which to build new high schools. The problem of cost pointed to park land as the solution, so it became necessary for the Board of Education to ask the Park Board to release some land for this purpose. Protracted negotiations ensued over what park land this was to be.

While all the boards in New Haven's government are to a certain extent autonomous, the Park Board is especially so because it consists in part of the high-status descendants of donors of park land to the city, who sit on the Board by legal right. Thus several high-status individuals, by virtue of their membership on the Park Board, participated significantly in the negotiations over the location of the new high schools.

The Board of Education asked for two sites which they thought were ideally located. An even more important consideration was that these sites, Edgewood Park to the west and Rice Field to the east, would require little or no expensive site preparation. The Park Board refused to give up these locations, however, and proposed alternative sites. The Board of Education, on the advice of the Mayor, accepted Beaver Pond in the west, hoping for a concession by the Park Board on the eastern

15. A stratification analyst, Floyd Hunter, has referred to Lee as a businessman-mayor in a review of Dahl, *Who Governs?*, in *Administrative Science Quarterly, 6* (March 1962), 517–19. It may be well in view of this to quote Dahl (p. 118) on Lee's background: "He came from a Catholic working-class family of mixed English, Scottish and Irish origins . . . went to New Haven public schools, worked as a reporter on the *Journal Courier*, served as an officer in the Junior Chamber of Commerce, had a brief spell in the army, and from 1943 until his election as mayor was in charge of Yale's public relations."

location. Instead the Park Board suggested three possibilities in succession. The first abutted a rundown and patently undesirable neighborhood. The second would have wiped out a large section of the most used park land in the city and would have provoked a great outcry. The third alternative, which the Board of Education finally accepted with reluctance, was a rather swampy wasteland which required over a million dollars in site preparation before construction could begin. This was unquestionably a major defeat for the Mayor and the Board of Education.

Finally, one of Mayor Lee's appointees to the Board of Education was a member of the status elite. This was Maynard Mack, professor of English at Yale. Mack was recruited to educational policy-making when he became active in the PTA in the neighborhood grammar school where three of his children were enrolled. The physical condition of this particular school was, in his words, "really dreadful," so parents in the area formed a committee to persuade the city to rehabilitate the school. This movement coincided with an election campaign, with the result that many improvements were actually made in the school building. As a PTA president and a leader in this controversy, Mack came to Mayor Lee's attention, and when Lee was elected and formed a Citizens Advisory Council for Education—a forerunner of other citizens action committees—Mack was asked to join. About six months after Mayor Lee took office in 1953, two seats on the school board fell vacant. In one case a member's term had expired, and in the other the Mayor succeeded in forcing a sitting member to resign. Mack and a labor leader, Mitchell Sviridoff, were then appointed to the Board, where they formed the nucleus of the activist coalition described earlier.

In urban redevelopment, several members of the economic or status elite performed vital tasks in aid of the Mayor. In particular, the bankers Carl Freese and Frank O'Brion (who headed the Redevelopment Agency) were instrumental in soliciting the support or at least the acquiescence of business leaders, a few of whom were opposed to the urban redevelopment program. Freese's successor as chairman of the CAC, utility executive Lucius Rowe, also actively supported the redevelopment program. Rowe was especially vigorous in his support of the main precondition of the program's continued success, namely, the continued electoral success of Mayor Lee. As many as 15 per cent of the names appearing on the literature of the Citizens Action Commission as members of the Commission or subsidiary committees could also be found on the list of the economic or status elite, but very few members of the

system, is perhaps the hardest area of all for an upper-class elite to control from behind the scenes because of the demands made by party organizations for candidates who can win. As I have indicated, we could find no instance of economic or status leaders dictating political nominations to suit themselves, aside from the leadership of John Golden, who is a party man first and only incidentally a member of the economic elite.

Thus we must reject the second proposition of the stratification theory.

The remaining three propositions fare no better. Is there a single power elite in the community? In each of the three issue-areas studied, entirely different decision-making processes could be identified. In urban redevelopment, a broadly based coalition consisting of civic leaders and municipal bureaucrats headed by a democratically elected official, the mayor, undertook sweeping innovations. In public education, some outcomes were achieved through the negotiations of the mayor, some through the efforts of a group of activists on the school board, some through the demands of interest groups, and most through the day-to-day workings of the school system bureaucracy, whose most significant actor was the superintendent. Political nominations were determined in part by custom and in part by strategic considerations between factions within the parties and between the two parties. In each issue-area different actors appeared, their roles were different, and the kinds of alternatives which they had to choose among were different. A very few actors appeared in more than one issue-area. Of these by far the most important was the mayor. The others had major roles in only one issue-area and played bit parts in a second. For example, President A. Whitney Griswold agreed to buy the high schools for Yale, a major decision in public education. In urban redevelopment, President Griswold appeared as the vice-chairman of the Citizens Action Commission, where he lent his prestigeful presence to several public meetings devoted to the discussion of the program.

In order to say that New Haven was ruled by a single power elite, we must find a small group, not selected by some democratic means, which was united in its policy aims and consistently got its way in more than one significant policy area. We could not find such a group in New Haven.

Even though there was no upper-class power elite, it still might be true that the outcomes of major decisions tended nonetheless to benefit members of the upper class more than any other group, thus favoring the long-run maintenance of this group.

But this is a difficult assertion to test. For example, are all owners of land in downtown New Haven similarly situated with respect to urban redevelopment decisions? Some landowners whose property was included regretted the fact, and one fought the redevelopment program. Others regretted *not* being included, and one of these fought the program. Still others were, in varying degrees, satisfied with the situation.

Whom did the new high schools benefit? The benefits and costs to any individual of these steel-and-concrete policy outcomes are diffuse and intangible and perhaps impossible to evaluate sensibly without making all sorts of highly questionable assumptions. The same is true of most other policy outcomes.

The only outcomes presenting a less ambiguous aspect are those actively espoused by a united upper class in opposition to others in the community. But we could find no decisions where even a substantial proportion of the upper class was active, where that portion of the upper class that was active was wholly united, or where they were substantially in less agreement with members of other classes than they were among themselves.

Thus we must also reject the proposition that major social conflicts in New Haven took place between the upper class and those below. In rejecting this last of the five key propositions of stratification theory as suitable for explaining decision-making events in New Haven, must we also, as well, reject the notion that indulgences and deprivations were distributed unevenly in the community? Did no one therefore rule? Was there no social conflict?

It would, as a matter of fact, be quite impossible to disprove the assertions of the stratification theory in a situation where there was no social conflict, just as it would be impossible to prove them. In New Haven there were many conflicts, some of them quite serious. But different patterns of conflict prevailed in different policy areas.

This is perhaps easiest to see in the area of public education, where the major conflict was a subdued antagonism between the superintendent and his supporters within the system, on the one hand, and the dominant faction on the Board of Education and its supporters, on the other.

This major conflict was superimposed upon the historical remains of two others: the original alignment of factions within the school system which supported and opposed the ouster by the present superintendent of his immediate predecessor; and, secondly, a continuing struggle by professionals in the school system to free personnel policies from "meddling" by party chieftains.

Often at stake as well were concrete matters of policy in which professionals disagreed with professionals, as in a running controversy over the testing program in the elementary schools. The Board of Education divided on the question of the wholesomeness of the high schools' annual Harvest Festival. Concrete issues such as these, and the advocates of the various sides of these issues, provided the bases for the significant conflicts in the field of education. Partisans could be identified not by their status characteristics, but only by their words and deeds relevant to actual controversies in the making of educational policy.

Urban redevelopment was an issue-area in which social conflict was held to a minimum by the strenuous efforts of the Mayor and his staff. On the original slum clearance, known as the Oak Street Project, and in the renewal of the Wooster Square section, which was the third phase of the city-wide program, opposition to the Mayor's plans was slight. This was true because most members of the community were wholly apathetic until aroused and educated by the Mayor to the possibilities of urban renewal. In addition, a few leaders in the community had recognized for years that something approximating these projects would be desirable if it could be achieved; and Mayor Lee achieved it cheaply by taking advantage of federal funds. No corporate group, save a scattering of disorganized slum landlords, stood to lose from the removal of the Oak Street eyesore, and the introduction into the adjacent area of the Connecticut Turnpike and feeder roads, built this time with state funds, was used by Mayor Lee as the occasion for accomplishing this project. In order to facilitate the Oak Street slum removal, it was necessary for Mayor Lee and his redevelopment staff to persuade the state highway department to change its original proposals, so as to bring the roads into conformity with plans for redevelopment. In this sense, the Mayor not only used the Turnpike as an opportunity for redevelopment, but also created this opportunity by negotiating for an extension of feeder roads through the worst of the slum area.

The second phase of urban redevelopment, the Church Street Project, was by far the most ambitious part of the program. This project involved razing a substantial portion of the city center, in which numerous retail stores were located. A group of small merchants who were directly affected objected strenuously to being removed from their places of business. Some of them were unable to sustain the loss of good will and improvements and were forced out of business. This group never attacked the redevelopment program per se, however; they only objected to its untoward effects on themselves. The city administration attempted to handle these objections by devising palliatives. It underwrote a 10 per cent reduction on rentals offered by the redeveloper to all displaced businesses taken into the new project;[19] it set up a business relocation office which turned out to be largely ineffectual, but which was designed to assist displaced merchants in finding suitable space; and, finally, the city aided financially in the construction of temporary housing for displaced businesses on cleared land in the downtown area.

The small merchants' objections to the redevelopment program were aired primarily at public hearings. The city administration always took these public occasions seriously and generally succeeded in offsetting the testimony of dissidents by producing a tidal wave of support for the program in the form of public statements by leaders from all conceivable segments of the community: business, banking, real estate, labor, religious and human welfare civic groups, PTA's, ethnic minorities, and so on.

Other objections came from two retailers in the community, one of middling size, the other quite important. In dealing with these and one or two other economically powerful dissidents, the Mayor brought other economic leaders in on behalf of the city in private negotiations. Thus conflict in urban redevelopment found members of the upper class on both sides.

One major group in the community which was severely damaged by the success of redevelopment was the Republican party. Mayor Lee put a nonpartisan gloss on his redevelopment activities by soliciting and receiving the endorsement and support of prominent New Haven Republican businessmen. Logue ran a clean and efficient operation, generally free of the City Hall patronage system.

Republican politicians did their best to exploit dissatisfactions they could find. They charged that redevelopment plans were put through with callous and undemocratic haste. They accused the Board of Aldermen of being a rubber stamp. They criticized the sale of the high schools and of redevelopment land to Yale and attacked the city administration for delays in rebuilding on cleared land. Since party membership cuts across classes, it can be said that the rather important cleavage between Democrats and Republicans also tends to weaken the proposition that social conflict is primarily a matter of interclass warfare.

Intraparty conflict in New Haven over political nominations seldom occurred along class lines. There was sometimes disagreement over who was "entitled" to what position on a party ticket, and this conflict may

19. However, the redeveloper was not obliged (and was not likely) to take into his project all those displaced businessmen who wanted to come in—nor were the actual costs of rentals in the new project made known to the public or to the displaced merchants.

have involved representatives of different ethnic groups, but it was un-
thinkable in a city with New Haven's large, well-organized, ethnically
diverse population for either party purposefully to alienate any substantial
segment of the population.

In fact, New Haven politics shows a record of hospitality especially to
the numerous members of lower-status groups, such as the Italians, who
were courted in earlier years, in particular, by the Ullman brothers,
long-time leaders of the Republican party.[20]

As I have indicated, conflict between and within the parties reflected
cleavages between individuals having commitments to different factions
rather than to different classes, and in fact even party factions often
attempted to achieve as socially heterogeneous a popular following as
they could possibly muster.

It is, however, fair to say that there was some residue of ethnic conflict in the slight tendency for the Irish voters to cluster in the Democratic party and the Italians in the Republican party. Nonetheless, both
parties continuously strove to appeal to the entire electorate, and men of
both Irish and Italian descent occupied positions of leadership in both
parties.

While the Irish-Italian split was the most obvious large-scale cleavage
along social lines in New Haven politics, I have the impression that
stratification writers would hesitate to call intramural battles between
such recent immigrants true class conflicts. They seem to have had in
mind conflicts between the economic and social elite and those below,
and, in this respect, the New Haven political record is almost totally
barren. The only instance which may fit this theory was the contest for
president of the Board of Aldermen a few years ago between two Republicans: a man of Italian extraction, who later became Republican city
chairman, and a prominent Yankee.

Mayor Celentano favored the Yankee, on the ground that he was ap-
pointing a tremendous number of Italians to high posts in the city government and felt that the Yankee segment of the Republican city coalition
deserved the recognition of the presidency. Republican aldermen declined to cooperate, however, and the gavel passed to the Italian candidate. In fact, what looks on the surface like a Yankee vs. Italian conflict
was actually a disagreement between the Celentano–DiCenzo (mostly
Italian-led) wing of the Republican party, which sponsored the Yankee,
and the Lynch (mostly Irish and Yankee-led) wing of the party, which
backed the Italian candidate who eventually won.

20. Dahl, *Who Governs?*, p. 39.

We must conclude, first, that the five propositions of the stratification theory were not validated by the New Haven research. Insofar as they could have been rejected, they were, I think, rejected. Moreover, they do not seem to have been overly helpful in eliciting a description of how decision-making in New Haven took place. This suggests once again a notion originally discussed in the course of the earlier close examination of the stratification studies of specific communities. It may be that in communities where the stratification theory guided research, significant decision-making events and activities were unintentionally but systematically neglected.

## APPENDIX: DID THE NEW HAVEN STUDY ADEQUATELY TEST THE STRATIFICATION THEORY?

It seems appropriate at this point to digress from the main thrust of my argument long enough to consider certain methodological issues raised by this approach to the problems of testing the propositions of the stratification theory with New Haven data. There are a great many difficulties associated with making a test of this kind. The key propositions themselves change slightly in their empirical references from study to study and it may be that, despite my best efforts, I have failed to capture the intentions of some stratification writers in the operations by which I sought to validate or invalidate the propositions. In Chapter 6, a systematic comparison is made of the methods used in New Haven and the methods used by stratification writers. In this appendix, I want to deal only with the question: is the method employed here adequate to accomplish its avowed purpose of making an empirical test of the stratification theory?

I would argue that the method is adequate if certain simplifications, designed to make the propositions accessible to a test, are allowed. It is generally understood that without some sort of arbitrary simplifications research is impossible. A suitable criterion by which the adequacy of a test can be judged is whether or not the simplifications introduced by the research design seem likely to prejudice the outcomes of the research.

The first simplification I made was to stipulate that to "rule" meant to initiate, modify, veto, or in some visible manner act so as to change outcomes of selected community decisions. How were these decisions selected? Two alternative strategies initially seemed feasible. I could have designated as "rulers" of New Haven those who prevailed on "representative" decisions. In pursuing the strategy of examining "important" decisions, I imposed a drastic simplification upon the complexity of the world, but the reasons for doing so seemed compelling.

We can, I think, in principle rank decisions according to their importance by making use of one or another, or a combination, of at least four criteria:

1. How many people are affected by outcomes,
2. How many different kinds of community resources are distributed by outcomes,
3. How much in amount of resources are distributed by outcomes,
4. How drastically present community resource distributions are altered by outcomes.

Presumably decisions vary greatly in their importance, and fewer decisions will be important than unimportant. Furthermore, it is entirely possible, indeed likely, that, taken together, all "unimportant" community decisions affect more people and more resources than the few "important" community decisions. This would argue, then, that the best strategy for studying community power would have been to pick "representative" decision-making processes and study them. However, this argument leaves aside certain grave empirical difficulties. While it may be a reasonably simple matter to identify the most significant decisions in community life at any given time, the problem of assessing the comparative importance of decisions becomes hopelessly snarled as one attempts to measure the comparative importance of "middle" and "low" importance decisions whose ratings may vary only slightly one from another on a single scale or fall differently among the different criteria. In decisions of "low" importance, there is also an empirical problem of deciding what constitutes a "decision." Hence the universe of decisions is an expanding one. If this is the case, then it is in fact impossible to assess the representativeness of any given set of decisions.

If it is impossible to determine the extent to which a decision is representative of other decisions in a community, or of decisions which may come afterward, and if, as I suppose, it is about equally taxing on the researcher to study an important decision as an unimportant one, then it seems clear that it is possible to learn more about how community outcomes are achieved per unit of research resources by studying how "big" decisions are arrived at, and what the necessary and sufficient conditions are for the maintenance and change of these patterns.

This, then, is one rationale for studying "important" decisions. There seem to be no satisfactory criteria which would identify a universe of all decisions in the community so that a sample of "typical" or "representative" decisions could in principle be drawn.

The reader will recall that the goal of the New Haven study was given as "to explain certain events," identified as policy-making events. It has been pointed out to me that sometimes decisions that are *not* made are every bit as significant in determining policy outcomes as decisions that are made. Indeed, it has been suggested that non-events make more significant policy than do policy-making events. This is the kind of statement that has a certain plausibility and attractiveness but that presents truly insuperable obstacles to research. We can sound the depth of the abyss very quickly by agreeing that non-events are much more important than events, and inquiring precisely *which* non-events are to be regarded as most significant in the community. Surely not *all* of them. For every event (no matter how defined) that occurs there must be an infinity of alternatives. Then which non-events are to be regarded as significant? One satisfactory answer might be: those outcomes desired by a significant number of actors in the community but not achieved. Insofar as these goals are in some way explicitly pursued by people in the community, the method of study used in New Haven has a reasonable chance of capturing them. A wholly unsatisfactory answer would be: certain non-events stipulated by outside observers without reference to the desires or activities of community residents. This answer is unsatisfactory because it is obviously inappropriate for outsiders to pick among all the possible outcomes that did not take place a set which they regard as important but which community citizens do not. This approach is likely to prejudice the outcomes of research—as indeed, I believe I have shown it does.

Another methodological problem: assuming the findings from New Haven presented here are correct, what can we infer from them about other cities? About New Haven ten years from now? Strictly speaking, the answer is little or nothing. New Haven bears certain similarities to other cities, but our theory has not yet progressed to the point where we know with any degree of confidence *which* other similarities predict political similarities. Similarly, aside from some primitive notions of "habit" or "inertia," [21] we have little to go on which helps us predict the effects on future decision-making processes of present ones. Apparently one fact of life which must be reckoned with is the relatively rapid turnover of decision-makers in many issue-areas. For example, almost all the main actors in New Haven's urban redevelopment in 1958 had disappeared by 1962. Although Mayor Lee, the most essential actor of all, was still on the scene, who could tell how long he would remain?

Finally, are the arrangements I described a "power structure"? It seems to me arbitrary whether we call the various political processes described in New Haven a "power structure" or not. The disadvantages of doing so involve two inconvenient connotative meanings of the term: first, that power and the class or status structure of the community are linked in a certain way (i.e. the way the stratification writers describe) and, second, that the power distributions which prevail at the time of the study are so ingrained and likely to be repeated that they can be referred to as "structural" properties of the community's social life, that is, permanently fixed in some sense. The latter is an empirical question, but I am dubious that investigation would disclose an affirmative answer.

To conclude: if we are modest in the conclusions to be drawn from the New Haven study and if the simplifications introduced to make research possible are accepted as reasonable, then I believe the adequacy of the test of the five key propositions is demonstrated.

21. As suggested, for example, in James S. Coleman's exemplary monograph, *Community Conflict* (Glencoe, Free Press, 1957), p. 2 and passim.

# 5. Power and Social Stratification: Theory or Ideology?

If the key propositions of stratification theory were irrelevant and untrue in New Haven, and at the least misleading and questionable in other communities, why are they so widely used, defended, and "discovered" in community studies? It is not enough to say that these other community studies are wrong, because, although this may be the case, it is also true that they are all wrong in the same or closely similar ways. This phenomenon invites investigation, for social science demands not merely identification of errors, but, if possible, the diagnosis and correction of these errors in future research.

In this chapter, three possible explanations will be advanced for the fact that the political theory of so many students of community power led them seriously astray. One explanation is that their political tastes and preferences made them want to believe that the five key propositions were true of American communities, and they were therefore victims of their personal biases. Another explanation holds that the basic axioms and presuppositions of stratification theory are such that the five key propositions can be deduced logically from them, so that by accepting the basic axioms of stratification theory researchers were unwittingly led to accept the five propositions. A third line of argument, supplementary to the second, holds that researchers were deceived by the entire intellectual framework of stratification theory. This explanation suggests that, embedded in the literature of social stratification, there are criteria governing the applicability of stratification analysis to society, and, by violating these criteria, students of community power made it highly probable that their findings would be faulty.

Let us consider the third explanation first. We can treat stratification theory, in its broadest outline, as an intellectual perspective which views society as an organism analogous in its structure to a layer cake. Writers on social stratification discuss such matters as who belongs in what layer and why, what goes on in each layer, and what relations are like between people in different layers. Stratification itself refers to the distributions of values in society. The way in which these values are distributed is critical: inequalities must exist, and, more than that, must persist if we are to say that stratification has taken place in a social system. Let us examine the rules of stratification analysis implied in this characterization.

We can think of values as things or events desired by individuals and groups in society. The values most often employed in modern stratification analysis are variants of the following three: life chances, prestige, and power. It is asserted—and, where not asserted, implied—in stratification analysis that these three values are distributed unequally in society, that they can be quantified at least roughly by the observer, and that individuals, or at least "classes" of individuals, are ordered transitively with respect to their possession of each value, so that it can be said that if A has more of value X than B and B than C, then A has more of value X than C. This third step gives an element of the stability mentioned above; it is also presumed in stratification analysis that everyone in a nuclear family will enjoy the same value-position with respect to each value and that these value-positions will tend to be passed on from generation to generation in the same family.[1]

1. Some of the general and theoretical works from which these criteria are drawn include Bernard Barber, *Social Stratification* (New York, Harcourt, Brace, 1957); Walter Buckley, "Social Stratification and Social Differentiation," *Am. Soc. Rev., 23* (Aug. 1958), 369–75; Reinhard Bendix and Seymour Martin Lipset, eds., *Class, Status and Power* (Glencoe, Free Press, 1953); John F. Cuber and William F. Kenkel, *Social Stratification in the United States* (New York, Appleton, 1954); Kingsley Davis, *Human Society* (New York, Macmillan, 1949); Davis and Wilbert E. Moore, "Some Principles of Stratification," *Am. Soc. Rev., 10* (April 1945), 242–49; Hans H. Gerth and C. Wright Mills, *Character and Social Structure* (New York, Harcourt, Brace, 1953); Milton M. Gordon, *Social Class in American Sociology* (Durham, Duke Univ. Press, 1958); Gordon, "A System of Social Class Analysis," *Drew Univ. Bulletin, 39* (Madison, N.J., Aug. 1951); Paul K. Hatt, "Social Stratification in the Mass Society," *Am. Soc. Rev., 15* (April 1950), 216–22; Joseph A. Kahl, *The American Class Structure* (New York, Rinehart, 1957); Harold F. Kaufman, Otis Dudley Duncan, Neal Gross, and William A. Sewell, "Problems of Theory and Method in the Study of Social Stratification in Rural Society," *Rural Sociology, 18* (March 1953), 12–24; Kurt B. Mayer, *Class and Society* (Garden City, Doubleday, 1955); Mayer, "The Theory of Social Classes," *Harvard Educational Review, 23* (Summer 1953), 149–67; Harold W. Pfautz, "The Current Literature on Social Stratification: Critique and Bibliography," *Am. J. Soc., 58* (Jan. 1953), 391–418; Harold W. Pfautz, "Social Stratification and Sociology," *Transactions of the Second World Congress of Sociology, 2* (1954), 311–20; Edward A. Shils, *The Present State of American Sociology* (Glencoe, Free Press, 1948); Melvin W. Tumin, "Some Principles of Stratification," *Am. Soc. Rev., 18* (Aug. 1953) (and Replies and Comments from Davis and Moore), pp. 387–97; Barber, Davis and Moore, and Talcott Parsons (in Bendix and Lipset, *Class, Status, and Power*, pp. 92–128) represent a school of theory which attempts to explain relative stabilities in the unequal prestige rankings of socially differentiated positions by positing a socially functional system

These are presumptions about empirical reality, hence criteria are immediately available for judging the conditions under which stratification analysis is appropriate. That is, insofar as conditions in the real world actually approximate the characteristics imputed to them by stratification analysts, the discussion of interclass relations and the life-styles, behavior, and attitudes of individuals as members of social classes is meaningful. But insofar as this is not the case stratification analysis may lead to great errors in describing social reality.

Let us turn to the three commonest dimensions of stratification theory and discuss briefly their appropriateness as variables in an analysis of modern American society. We shall be asking of each variable[2] in turn: (1) can it be quantified by an observer?[3] (2) is it distributed unequally in society? (3) are individuals and groups ordered transitively with respect to it? (4) does everyone in the nuclear family enjoy the same amount of it? (5) is it passed on from generation to generation in the same family?

A recent text in social stratification says of life chances:

> In modern industrial societies members of the same economic class
> have similar chances to obtain certain values and opportunities which

of rewards and penalties attaching in varying degrees to positions of more and less social responsibility and importance. Critics of this so-called "functional" approach (e.g. Buckley, Pfautz in *Transactions,* Tumin) charge that stratification implies greater stability than can be explained in this fashion; hence functionalists are explaining at most "social differentiation." Functionalists seem willing to accept this characterization cheerfully enough, if it is purged of its pejorative overtones (see Kingsley Davis, "The Abominable Heresy: A Reply to Dr. Buckley," *Am. Soc. Rev.,* 24 [Feb. 1959], 82–83). The rather more elaborate criteria of stability proposed here follow what seems to be the majority, nonfunctionalist approach; hence functionalist treatments of power are exempted from my criticism of stratification analyses at the appropriate points. I should point out, however, that functionalist treatments of power can be criticized on other grounds: e.g., they posit a central, society-wide value system according to which positions are ranked. But power in American society is decentralized in a variety of ways as, for example, by scopes (or issue-areas) and by constitutional entities, or jurisdictions; hence describing power in America by making reference to a central value system is bound to be unwieldy and inconvenient. See also Dennis H. Wrong, "The Functional Theory of Stratification: Some Neglected Considerations," *Am. Soc. Rev.,* 24 (Dec. 1959), 772–82.

2. Note that "variables" of stratification analysis are socially valued. In principle, hair color and foot size can be analyzed in the same way, but societies are not thought to be stratified on these bases because these human characteristics are not socially valued in any clearly recognizable fashion. See Robin M. Williams, Jr., *American Society* (New York, Knopf, 1951), 79–80.

3. Quantification does not necessarily refer to exact counting. It may equally well refer to rough estimates of "more or less," provided only that some relatively stable empirical indices of the value quantified are available, so that estimates can be checked for their validity.

are of primary importance for life and survival. "Everything from the chance to stay alive during the first year after birth to the chance to view fine arts, the chance to remain healthy and grow tall, and if sick to get well again quickly, the chance to avoid becoming a juvenile delinquent—and very crucially, the chance to complete an intermediary or higher educational grade"—all these *life chances* are crucially influenced by one's position in the economic class structure.[4]

The economic structure in turn refers to the amount and source of income:

> Individuals of the same or similar economic position have identical or similar goods and services to offer in the system of production and distribution and therefore receive identical or similar monetary rewards in the market place.[5]

It is, of course, easy to quantify income amounts, and this is the baseline of economic stratification. The source of income is an ambiguous variable, used in conjunction with the first to make predictions (or inferences) about the consumption patterns of individuals and about how they spend their time, and these variables in turn are also subject to measurement. The fact that income *source* is called an economic variable, may, however, produce spurious correlations between the economic and status hierarchies.

There are additional problems in quantification. Some income is received in kind—traditionally in the form of home-grown produce, but more recently in the form of fringe benefits. The availability of tax-supported public services, e.g. public housing, free welfare clinics, and public libraries, also makes a difference in real income. There are, finally, regional differences in purchasing power and various forms of taxation having differential impacts, and they too must be taken into account in order to give a strictly accurate measure of an individual's comparative economic position.[6] However, all of these obstacles can be overcome in principle, and a satisfactory quantification of economic positions can be achieved.

It is an easily defended proposition that wealth, and hence purchasable advantages of various kinds, is unequally distributed in society. That these unequal relations can be ordered transitively seems intuitively ob-

4. Mayer, *Class and Society*, p. 23, quoting Gerth and Mills (*Character and Social Structure*), p. 313.
5. Ibid.
6. Cf. Gideon Sjoberg, "Are Social Classes in America Becoming More Rigid?" *Am. Soc. Rev., 16* (Dec. 1951), 775–83.

vious. It is also obvious that, in normal circumstances, a spouse and child enjoy life chances which correspond with those of the head of their household. Finally, wealth, therefore life chances, can pass through inheritance from generation to generation.

Much the same story can be told, with perhaps a few more reservations, of the distribution of social status in society. The social status structure implies that there is a pattern of deference in society in which individuals recognize others as being "above" or "beneath" them, or "on the same level," for purposes of sociability. These inequalities are observed and quantified in a variety of ways: social scientists have recorded numerous sets of self-and-other ratings by individuals in communities, by panels of especially knowledgeable citizens, and by participant observers.[7] Numerous objective criteria are used in the rating process by citizens themselves and by observers. These criteria have included: family background, residence location, occupation, education, social participations (kinds and numbers of social memberships), and "style of life," which subsumes patterns of consumption and adherence to various canons of "taste" and/or "fashion."[8]

Congruence among these various measures of status is not always high, hence instabilities in status are not uncommon.[9] This occasionally prevents a strict transitive status ordering of individuals. A may successfully claim deference from B and B from C in a small town, on account of superiority in family connections. But when they are placed in a metropolitan environment, their consumption patterns may reverse this order or possibly render the exchange of deference entirely unpredictable.

However, the status positions of many families in many communities are apparently relatively well fixed. The fact that this applies to entire families is deemed so well established as to preclude the necessity for empirical testing.[10] In fact, it is generally argued that, while the breadwinner establishes the status of a family, it is his wife who enforces

7. See, for example, Hollingshead, *Elmtown;* Harold F. Kaufman, "Prestige Classes in a New York Rural Community," Cornell Univ. Agricultural Experiment Station, *Memoir 260* (Ithaca, March 1944); W. Lloyd Warner, Marchia Meeker, and Kenneth Eels, *Social Class in America* (Gloucester, Peter Smith, 1957); Gerhard E. Lenski, "American Social Classes: Statistical Strata or Social Groups?" *Am. J. Soc., 58* (Sept. 1952), 139–44.

8. See Joseph A. Kahl and James A. Davis, "A Comparison of Indexes of Socioeconomic Status," *Am. Soc. Rev., 20* (June 1955), 317–25.

9. See ibid. and Gregory P. Stone and William H. Form, "Instabilities in Status," *Am. Soc. Rev., 18* (April 1953), 149–62.

10. However, works such as Hollingshead's *Elmtown* bear out the conclusion that members of different generations in the same nuclear family have similar status positions.

the maintenance of status boundaries and his children who perpetuate these arrangements through their social participations, the most important of which is the marriage market.

All of the foregoing is elementary doctrine of social stratification analysis, to be found in any textbook on the subject.[11] It is mentioned only as an introduction to what should be a surprising observation: that the third famous dimension of stratification analysis, power, fits only one of the criteria of stratification analysis at all well. It is in no wise comparable to the variables class and status in its fit with the criteria of stratification analysis.

Let us consider the first criterion: is it possible for an observer, through empirical observations, to arrive at an estimate of who has more and who has less power? This has never been done in stratification studies except by definition. Thus C. Wright Mills *defines* as America's power elite those occupying specified positions in military, economic, and political hierarchies.[12] Milton Gordon cites power as a dimension of social stratification, owing to the fact that power distributions are "inherently hierarchical."[13] But we must reject the substitution of definition for observation because obviously a construct which exists in language need not exist in the real world, and the task of stratification analysis is to clarify man's social behavior, not to indulge in circularities.

Another attempt to satisfy the first criterion holds that power can be observed empirically, but suggests as evidence the identical observations which were used as indices of economic or status positions. As an example of this, Kurt B. Mayer says in his text:

> We have defined power as the ability to control the behavior of others. Sociologically, power refers especially to the control which certain groups and individuals are able to exercise over the life chances of others.[14]

The difficulty with this formulation is that the "life chances" of an individual refers to the characteristic which defines his *economic* position,

11. E.g. Barber, *Social Stratification*, p. 74; Cuber and Kenkel, *Social Stratification in the U.S.*, pp. 71–73, 176–78; Kahl, *American Class Structure*, pp. 142 ff., 190; Warner, Meeker, and Eels, *Social Class in America*, p. 10; Talcott Parsons, *Essays in Sociological Theory* (rev. ed., Glencoe, Free Press, 1954), p. 422.

12. C. Wright Mills, *The Power Elite* (New York, Oxford Univ. Press, 1956), passim, esp. chap. 1.

13. Gordon, *Social Class in American Sociology*, pp. 238–39, 243 ff. See also Cuber and Kenkel, *Social Stratification in the U.S.*, p. 322.

14. Mayer, *Class and Society*, p. 26.

as we have seen.[15] When one individual controls the life chances of another, this is usually an indication of his superior *economic* position (e.g. boss vs. employee). Thus "control over the life chances of others" is at best a highly ambiguous criterion for use as an index of the power of actors, and, at worst, the observations suggested by this criterion are identical with those one would make to ascertain the economic class position or life chances of an individual. Others make an analogous mistake with respect to social status.[16] As long as we adhere to the notion that power is an empirically separable variable of social stratification, we must reject these as improper, and search for specific, separate empirical indices by which power can be measured. Stratification analysis has so far failed to fulfill this criterion.

As for the second criterion, it seems intuitively obvious that power is distributed unequally in society. But this most basic of criteria merely invites us to state the shape and durability of the inequality.

The difficulty of making such a statement becomes plain when we attempt to satisfy the criterion of transitivity. Robert Dahl states the dilemma nicely:

> With an average probability approaching one, I can induce each of 10 students to come to class for an examination on a Friday afternoon when they would otherwise prefer to make off for New York or Northampton. With its existing resources and techniques, the New Haven Police Department can prevent about half the students who park along the streets near my office from staying beyond the legal

15. Ibid., p. 23. Neal Gross, arguing from evidence in Mayer's "The Theory of Social Classes," comes to a similar conclusion. He also confirms my impression that Mayer's work ably represents the current central tendency in stratification theorizing. Gross, "A Critique of 'Social Structure and American Educaton,'" *Harvard Educational Review*, 23 (Fall 1953), 298–329. The one significant attempt to overcome the disabilities of presuming, without a further attempt at empirical confirmation, that power is an epiphenomenon of class and status position is the so-called "influence attribution" method used by Floyd Hunter and others. Hunter, *CPS*. But this method also presumes that power is coextensive with class and status, and thus suffers from the same methodological handicap as studies which do not use this device. See especially Raymond E. Wolfinger, "Reputation and Reality in the Study of 'Community Power,'" *Am. Soc. Rev.*, 25 (Oct. 1960), 636–44; also Dahl, "Critique," 463–69; Nelson W. Polsby, "Three Problems in the Analysis of Community Power," *Am. Soc. Rev.*, 24 (Dec. 1959), 795–803.

16. See, for example, Baltzell, *Philadelphia*, pp. 32 ff. Warner, Meeker, and Eels, *Social Class in America*, p. 8. David Riesman makes the following pungent comment: "All the arguments which go on so tiresomely . . . between Warner and the Marxists seem to me an argument as to which status system runs the country, when, in fact, neither does"; "Some Observations Concerning Marginality," *Phylon*, 12 (June 1951), 117.

time limit. Which of us has the more power? The question is, I believe, incapable of being answered unless we are ready to treat my relationships with my students as in some sense comparable with the relations of the Police Department with another group of students. Otherwise any answer would be arbitrary, because there is no valid way of combining the three variables—scope, number of respondents and change in probabilities—into a single scale.[17]

The question of transitivity merely compounds the comparability problem outlined by Dahl. If there is no satisfying way of comparing A's power with B's, then how much less likely it is that we can arrive at some agreement with respect to all three relationships, A-B, B-C, and A-C!

As for the fourth criterion, Robert Schulze has urged that we regard power exercise as a relationship not merely between persons, but between persons occupying particular positions.[18] Thus Professor Dahl's chances of seeing me in an examination on any hypothetical Friday declined precipitously when I completed his courses. This common-sense formulation of the power relation also reveals that the members of a power-holder's family seldom have anything to do with his power exercise, except insofar as they can influence the power-holder directly. Ellen Dahl's ability to detain one or several Yale students in New Haven should not be confused with the comparatively futile efforts her father might make in the same direction.

There are occasional examples in American history where the power of one member of a family was shared among members of his household. The activities of Mrs. Woodrow Wilson during her husband's sickness in office is perhaps the most striking case in point. But no one is likely to mistake an historical rarity for a social pattern.

The final criterion has to do with the inheritance of power by the children of the powerful. No one will deny that there is a tradition in American politics according to which certain families enter public service; several generations of these families have unquestionably been prominent in positions of power and public trust. One thinks, for example, of the Byrds of Virginia, the Longs of Louisiana, Lodges of Massachusetts, and Frelinghuysens of New Jersey. But additional facts must be kept in mind. These positions of public trust are not inherited as a matter of course, but rather must be achieved by some kind of personal accomplishment

17. Robert A. Dahl, "The Concept of Power," *Behavioral Science*, 2 (July 1957), 206.
18. Schulze "Bifurcation."

even by inheritors of a long family tradition of public service. Family background often provides extremely good opportunities for the sons of political notables to display their talents, but their personal accomplishments are by no means irrelevant to their subsequent rise to positions of power in their own right. This of course does not mean that political leaders from politically prominent families necessarily possess unusual competence at the tasks they perform, since those qualities that may be necessary to achieve public office or political leadership—e.g. popularity —are not always useful in the day-to-day conduct of business. In any event, it should be noted that far from a majority of the powerful are children of the powerful, as can be seen by even a casual census of, let us say, current chief executives of American cities and states. And it is also obvious that only a minority of the offspring of the powerful go on to become politically notable themselves.[19] This provides a vivid contrast with the dimensions of class and status, where, as a matter of course, children inherit the positions of their parents. The passage of power by inheritance alone in modern America, while it is not unheard of, is surely a deviant, not a dominant pattern.

If the argument is persuasive that modern American community life is a relatively inappropriate setting for the application of a stratification analysis, then it follows that those who try to make such an analysis run certain risks. The two characteristic pitfalls are similar to those confronting a man doing a jigsaw puzzle. On the one hand, he must not force pieces into places they do not fit. On the other, he must not have any odd pieces left over when he completes his work. As we have seen,

19. Cf. Donald R. Matthews, *The Social Background of Political Decision-Makers* (Garden City, Doubleday, 1954). This book contains at least five methodological difficulties which sharply limit its usefulness in the present context: first, it depends in part for confirmation of its thesis on the community studies whose findings about power have been questioned in this book and elsewhere. Second, Matthews presents data on the occupational distributions of legislators as compared with gross occupational figures for the total American population, without controlling for the systematic constitutional over-representation of rural areas in legislatures, which ought in turn to produce skews in the occupations of legislators: e.g., over-representation of farmers, under-representation of urban workers. Third, Matthews' data are often skimpier than they appear: e.g., there are several tables showing percentage distributions where N's are fewer than 100 and in one case as low as 2. Fourth, social backgrounds have been found to be insufficient data for predicting policy positions in decision-making. See W. W. Charters, Jr., "Social Class Analysis and the Control of Education," *Harvard Educational Review, 23* (Fall 1953), 268–83, and C. Arnold Anderson, "The Need for a Functional Theory of Social Class," *Rural Sociology, 19* (June 1954), 152–60. A final point: Matthews presents no data on the *power* positions of parents of political decision-makers, concentrating instead on *economic* positions. Therefore his data fail to test the hypothesis suggested.

stratification studies of community power have on occasion both forced their data and ignored contrary evidence. But this is understandable, since stratification analysis presumes the existence of stable, significant inequalities. Stratification writers have stated this as a finding, but in reality these inequalities are a *presumption* without which stratification analysis is impossible.

But why was stratification theory employed at all? A hypothesis worth exploring is that stratification theory somehow fits the policy preferences or the personal, emotional needs of researchers. This argument is hard to sustain if for no other reason than that stratification writers have in general eschewed direct expositions of their social and political values. In the three instances in which this has not been the case, however, there has been a disparity of views. C. Wright Mills has indicated his distress at the pattern of dominance he detects in modern society, characterizing it as conducive to a "higher immorality." [20] Digby Baltzell, on the other hand, celebrated the identical pattern in Philadelphia as a necessary check on the abuse of power by leaders unacculturated to upper-class *noblesse oblige*.[21] The Lynds expressed great discontent at the low standards of administrative morality and efficiency which prevailed in Middletown as the result of the alleged withdrawal of the "better" people from political life, but they also decried the antidemocratic hegemony of the business class, thus placing themselves on both sides of the question.[22]

We can say, then, that diametrically opposed policy positions are supported equally well by the stratification analysis of community power. The five key propositions can be deduced from the social values of neither Mills nor Baltzell. Nor can either set of values be deduced from their "findings" about power. It is possible that several researchers were led to the same false conclusion each for a different reason. But I am proceeding on the assumption that this was not the case and that a common source of error exists.

20. Mills, *The Power Elite*, passim, esp. chap. 15. See also Mills, *White Collar* (New York, Oxford Univ. Press, 1953); Mills, "The Power Elite: Comment on Criticism," *Dissent*, 4 (Winter 1957), 22–34; Mills, "The Middle Classes in Middle-sized Cities," *Am. Soc. Rev.*, 11 (Oct. 1946), 520–29; Mills and Melville Ulmer, *Small Business and Civic Welfare: Report of the Smaller War Plants Corporation*, U.S. Senate Document 134, 79th Cong., 2d Sess. (Washington, Government Printing Office, 1946).
21. Baltzell, *Philadelphia*, pp. 4–5, 60–63.
22. See Lynd, *M*, e.g. pp. 414, 425–29 and Lynd, *MIT*, e.g. pp. 123, 322, 364. This point is elaborated in Polsby, "Power in Middletown: Fact and Value in Community Research," *Canadian Journal of Economics and Political Science*, 26 (Nov. 1960), 592–603.

If the political views of researchers do not provide a suitable rationale for the employment of stratification theory, one may hypothesize that the intellectual framework of stratification theory was a natural one for sociologists to use. According to one prevailing opinion among sociologists, stratification theory was erroneously supposed by researchers to have been inappropriate for the study of American life until certain twentieth-century events—notably the depression—reawakened interest in the study of social inequality and in the Marxian prophecy of capitalist self-destruction.[23] By the time most of the studies discussed in this book were written, stratification theory was enjoying great popularity, and it is not too much to say that today stratification analysis is one of the commonest, most conventional perspectives from which sociologists view social life.

I turn, finally, to certain basic presumptions, axioms, and definitions of stratification theory itself, for the light they may throw on the source of common error. The first hypothesis suggested reasons why the application of stratification theory might have been expected to produce errors in describing social reality. The present discussion attempts to discover why these particular errors, embodied in the five key propositions, were made.

Stratification means, of course, the division of the community into strata, or layers, one on top of the other. Each individual in the community can in principle be located in a layer, and no one is found in more than a single layer at any point in time. This suggests that by some criterion or other there is always an identifiable top layer in the community, whose members are more or less firmly fixed in place.

Power, in stratification theory, consists of the *capacity* to realize one's will, even over objections.[24] The emphasis upon capacity is important,

23. It is interesting to note that the depression intervened between the writing of the first and the second Middletown books. The second, *Middletown in Transition*, contains by far the more elaborate discussion of power in Middletown and shows a distinct Marxist influence hardly visible in *Middletown*. See also Kingsley Davis, "Introduction" to Kahl, *American Class Structure*, Shils, *Present State of American Sociology*, p. 15; Robert E. L. Faris, "American Sociology" in G. Gurvitch and W. E. Moore, eds., *Twentieth Century Sociology* (New York, Philosophical Library, 1945), pp. 558–59; Gordon, *Social Class in American Sociology*, pp. 8–9; Howard E. Jensen, "Editorial Note," in ibid., pp. viii–ix. Cf. Leonard Reissman, *Class in American Society* (Glencoe, Free Press, 1959), p. 30; Irving Kristol, "The Study of Man: Class and Sociology," *Commentary, 24* (Oct. 1957), 358–63.

24. This is Max Weber's famous definition. See H. H. Gerth and C. Wright Mills, eds., *From Max Weber, Essays in Sociology* (New York, Oxford Univ. Press, 1946), pp. 180–95. Weber's framework for the study of power as an aspect of stratification is widely accepted among sociologists. See, for example, Mayer, *Class and Society*, p. 18;

because it signifies the stratification writers' attempt to find some relatively unambiguous set of resources which unfailingly index this capacity successfully (i.e., which predict the outcomes of conflicts). As we saw earlier, stratification writers customarily fall back on the indices of high class or status position as indices of power. Given these presumptions, one might deduce the first proposition: the upper class rules because the upper class is at the top of the economic and status hierarchy, and capacity to realize one's will (or to rule or prevail in decision-making) is indexed by class and status position.

Another characteristic of stratification analysis is to blur the distinction between values accruing to an individual and those accruing to a group. This is a serious matter when collective activity is involved; less so when individuals deal directly with individuals. In the latter case, let us say that the middle class, with 40 per cent of the nation's population, has $100 million in wealth, while the upper class, with 3 per cent of the population, has $50 million. We would say, then, that the per capita wealth of the upper class was greater, but that the collective wealth of the middle class was greater. In assessing the life chances of an individual, it is clearly his per capita value position which is relevant, and not the aggregate value position of all the members of his class.

But in order to maintain the proposition that the upper class rules, stratification theory must make the assumption that per capita power is irrelevant. Rather, the power position of a class must be considered a collective property, and the upper class always must have more of the total amount of power in the community than any other group.[25] Without this proviso, we could conceive of situations in which all the members of the more numerous lower classes got together and outvoted the upper class; hence, the upper class would not rule. The fact that this sometimes happens suggests one limitation on the utility of the assump-

---

Kaufman, Duncan, Gross, and Sewell, "Problems of Theory and Method," Schulze, "Bifurcation"; Herbert Goldhamer and Edward Shils, "Types of Power and Status," *Am. J. Soc.*, 45 (Sept. 1939), 171–82; Robert Bierstedt, "An Analysis of Social Power," *Am. Soc. Rev.*, 15 (Dec. 1950), 730–38; Talcott Parsons, "A Revised Analytical Approach to the Theory of Social Stratification," in Bendix and Lipset, eds., *Class, Status and Power*, pp. 92–128; Bendix and Lipset, "Introduction" in ibid., p. 13; Hans Gerth and C. Wright Mills, review of W. Lloyd Warner and Paul S. Lunt, *The Social Life of a Modern Community*, in *Am. Soc. Rev.*, 7 (April 1942), 263–71; Floyd Hunter, *Top Leadership: U.S.A.* (Chapel Hill, Univ. of North Carolina Press, 1959).

25. As I have said, stratification writers do not make these distinctions clear. However, see Gerth and Mills, *Character and Social Structure*, pp. 328 ff., esp. 339–41; Gordon, *Social Class*, pp. 240–45; Mayer, *Class and Society*, pp. 5–6.

tion. But a more serious objection may be raised: how can the power of the class a man belongs to be revealed by his individual life chances? The set of logical leaps which by implication establishes the identity of individual and collective value-positions is an unfortunate aspect of stratification theory. Once accomplished, they enable us to observe that political and civic leaders are subordinate to economic and social leaders because the latter group occupies the top, and no matter how numerous or powerful civic leaders become they can never, by the rules of stratification analysis, collectively exceed the power of the upper class.

A single power elite is seen to rule in American community life because stratification theory provides for differentiation only between ranks in a hierarchy; hence those who belong to some group other than the top group are nonrulers, and all those who belong to the top group are rulers.

The interests of a group may be defined as maximizing its long-run share of values. In stratification theory, every group is presumed to be pursuing its own interests. Insofar as a group fails to do so, it is presumed to lack information and organization. The upper class is presumed to be uniquely endowed with information, organization, and all other conceivable means for pursuing rational activity, i.e., maximizing its long-run share of values.[26] Therefore, the conclusion must be that the upper class rules in its own interests.

A final set of stratification theory presumptions has to do with the scarcity of values in society.[27] This means that each class, in maximizing its own long-run share of values, runs up against other classes bent on the same end. Conflict takes place because values demanded exceed values supplied, and this scarcity sets off class conflict. Again, groups other than classes are not seen as conflicting for values because stratification theory differentiates clearly only between classes; other groups, lacking a place in the basic language of stratification analysis, are not unimportant so much as invisible.

The key propositions of the stratification analysis therefore follow from the basic axioms and definitions of stratification theory. It seems highly improbable that propositions different from those given would appear

26. See Kahl, *American Class Structure*, pp. 159–60; Gordon, *Social Class*, pp. 193 ff.; Mayer, *Class and Society*, pp. 24, 61–68.

27. See Seymour M. Lipset, "Political Sociology," in R. K. Merton, L. Broom, and L. S. Cottrell, Jr., eds., *Sociology Today* (New York, Basic Books, 1959), pp. 105–06; Talcott Parsons, "The Distribution of Power in American Society," *World Politics, 10* (Oct. 1957), 139; Robert S. Lynd, "Power in American Society as Resources and Problem," in Arthur Kornhauser, ed., *Problems of Power in American Society* (Detroit, Wayne State Univ. Press, 1957), pp. 9–10.

as findings in stratification studies, given the assumptions that (1) the community is divided horizontally, into ranked layers, with a single layer on top; (2) power is a collective attribute of classes indexed by the per capita economic and status value positions of class members; (3) classes are oriented to the goal of maximizing their long-run share of values; (4) the total supply of values in the community is smaller than the demands of the various classes. Since each of these conditions is postulated, explicitly or implicitly, in stratification theory, it seems legitimate to conclude that the key propositions could have been deduced from basic axioms. This may explain why stratification writers have advanced similar propositions about community power despite the fact that the propositions were not justified by the facts in the communities they studied.

# 6. How to Study Community Power: The Pluralist Alternative

In criticizing the stratification approach to the study of community power, I have suggested, among other things, that this approach encourages research designs which generate self-fulfilling prophecies, that it leads to the systematic misreporting of facts and to the formulation of vague, ambiguous, unrealistic, and unprovable assertions about community power. I now want to discuss an alternative method of studying community power which appears to have successfully avoided these undesirable by-products in a number of community studies.

This alternative research strategy can be called the "pluralist" approach. Old, familiar pluralistic presumptions[1] about the nature of American politics seem to have given researchers strategies for the study of community power which are both feasible to execute and comparatively faithful to conditions in the real world.[2] What follows is an attempt to

1. I am well aware that for other purposes the "pluralist" approach can be divided into several schools of thought. However, all variations of pluralist theory contrast effectively with stratification theory. Pluralist presumptions can be found, for example, in the writings of Tocqueville and Madison and in Arthur Bentley, *The Process of Government* (Chicago, Univ. of Chicago Press, 1908); Pendleton Herring, *The Politics of Democracy* (New York, Rinehart, 1940); David B. Truman, *The Governmental Process* (New York, Knopf, 1953); V. O. Key, Jr., *Politics, Parties and Pressure Groups* (New York, Crowell, 1942 and 1959). More formal treatments of propositions contained in many of these works can be found in Anthony Downs, *An Economic Theory of Democracy* (New York, Harper, 1957); David Braybrooke, "Some Steps toward a Formal System of Political Science," a report prepared for the Committee on Political Behavior of the Social Science Research Council, Sept. 1957; James S. Coleman, "An Examination of Arthur F. Bentley's Theory of Government," ibid., July 1957; and Robert A. Dahl, *A Preface to Democratic Theory* (Chicago, Univ. of Chicago Press, 1956).

2. Among the researchers who have found pluralist presumptions about the nature of the political system useful are Robert A. Dahl (see his "The New Haven Community Leadership Study," Working Paper Number One, Dec. 1957, mimeo.; and *Who Governs?*); Harry Scoble ("Yankeetown"); and George Belknap and Norton E. Long (see Long, "The Local Community as an Ecology of Games," *Am. J. Soc.*, 64 [Nov. 1958], 251–61; Long and Belknap, "A Research Program on Leadership and

explain why this seems to be the case for pluralist studies, but not for stratification studies.

The first and perhaps most basic presupposition of the pluralist approach is that nothing categorical can be assumed about power in any community. It rejects the stratification thesis that *some* group necessarily dominates a community. If anything, there seems to be an unspoken notion among pluralist researchers that at bottom *nobody* dominates in a town, so that their first question to a local informant is likely to be not "Who runs this community?" but rather "Does anyone at all run this community?" It is instructive to examine the range of possible answers to each of these questions. The first query is somewhat like "Have you stopped beating your wife" in that virtually any response short of total unwillingness to answer will supply the researcher with a "power elite" along the lines presupposed by stratification theory.[3] On the other hand, the second question is capable of eliciting a response which *could* lead to the discovery of a power elite (i.e., "Yes"), or any of an infinite number of stable, but nonelitist patterns of decision-making (i.e., "No, but . . . ," "Yes, but . . .") or total fragmentation, or disorganization (i.e., "No").

What sort of question is likely to follow "Who runs the community?" in a questionnaire? Obviously, something like "*How* do the people named in the above response run the community?" This entirely probable pattern of investigation begs the question whether or not those said to rule actually do rule. In the pluralist approach, on the other hand, an attempt is made to study specific outcomes in order to determine who actually prevails in community decision-making. Because the study of actual outcomes requires arduous and expensive field work, outcomes in a few (but for reasons of expense usually only a few) issue-areas are studied closely. More than a single issue-area is always chosen, however, because of the presumption among pluralist researchers that the same pattern of decision-making is highly unlikely to reproduce itself in more than one issue-area. In this expectation, pluralist researchers have seldom been

Decision-making in Metropolitan Areas," [mimeo., New York, Governmental Affairs Institute, Aug. 1956]; Belknap and John H. Bunzel, "The Trade Union in the Political Community," *PROD, 2* [Sept. 1958], 3–6; Belknap, "A Plan for Research on the Socio-political Dynamics of Metropolitan Areas," presented before a seminar on urban leadership of the Social Science Research Council, New York, Aug. 1957). See also a paper presented to this seminar by Peter H. Rossi, "The Study of Decision-making in the Local Community."

3. See Herbert Kaufman and Victor Jones, "The Mystery of Power," *Public Administration Review, 14* (Summer 1954), 205–12.

disappointed.[4] They recognize, however, the possibility that the same pattern *could* reproduce itself in more than one issue-area. Since actual behavior is observed or reconstructed from documents, witnesses, and so on, it is possible to determine empirically whether or not the same group rules in two or more issue-areas. The presumption that a power elite is unlikely does not, in other words, prevent finding one.

A superficially persuasive objection to this approach might be phrased as follows: "Suppose research in a community discloses different patterns of decision-making in each of three issue-areas. This does not rule out the possibility that all other issue-areas in the community are dominated by a single power elite." How can pluralists meet this objection? First, it is necessary to acknowledge the *possibility* that this is the case. However, pluralists can (and do) protect themselves in part by studying significant issues. In New Haven, for example, Dahl, Wolfinger, and I studied nominations by the two political parties (which determined who held public office), the urban redevelopment program (the largest in the country, measured by past and present outlays per capita), public education (the most costly item in the city's budget), and a campaign to revise the city charter. In Bennington, Scoble studied political nominations and elections, the issue of consolidation of various municipal governments, the formation of a union high school district, and the construction of a new high school building.[5] A Long and Belknap pilot study of a large eastern city embraced the problems of transportation, race relations, traffic, urban redevelopment, and recreation,[6] and Belknap studied the issues of urban redevelopment, transportation, and race relations in the San Francisco Bay area.[7]

None of these issues is trivial, and a case can be made for the proposition that they were in fact the most important issues before these communities during the time the studies were being carried out. What sort of power elite asserts itself in relatively trivial matters, but is inactive or ineffective in the most significant areas of community policy-making?

Stratification theory holds that power elites fail to prevail only on trivial issues.[8] By preselecting issues generally agreed to be significant,

4. Raymond E. Wolfinger, "Reputation and Reality in The Study of 'Community Power,'" *Am. Soc. Rev.*, 25 (Oct. 1960), pp. 636–44, has summarized findings on this point. See also below, chap. 7.

5. "Yankeetown."

6. "A Research Program."

7. "A Plan for Research."

8. See, for example, Roland J. Pellegrin and Charles H. Coates, "Absentee-owned Corporations and Community Power Structure," *Am. J. Soc.*, 61 (March 1956), 413–19; and Lynd, *MIT*, p. 89.

pluralist researchers can test stratification theory without searching endlessly in issue-area after issue-area in order to discover some semblance of a power elite. After all, we cannot reasonably require of researchers that they validate someone else's preconceived notion of community power distributions. If the researcher's design is such that any power distribution has an equal chance of appearing in his result, we may not properly criticize his result on the ground that it did not conform to expectations. The burden of proof is clearly on the challenger in such a case to make good his assertion that power is actually distributed otherwise.[9]

Another presumption of the pluralist approach runs directly counter to stratification theory's presumption that power distributions are a more or less permanent aspect of social structure. Pluralists hold that power may be tied to issues, and issues can be fleeting or persistent, provoking coalitions among interested groups and citizens ranging in their duration from momentary to semi-permanent. There is a clear gain in descriptive accuracy in formulating power distributions so as to take account of the dimension of time, as pluralists do.[10] For it is easily demonstrated that coalitions *do* vary in their permanency, and to presume that the set of

9. See Dahl, "Critique."

10. See, for example, Belknap ("A Plan for Research"), who discusses this explicitly. One stratification writer who has attempted to take account of the time factor is Jerome K. Myers, "Assimilation in the Political Community," *Sociology and Social Research*, 35 (Jan.–Feb. 1951), 175–82. Myers plots a secular trend which indicates slow increases in the number of Italians and Italian-descended employed by New Haven municipal government over a 50-year period ending in 1940. He claims to have discovered "discrimination" against Italians, because they did not participate in city government to an extent proportional with their representation in the total population of the city. His conclusion in 1951 was that "the early or quick assimilation of New Haven Italians in the political system does not seem very probable. . . . All indications are that political assimilation is inevitable, although it is at least several generations away." By taking account of shorter-term cyclical movements within the allegedly "basic" structure, we may be able to explain the delay in the political assimilation of Italians. As I have mentioned, New Haven Italians were and are predominantly Republican in local politics. From 1920 to 1940, years in which the Italians would "normally" have been expected to come into their own as a politically significant minority group, the city government was in Democratic hands twice as much as Republican, and this would lead one to expect Italians to be less well represented among office-holders than if this situation were reversed. However, in 1945, when William Celentano, a Republican of Italian descent, was elected mayor, Italians entered the top echelons of city government in large numbers. There is, of course, no sure way of telling what a "normal" rate of absorption into political positions would be. More or less comparable data indicate that in New Haven Italians were perhaps a bit swifter in their rise to political leadership than in Providence, Rhode Island. See Elmer E. Cornwell, Jr., "Party Absorption of Ethnic Groups: The Case of Providence, Rhode Island," *Social Forces*, 38 (March 1960), 205–10.

coalitions which exists in the community at any given time is a time-lessly stable aspect of social structure is to introduce systematic inaccuracies into one's description of social reality.

Why do pluralists reject the idea that *some* group necessarily dominates every community? The presumption that communities are likely to be less rather than more permanent in their patterns of decision-making is no doubt part of the answer, but another part is an even more fundamental presumption that human behavior is governed in large part by inertia. This notion leads pluralists to look upon overt activity as a more valid indication of involvement in issues than mere reputations for leadership.[11]

Pluralists refuse to regard particular groups as necessarily implicated in decisions when the groups themselves reject such involvement.[12] For pluralists, the imputation of "false class consciousness" suggests that the values of analysts are being imposed arbitrarily on groups in the community. They reject the idea that there is any particular issue or any particular point in the determination of an issue when a group *must* assert itself in order to follow its expressed values. Rather, the pluralist assumes that there are many issues and many points at which group values can be realized. Further, pluralists presume that there are certain costs in taking any action at all. This refers not simply to the possibility of losing, of making political enemies, and so on, but also to the costs in personal time and effort involved in political mobilization, in becoming informed, in lobbying or campaigning, and in taking the trouble to vote.[13]

It is a demonstrated fact that public activity of all kinds is a habit of the middle and upper classes.[14] Vidich and Bensman, in their community study, depicted the life of the lowest-class groups in the community sufficiently well so that the personally functional aspects of withdrawal from the community were revealed.[15] The presumption of inertia permits

11. See the previous critique of Hunter in Chap. 3, and Wolfinger, "Reputation and Reality."

12. See C. Wright Mills, "The Middle Classes in Middle-sized Cities," *Am. Soc. Rev.*, 11 (Oct. 1946), 520–29, for the stratification theory view.

13. See Downs, *Economic Theory of Democracy*; see also Samuel Stouffer, *Communism, Conformity and Civil Liberties* (Garden City, Doubleday, 1955), pp. 58 ff.

14. Robert E. Lane, *Political Life: How People Get Involved in Politics* (Glencoe, Free Press, 1959), pp. 220–34; Angus Campbell, Gerald Gurin, and Warren E. Miller, *The Voter Decides* (Evanston, Row, Peterson, 1954), pp. 70–75.

15. Arthur J. Vidich and Joseph Bensman, *Small Town in Mass Society* (Princeton, Princeton Univ. Press, 1958), pp. 69–70, 290–91. Studies of social status have been hampered by a similar problem of upper-class-centeredness. See the criticism of Warner on this point by Seymour Martin Lipset and Reinhard Bendix, "Social Status and Social Structure," *British Journal of Sociology*, 2 (June 1951), esp. 163 ff.

the researcher to regard the public sector of activity as but one facet of behavior capable of giving people satisfaction and discourages the inappropriate and arbitrary assignment of upper- and middle-class values to all actors in the community.

The presumption of inertia also helps put economic and social notables into perspective. If a man's major life work is banking, the pluralist presumes he will spend his time at the bank, and not in manipulating community decisions. This presumption holds until the banker's activities and participations indicate otherwise. Once again, it is very important to make the point that this assumption is not scientifically equivalent to its opposite. If we presume that the banker is really engaged in running the community, there is practically no way of disproving this notion even if it is totally erroneous. On the other hand, it is easy to spot the banker who really *does* run community affairs when we presume he does not, because his activities will make this fact apparent. In the absence of the requisite activities, we have no grounds for asserting that the banker in fact does run the community.[16]

The pluralist emphasis on the time-bounded nature of coalitions and on the voluntary aspect of political participation leads to a further contrast with stratification theory, since pluralists hold that the "interest group" and the "public" are the social collectives most relevant to the analysis of political processes. In the sociologist's patois, politically important groups would be called phenomena of "collective behavior" rather than of "social structure."[17] Social classes in stratification theory are populations differentially ranked according to economic or status criteria, which embrace the entire community. Everyone in a community is a member of at least one but no more than one class at any given moment, and no one in the community falls outside the system. This is a legitimate heuristic construction; however, it is a mistake to impute to the apparently inescapable fact of class membership any sort of class consciousness. This

16. See Bentley, *Process of Government,* pp. 175–222, and note at p. 202: "If we can get our social life stated in terms of activity and of nothing else, we have not indeed succeeded in measuring it, but we have at least reached a foundation upon which a coherent system of measurements can be built up. . . . We shall cease to be blocked by the intervention of unmeasurable elements, which claim to be themselves the real causes of all that is happening, and which by their spook-like arbitrariness make impossible any progress toward dependable knowledge."

17. Only one sociologist seems to have realized what this implies for the methods and conclusions of political analysis. See Rudolf Heberle, *Social Movements* (New York, Appleton, 1951). The relevant theory is compactly expounded by Herbert Blumer in "Collective Behavior," which appears in Alfred M. Lee, ed., *Principles of Sociology* (New York, Barnes and Noble, 1953), pp. 167–220.

sociologists have long recognized.[18] But they seem less willing to grant that it is equally incorrect to presume that those sharing similar market or status positions are also equidistant from all the bases of political power, or in fact share class interests. American society has never been noted for its interclass warfare, a fact often reported with great surprise in stratification studies of American communities.[19]

Pluralists, who see American society as fractured into a congeries of hundreds of small special interest groups, with incompletely overlapping memberships, widely differing power bases, and a multitude of techniques for exercising influence on decisions salient to them,[20] are not surprised at the low priority Americans give to their class memberships as bases of social action. In the decision-making of fragmented government—and American national, state, and local governments are nothing if not fragmented—it is the claims of small, intense minorities that are usually attended to.[21] Hence it is not only inefficient but usually unnecessary for entire classes to mobilize when the preferences of class members are pressed and often satisfied in piecemeal fashion. The empirical evidence supporting this pluralist doctrine is overwhelming,[22] however stratification theorists may have missed its significance for them; the fragmentation of American governmental decision-making and of American society makes class consciousness inefficient and, in most cases, makes the political interests of members of the same class different.

Pluralist research is not interested in ascertaining an actor's ranking in a system presumed to operate hierarchically. Rather, pluralists want to find out about leadership *roles*, which are presumed to be diverse and fluid, both within a single issue-area over time and between issue-areas. Long and Belknap, for example, identify the following leadership roles

18. Indeed, Max Weber, the most important founding father of modern stratification analysis, makes just this point. See Weber's "Class, Status, Party," in H. H. Gerth and C. W. Mills, ed., *From Max Weber: Essays in Sociology* (New York, Oxford Univ. Press, 1946), pp. 180–95, esp. p. 184.

19. See, for example, Lynd, *MIT*, pp. 454–55, 509; Alfred Winslow Jones, *Life, Liberty and Property* (Philadelphia, Lippincott, 1941), pp. 336–54; Warner, *Jonesville*, p. 27; C. Wright Mills, "The Middle Classes." Cf. also Richard Centers, *The Psychology of Social Classes* (Princeton, Princeton Univ. Press, 1949), and note the extent to which his conclusions outrun his data.

20. See, for example, Truman, passim; Alexis de Tocqueville, *Democracy in America* (New York, Vintage, 1952), esp. *1:* 181–205, 281–342; *2:* 114–35.

21. See Dahl, *Preface to Democratic Theory.*

22. Truman (*Governmental Process*) summarizes a tremendous amount of this material. For a recent treatment of the same theme in a case study, see Aaron B. Wildavsky, *Dixon-Yates: A Study in Power Politics* (New Haven, Yale Univ. Press, 1962).

in community decision-making: initiation, staffing and planning, communication and publicity, intra-elite organizing, financing, and public sanctioning.[23]

By describing and specifying leadership roles in concrete situations, pluralists are in a position to determine the extent to which a power structure exists. High degrees of overlap in decision-making personnel among issue-areas, or high degrees of institutionalization in the bases of power in specified issue-areas, or high degrees of regularity in the procedures of decision-making—any one of these situations, if found to exist, could conceivably justify an empirical conclusion that some kind of power structure exists. By specifying leadership roles and activities, the pluralist research strategy makes possible an empirical determination and description of the bounds and durability of a community power structure—if there is one, and the stratification theory presumption that community power is necessarily general and relatively immutable can be discarded as arbitrary.

The final contrast I want to make between the pluralist and stratification methods has to do with their differing conceptions of what is meant by "power." As we have seen, stratification theorists emphasize the cataloguing of power bases, or resources available to actors for the exercise of power.[24] Pluralists, on the other hand, concentrate on power exercise itself. This leads to two subsidiary discoveries. First, there are a great many different kinds of resources which can be put to use in the process of community decision-making—many more resources, in fact, than stratification theorists customarily take into account. One list, for example, might include:

1. Money and credit
2. Control over jobs
3. Control over the information of others
4. Social standing
5. Knowledge and expertness
6. Popularity, esteem, charisma
7. Legality, constitutionality, officiality, legitimacy
8. Ethnic solidarity

23. Long and Belknap, "A Research Program," 9–11; See Polsby, "The Sociology of Community Power: A Reassessment," *Social Forces*, 37 (March 1959), 232–36; and Edward C. Banfield, "The Concept 'Leadership' in Community Research," delivered at the meetings of the American Political Science Association, 1958, for similar lists.
24. See above, Chap. 5.

9. The right to vote
10. Time
11. Personal (human) energy[25]

Second, resources can be employed with greater or less skill. The elaboration of the ways in which resources are employed enables the pluralist researcher to pay attention to what practical politicians customarily see as the heart of their own craft: the processes of bargaining, negotiation, salesmanship and brokerage, and of leadership in mobilizing resources of all kinds. It is also possible using this approach to make a more realistic evaluation of the actual disposable resources of actors. A corporation may be worth millions, but its policies and liquidity position may be such that it cannot possibly bring these millions into play to influence the outcome of a community decision—even one in which the corporation is vitally interested. And interest itself, as noted above, is differentially distributed in a pattern which pluralists assume is rational for most actors most of the time. For example, Long and Belknap observe:

> Just as business organizations may be disinterested in community affairs because of the national scope of [their] operations, individual businessmen who move or are shifted from city to city may have little opportunity or incentive to participate in community affairs. Some businesses have strong pressures on them to give attention to community and metropolitan problems. Large department stores are particularly tied up with the destiny of the city and must decide whether to keep to the central city or decentralize in suburban shopping centers. Businessmen with a "metropolitan view" would thus be expected to be found here rather than in the branch office of a national corporation.[26]

What are the practical recommendations which emerge from this comparison of stratification and pluralist approaches to the study of community power? [27] First, the researcher should pick issue-areas as the focus of his study of community power. Second, he should be able to defend

25. See Robert A. Dahl, "The Analysis of Influence in Local Communities" (mimeo., May 1959), 10; Dahl, "Leadership in a Fragmented Political System: Notes for a Theory," presented to the Social Science Research Council Conference on Metropolitan Leadership, Evanston, Ill., April 1–3, 1960, p. 7.
26. Long and Belknap, "A Research Program," 13–14. This corresponds to the findings—but not the interpretations—of Robert O. Schulze, "The Role of Economic Dominants in Community Power Structure," Am. Soc. Rev., 23 (Feb. 1958), 3–9.
27. This presumes that the researcher wants to make some generalization about the "normal" distributions of power in community decision-making.

these issue-areas as very important in the life of the community. Third, he should study actual behavior, either at first hand or by reconstructing behavior from documents, informants, newspapers, and other appropriate sources. There is no harm in starting with a list of people whose behavior the researcher wishes to study vis-à-vis an issue-area. The harm comes, rather, in attributing some mystic significance to the list, so that the examination of activity and of actual participation in decision-making becomes superfluous. This recommendation is not meant to discourage the researcher from collecting information about the reputations of actors, or their intentions with respect to community issues, or their evaluations about the meanings of community incidents. All of these kinds of data are of immeasurable value in tracing patterns of decision-making. However, they must be accompanied by information about behavior so that the researcher has some way of distinguishing between myths and facts.

The final recommendation is of the same order: researchers should study the outcomes of actual decisions within the community. It is important, but insufficient, to know what leaders want to do, intend to do, and think they can do. The researcher still has to decide on the basis of his own examination of the facts what the actual upshot is of these various intentions, and not conclude prematurely that intentions plus resources inflexibly predetermine outcomes.

# 7. Notes for a Theory of Community Power

In suggesting that the pluralist approach to the study of community power avoids mistakes which can seriously damage the results of research, I do not mean to imply that a pluralist theory has emerged which successfully explains the shaping and sharing of values in American local life. In fact pluralist writers have thus far attempted only tentatively to construct a theory of community power and decision-making. Yet theory is necessary if substantial progress in the state of knowledge is to take place.[1] Its desirability is not lessened by the fact that it can be converted

1. At least two substitutes for theory are in common use among pluralist researchers who study community power and politics. One substitute is the case method, which focuses research attention upon those features of political life that seem dramaturgically most compelling, or most historically accidental, or unique, or employs some other, similar criterion of reportorial selection. Examples of excellent case studies of decision-making in local communities are: Herbert Kaufman, "Gotham in the Air Age" in Harold Stein, ed., *Public Administration and Policy Development* (New York, Harcourt, Brace, 1952), pp. 143–97; Herbert Kaufman, *The New York City Health Centers*, Inter-University Case Program (University, Ala., Univ. of Alabama Press, 1959); William K. Muir, Jr., *Defending "The Hill" Against Metal Houses*, Inter-University Case Program (University, Ala., Univ. of Alabama Press, 1958); Louis Menand, III, *Hanover Builds a High School*, Inter-University Case Program (University, Ala., Univ. of Alabama Press, 1959). See also Martin Myerson and Edward Banfield, *Politics, Planning and the Public Interest* (Glencoe, Free Press, 1955); Peter B. Clark, *The Chicago Big Businessman as a Civic Leader* (mimeo., New Haven, Sept. 1959); James Q. Wilson, "Negro Leaders in Chicago" (unpub. doctoral dissertation, Univ. of Chicago, Aug. 1959). A second substitute for theory is the use of metaphors, such as those which currently describe the local community as an "ecology of games" or a "contest for prizes." See Norton E. Long, "The Local Community as an Ecology of Games," *Am. J. Soc.*, 64 (Nov. 1958), 251–61; Herbert Kaufman, "Metropolitan Leadership: The Snark of the Social Sciences," presented to the Social Science Research Council Conference on Metropolitan Leadership, Evanston, Ill., April 1–3, 1960. See also Wallace S. Sayre and Herbert Kaufman, *Governing New York City* (New York, Russell Sage, 1960). Neither of these substitutes for theory systematically misguides research as stratification theory apparently does. The major criticism to be leveled against these devices is that they do not go far enough in organizing data. (Cf. Anatol Rapoport, "Various Meanings of 'Theory,'" *Am. Pol. Sci. Rev.*, 52 [Dec. 1958], 972–88). Case studies leave to their readers the task of determining how findings add to previous knowledge. When findings are not explicitly stated so that they relate to previous information, they may be lost altogether. This, on the whole, seems more wasteful than if case writers were to advance general propositions which accurately reflected their admittedly limited data, even if ultimately they proved to

by the unwary into ideology, thus imprisoning rather than disciplining thought.

If a theory of community power were to exist, what would it tell us? It might, perhaps, tell us who rules, and what the conditions are of ruler-ship. In the first chapter, I suggested that the question "who rules?" could be broken into three component parts, allowing us to speak of three characteristic problems which a theory of community power might help to solve: (1) the problem of identifying and characterizing participants in decision-making, (2) the problem of determining who gains and who loses from outcomes of decisions, (3) the problem of dis-covering what makes for successful participation in decision-making.[2]

## WHO PARTICIPATES?

One of the most common patterns of behavior to be observed in Amer-ican community life is that participation in the making of decisions is concentrated in the hands of a few. But this does not mean that Amer-

---

be wrong most of the time. A hypothesis (which sets forth conditions and conse-quences) even though incorrect is easier to relate to new experience than are collec-tions of unexceptionable, but unorganized anecdotes. See the similar comments by Kaufman in "The Next Step in Case Studies," *Public Administration Review, 18* (Winter 1958), 52–59. Metaphors have the advantage of sensitizing readers and re-searchers to certain orders of data, but provide little information about the conditions necessary for their proper application. The circumstances under which a community is not an ecology of games or a contest for prizes are worth knowing. We also would like to know when one or another kind of ecology or contest is held to exist; but directions on how to use the metaphor are not given on the package. One illustration of the ease with which these metaphors can be applied to almost any situation has already cropped up in the literature. Klapp and Padgett discovered, by methods ap-parently similar to those employed by Delbert C. Miller, that there was a "power elite" in Tiajuana, Mexico, but that this "group" did not interact frequently nor did it have much to do with community decision-making or political activity. Klapp and Padgett decided that the "pyramid" metaphor originally sponsored by Hunter could not be used. They also rejected Miller's "concentric ring" image, for reasons not en-tirely clear to me. Instead, Tiajuana was labeled an "ecology of games" because, apparently, "Tiajuana has no government." Orrin E. Klapp and L. Vincent Padgett, "Power Structure and Decision-making in a Mexican Border City," *Am. J. Soc., 65* (Jan. 1960), 400–06. If the application of the metaphor to these confusing findings represents a gain in knowledge, it is not clear just what this gain might be. The widespread use of metaphors may have the deleterious effect of persuading researchers who employ them that they have something more than a case study with a label on it. But until the labels are so formulated as to discriminate among case studies, we may in fact have something less.

2. For alternative programmatic statements, see H. Douglas Price, "Research on Metropolitanism: Economics, Welfare and Politics" (mimeo., Columbia Univ., Sum-mer 1959); and Peter H. Rossi, "A Theory of Community Structure," delivered at the annual meeting of the American Sociological Society, Chicago, Sept. 1959.

ican communities are ruled by a single all-purpose elite, after the fashion suggested by stratification theory. At least three significant modifications to the finding of limited participation in decision-making must be made. First, different small groups normally make decisions on different community problems, and, likewise, the personnel of decision-making groups often change, even over the short run.[3] Second, the decisions made by small groups are almost always considered routine or otherwise insignificant by most other members of the community. Third, when small groups undertake innovation or decision-making in cases salient or likely to become salient to others in the community they must achieve special kinds of legitimacy or risk the likelihood of failure.

The finding that participants in decision-making are largely specialized to certain issue-areas has been confirmed by data gathered using both the methods prevalent in community power research. When citizens or "experts" were asked to nominate leaders in specific issue-areas (as against a more general "who's got the power around here" question employed by Hunter, Miller, and others), different leaders emerged in different issue-areas.

For example, Smuckler and Belknap report in a study of "Community A," Michigan,[4] that, despite severe limitations imposed by the influence attribution method, respondents indicated that most leaders tended to concentrate their efforts in one of a few issue-areas. Unfortunately, the population quizzed about leadership in specific issue-areas was quite restricted, and several of the issue-areas discussed were interrelated in community action programs, thus artificially muting the effects of issue-specialization in the community. Still, Smuckler and Belknap found that while there was a group of top leaders named which overlapped in several local issues,[5] different top leaders within the community were named as influential in local, state, and national affairs, people nominated as leaders in school problems were held to be inactive in community devel-

3. For evidence on this last point, see Donald Olmsted, "Organizational Leadership and Social Structure in a Small City," *Am. Soc. Rev., 19* (June 1954), 275–81.

4. Ralph H. Smuckler and George M. Belknap, *Leadership and Participation in Urban Political Affairs* (East Lansing, Governmental Research Bureau, Michigan State Univ., 1956), and Belknap and Smuckler, "Political Power Relations in a Mid-west City," *Public Opinion Quarterly, 20* (Spring 1956).

5. As well as being quizzed on leadership on specific issues, respondents were also asked to name the "most important people in town when it comes to making decisions about local public affairs here in Community A." This produced a top general elite of 15 names upon whom a relatively large number of respondents were agreed. For reasons given in Chapter 3, I regard this question as misleading, so my summary of findings in Community A emphasizes responses given to more specific questions.

opment programs, and, finally, different top leaders were nominated by
different groups in the population.

Scoble's findings in Yankeetown are similar.[6] Out of 69 individuals who
were nominated as leaders, roughly half were confined to a single issue-
area. Of 27 "general leaders," only 4 were considered influential in the
three issue-areas Scoble studied; 9 were named in two policy areas, 9 in
only one, and 5 in *none* of the areas Scoble studied.[7] Scoble attempted
to test the agreement of the influence attribution method with observed
behavior by constructing an "index of leadership activity," which correlated rather poorly with leadership nomination.[8] Scoble indicates that
high public visibility and office-holding rather than actual leadership activity is associated with "general leadership" nominations.[9] In fact, in the
two community controversies he studied, Scoble concluded that "different
sets of leaders were activated . . . however similar the controversies
seem."[10]

In an early study of influence attributions which did not take up questions relating to community decision-making, Merton reports that influentials in the town of Revere were specialized in their preoccupations and
orientations, either to matters of strictly local concern or to national and
international events.[11] "Locals" tended to hold political posts "ordinarily
obtained through political and personal relationships." "Cosmopolitans,"
on the other hand, more often appeared in public positions involving the
utilization of special skills and knowledge, e.g. on the Board of Health
or the Board of Education. Respondents to Merton's survey tended to
name as influential people close to themselves in overall amount of influence. Although interpersonal influence was reported to be concentrated
among a relatively few individuals, the bulk of all influence exerted in
the community was dispersed among a large number of relatively uninfluential persons. Finally, Merton suggests that the number of topics
upon which a citizen was influential varied considerably from person to
person.

Agger and Ostrom found that two out of three leaders held to be generally most influential by the population of a small Oregon village were actually restricted in their concerns: one to welfare policies, the other to
"seeking the amelioration of specific conditions in his [lower-class] con-

6. "Yankeetown."                           8. Ibid., 18.
7. Ibid., 12–13.                          9. Ibid., 26–27.
10. Ibid., 38.

11. Robert K. Merton, "Patterns of Influence," in Paul F. Lazarsfeld and Frank N.
Stanton, eds., *Communications Research, 1948–1949* (New York, Harper, 1949), pp.
180–219.

stituency."[12] This top trio was associated in a card-playing group with a few other men whose roles are characterized as "more specialized in terms of both their arena of activity and the function they performed." [13] Agger, presenting figures on leadership nominations, indicates that among seven top leaders named as "generally" most influential in the community, *all* were specialized to local government matters, school matters, or community welfare. An eighth top leader was named by nobody as generally influential, but he received 47 per cent of all nominations as most influential in community welfare problems. Only one of the top eight leaders received more than a few nominations in more than one issue-area. Twenty-eight out of thirty-four "advisors" in the community told Agger that they were asked for advice in only one issue-area.[14]

Agger and Ostrom conclude that "participation in policy-making at the local level tends to be specialized for most people in terms of the types of policies with which they concern themselves and in terms of the policy-making arena in which they act." [15]

Fanelli reports similar findings in his study of "Bakerville," Mississippi, where leaders were thought to be specialized to issue-areas on account of their occupations.[16] Leaders were rated both by respondents in the general population and by fellow-nominees according to their general and special influence, and by fellow-nominees alone according to their interactions on community issues. Fanelli suggests that leaders play different kinds of roles within issue-areas; some are considerably more active than others who are rated equally influential by the general population.

The same general finding of specialization of elites was also made by students who used research techniques more closely approximating the "total immersion" approach employed in New Haven. McKee, for example, reports that leadership in Lorain, Ohio, was divided in many ways.[17] "There is no single locus of decision-making, but rather a number

12. Robert E. Agger and Vincent Ostrom, "The Political Structure of a Small Community," *Public Opinion Quarterly*, 20 (Spring 1956), 84.

13. Robert E. Agger and Vincent Ostrom, "Political Participation in a Small Community" in H. Eulau, S. Eldersveld, and M. Janowitz, eds., *Political Behavior* (Glencoe, Free Press, 1956), p. 141.

14. Robert E. Agger, "Power Attributions in the Local Community," *Social Forces*, 34 (May 1956), 325–26.

15. Agger and Ostrom, "Political Participation," p. 140.

16. A. Alexander Fanelli, "A Typology of Community Leadership Based on Influence and Interaction within the Leader Sub-system," *Social Forces*, 34 (May 1956), 332–38.

17. James B. McKee, "Status and Power in the Industrial Community: A Comment on Drucker's Thesis," *Am. J. Soc.*, 58 (Jan. 1953), 364–70. For other more fragmentary, but generally corroborative, reports of industrial communities, see C. W. M.

of loci, each differently structured. Within the corporation is one, within the community are several, and there are other significant ones within the larger society." In Lorain, a single steel mill provided more than half the local jobs, making it a company town in many ways. Collective bargaining was not carried on in the local community, but in Pittsburgh. However this does not mean that the local union was weak. On the contrary, deprived of this central sphere of activity, union leaders moved into local politics and defeated an upper-class Republican coalition which had maintained itself by exploiting ethnic divisions among working-class voters.

The union was also instrumental in "wresting control of the educational system from the upper stratum. However . . . in contrast to municipal politics, the individuals who have sought leadership here . . . have been distinguished . . . on the basis of their policy toward the functioning of the school system." Finally, in the area of civic welfare, the upper stratum remained largely in control, but this control was legitimized by the presence on the requisite boards of directors of a small minority of union leaders who used these memberships not to influence welfare policy but to gain civic respectability for themselves and their union.

The pattern of decision-making by small minorities, largely specialized within issue-areas, is also reported by the Lynds in Middletown, as we have seen. This pattern apparently holds for New Haven and, as Sayre and Kaufman observe, for New York City as well. As Kaufman says:

> Decisions of the municipal government emanate from no single source, but from many centers; conflicts and clashes are referred to no single authority, but are settled at many levels and at many points in the system: no single group can guarantee the success of any proposal it supports, the defeat of every idea it objects to. Not even the central governmental organs of the city—the Mayor, the Board of Estimate, the Council—individually or in combination, even approach mastery in this sense.
>
> Each separate decision center consists of a cluster of interested contestants, with a "core group" in the middle, invested by the rules with the formal authority to legitimize decisions (that is to promul-

Hart, "Industrial Relations Research and Social Theory," *Canadian Journal of Economics and Political Science, 15* (Feb. 1949), 53–73; Charles R. Walker, *Steeltown* (New York, Harper, 1950); Alfred Winslow Jones, *Life, Liberty and Property* (Philadelphia, Lippincott, 1941); Joel Seidman, Jack London, and Bernard Karsh, "Political Consciousness in Local Unions," *Public Opinion Quarterly, 15* (Winter 1951–52), 692–702.

gate them in binding form) and a constellation of related "satellite groups" seeking to influence the authoritative issuances of the core group.[18]

Specialization of leadership within issue-areas is one important pattern of participation which modifies the stratification analysis picture of rule by small numbers of people. Another important pattern which modifies and constrains the rule of the few has to do with the grant of legitimacy made to these small groups, entitling them to make decisions. Careful examination of the evidence at hand seems to indicate that elites are freest in their power to commit the resources of the community when decisions are relatively routine and innocuous; other kinds of decision-making—of a nonroutine, unbureaucratized, or innovative variety—seems to require special consent by citizens who fall outside the small decision-making group.

If this pattern is correctly identified, certain propositions can be seen to follow from it. We might reasonably expect, for example, (1) that a general elite, where one is found to exist, would place great emphasis upon maintenance of sociability and contact with a wide range of citizens in the community and less emphasis upon accomplishment, "doing things," or innovation; that in fact these general elites would seek to restrict their own activities in various ways; (2) that elite groups which wanted to innovate would seek systematically to acquire consent from nonelite members of the community; (3) that attempts by elites to put programs into effect without achieving wider legitimacy in the community would fail; and (4) that nonelite members of the community would seek to bring elites under control in areas of concern to them.

The evidence which has begun to accumulate on each of these points indicates that they are true, and hence we can say that in a wide range of community situations participation in decision-making is limited to a relatively few members of the community, but only by the easily revoked consent of a much larger percentage of the local population.[19]

On the propensity of general elites to be self-limiting in their influence, we have the testimony of Scoble, Vidich and Bensman, and Merton, who

18. Kaufman, "Metropolitan Leadership," p. 5. More fully in Sayre and Kaufman, *Governing New York City*, pp. 710 ff.

19. Of course most political issues are entirely uninteresting to most people. Thus, the "larger percentage" I speak of here should not be interpreted as meaning "a majority," except in unusual circumstances. See Samuel Stouffer, *Communism, Conformity and Civil Liberties* (Garden City, Doubleday, 1955), pp. 58–69; and e.g. Raymond Bauer, Ithiel Pool, and Lewis A. Dexter, *American Business and Public Policy* (Atherton, New York, 1963).

speaks of their preoccupation with sociability rather than achievement.[20] Scoble points out that the "general leaders" of Yankeetown seemed to be able to reach the greatest amount of agreement among themselves on the least important issues but were split and competed with one another for the support of nonleaders on issues that were salient to "publics" in the community.[21] Even more striking than self-limitation by competition was the self-limitation by abdication which general leaders imposed upon themselves in "Springdale," where Vidich and Bensman report greater agreement among these leaders on the contents of public policy than seems to have been the case in Yankeetown. But about the exercise of power based on this agreement, Vidich and Bensman say:

> at almost every point in [their] seemingly broad . . . political domain the village and town boards adjust their·action to either the regulations and laws defined by state and federal agencies which claim parallel functions on a statewide or nationwide basis or to the fact that outside agencies have the power to withhold subsides to local political institutions. . . . The village board in Springdale accepts few of the powers given to it. . . . Town and village governments find it hard to act even when they have the power.[22]

Evidence gathered in New Haven, especially on the redevelopment issue, indicates the extent to which successful innovation depended upon the broadly based community consensus which was systematically built and nurtured by the mayor. When this sort of consensus is not sought or achieved, failure is not uncommon, as in the New Haven charter reform battle, and as Schulze demonstrates in recounting the painful lesson learned by the proponents of the new Cibola city charter, who had neglected to seek the consent of representatives of laboring and Negro groups.[23] Paul Miller cites figures which indicate that community attempts to build new hospitals were much more successful when they had the backing of local government leaders than when they were carried out strictly under private auspices.[24] As Ross and others have pointed out, private and semi-public charitable organizations and money-raising cam-

20. Merton, "Patterns of Influence."

21. Scoble, "Yankeetown," p. 39.

22. Arthur J. Vidich and Joseph Bensman, *Small Town in Mass Society* (Princeton, Princeton Univ. Press, 1958), pp. 98–100.

23. On New Haven charter reform, see Raymond E. Wolfinger, *The Politics of Progress*, pp. 357–90, and Dahl, *Who Governs?*, pp. 264–67. On Cibola charter reform, see Schulze, "Bifurcation."

24. Paul A. Miller, "The Process of Decision-making within the Context of Community Organization," *Rural Sociology, 17* (June 1952), 153–61.

paigns are generally controlled by the wealthy, so it is easy to deduce that one significant difference between public and private auspices in hospital fund-raising is the extent to which members of all segments of the community are allowed to participate.[25]

We can interpret the failure of elite-backed community programs from lack of popular support—either in votes or money—as one device through which members of nonelites seek to bring elites under control. Warner's data suggests that the unionization of the mills in Yankee City was an example of another such device, namely the promotion of counterelites.[26] A third device for bringing elites under control and enlarging the extent of community participation in decision-making is, as Coleman has indicated, the promulgation of controversy and conflict.[27]

Coleman has summarized numerous instances in which innovation by elites in community affairs was prevented because they lacked special grants of legitimacy. A typical pattern of community conflict identified by Coleman occurs when community leaders have failed to respond sympathetically to seemingly minor complaints by small groups of citizens. "Little" instances of administrative arbitrariness occasionally draw sympathy to the victims from other citizens who have quite different axes to grind; and the resulting public commiseration may lead to widespread and serious attacks on the legitimacy of many or all administrative activities. Coleman's work suggests the hypothesis that the more people become attentive to community policy-making, the more likely it is that anti-administration outcomes will ensue.

Striking evidence for this proposition is contained in a tabulation showing all available results of community referenda on the installation of fluoridation equipment (initiated by city administrations) between November 1951 and November 1955 in the United States.[28] The table suggests that most citizens are drawn into political participation when they have an objection to register, rather than when they have been sold on a political program they want to support. It also indicates that those who are only occasionally involved in community affairs prevail more often than not over those who are inclined to be regular in their participation,

25. Aileen D. Ross, "The Social Control of Philanthropy," *Am. J. Soc.*, 58 (March 1953), 451–60; Ross, "Philanthropic Activity and the Business Career," *Social Forces*, 32 (March 1954), 274–80; Ross, "Control and Leadership in Women's Groups: An Analysis of Philanthropic Money-raising Activity," *Social Forces*, 37 (Dec. 1958), 124–31; McKee, "Status and Power"; Lynd, *MIT*, pp. 79, 139, 140.

26. See Warner, YC 4, passim.

27. James S. Coleman, *Community Conflict* (Glencoe, Free Press, 1957).

28. Ibid., p. 19.

TURNOUT

|  | Under 10% | Over 30% |
|---|---|---|
| Fluoridation won | 58% | 37% |
| lost | 42% | 63% |
|  | 100% | 100% |
| Number of cases | 19 | 38 |

when those who are less involved turn out. But note that decision-makers
even in a conflict situation and for a referendum still typically are less
than a majority of the population. "High" turnout in Coleman's table
means "Over 30%." [29]

Another area of interest concerns the paths people travel in order to
become involved in decision-making. Information concerning leadership
recruitment is fragmentary in many community studies, but enough information exists for us to infer that few if any authoritative community
decision-making groups are made up of participants whose backgrounds
are entirely homogeneous. Contrary to the stratification theory assumption that leadership recruitment is a process whereby top leaders pull
into their midst congenial new blood, there is a good deal of evidence that
decision-makers become so by *self-selection*—pushing themselves into
the leadership group by showing interest, willingness to work, and competence.[30]

29. The table also underscores the relative rarity of the New Haven experience,
where the mayor sought to achieve special legitimacy for his redevelopment program
and succeeded for a time in increasing both turnout in mayoralty elections *and* his
margin of victory.

30. This was evidently the dominant pattern in New Haven (see above, Chap. 4;
Dahl, *Who Governs?*; and Wolfinger's *Politics of Progress*); in urban renewal on
the south side of Chicago (see Peter H. Rossi and Robert A. Dentler, *The Politics
of Urban Renewal* [New York, Free Press of Glencoe, 1961]); in Lorain (see
McKee, "Status and Power"); in Yankeetown (see Scoble); and in New York City
(see Sayre and Kaufman, *Governing New York City*). One supposes that in each
community a minimal amount of resources of some kind are necessary for participation in decision-making to be possible, but this minimum must vary tremendously
from issue to issue and depend less upon sheer amount than upon the skill and
dedication with which resources are manipulated. Clark (*Chicago Big Businessman*)
describes most Chicago big businessmen as relatively ineffective in community decision-making, and Wilson ("Negro Leaders in Chicago") paints a similarly pessimistic
picture of leadership in the Chicago Negro community. Yet Rossi and Dentler report
that the single actor who succeeded most consistently in getting what he wanted
from South Side Chicago urban renewal was an unprepossessing Negro dining-car
waiter named Victor Towns, who was not even a leader or high in status in the
Negro community. He was, however, extremely diligent in pressing claims on renewal
planners in behalf of the welfare of his block, which he legitimately represented. The

Presumably, a theory of community power would attempt to specify the conditions under which different patterns of participation—that is to say, of specialization, legitimacy, recruitment, and reciprocal controls between elites and nonelites—exist. A second major task for such a theory is the examination of the distribution of values in decision-making, which carries us into a discussion of the nature of community decisions.

## Who Gains, Who Loses?

If politics is who *gets* what, when, and how, then knowing who appears to receive indulgences and who appears to suffer deprivations from community decisions should presumably be helpful in identifying possessors of community power. Let us keep two different indices separate for the moment: simply *getting* things that are generally valued is the matter at hand; getting what one *wants* or *prefers* is quite another and will be discussed later. I am going to suggest reasons why knowing value distributions is insufficient and perhaps misleading in discovering who rules. Briefly, these reasons are: (1) value distributions occur without explicit decisions taking place, hence may tell us nothing about decision-making; (2) values within the community may be distributed in important ways as a by-product of decisions and nondecisions made outside the community; (3) there are many irrationalities in decision-making, which may lead to the distribution of values in unpredictable, unintended ways; (4) the powerful may intentionally distribute values to the nonpowerful.

We commonly speak of decisions as "choices among alternatives," [31] and immediately it becomes necessary to clarify the notion of "choice" when used to describe collective decision-making. It is easy enough (though, as I shall suggest below, misleading) to postulate an individual, or a small group of individuals, consciously considering an array of possible future events, consulting their list of goals, and picking a course of action which they calculate will lead to the most preferred state of affairs. This is in fact more or less the process advanced by stratification writers as descriptive of community decision-making. But the evidence indicates that decentralized, fragmented, constrained, reversible, and relatively uncoordinated (as among issue-areas) decision-making is the rule. This leads to the possibility that many outcomes, seen from the per-

possession of certain kinds of resources may, in fact, render leaders vulnerable to pressure, as in the case of prosperous retail businessmen who nonetheless remain dependent upon local good will. See Kenneth Wilson Underwood, *Protestant and Catholic* (Boston, Beacon, 1957).

31. See, e.g., Herbert A. Simon, *Administrative Behavior* (2d ed. New York, Macmillan, 1957), pp. 3–4.

spective of the entire community, are not intended by anybody, and consequently who "wins" indulgences in these cases cannot be construed as indicative of the *power* of actors, though it may correctly indicate some other of their value-positions.

Norton Long gives the example of a community which every day is collectively fed, clothed, employed, and sheltered, not as the result of a single program, but rather by the individual activities of myriad citizens, none of whom intend, or are concerned with, the collective outcome. [32] There is at least one sense, then, in which many payoffs of community life must be considered fortuitous and beyond the control of actors in the system.

A second instance in which this may be true is when the community is affected by forces from outside. National and international events of all kinds have their repercussions in community life: war industry in neighboring communities provoked the outmigration of the Morris, Illinois, labor force; the depression accentuated the dependence of Muncie upon the largesse of the Ball family; the war stopped school construction in New Haven, and postponed until 1945 the emergence of an Italian candidate for mayor, who rode to power on the school issue; the Federal Housing Act of 1949 provided essential resources for Mayor Lee's urban renewal venture. The list can be extended indefinitely. At most, actors within the community can take into account these larger forces in making their private calculations; they can only rarely alter the impact these events have on the life of the community. [33]

We can say, then, that many community "decisions" are unconscious, intended by nobody in the community, and yet have profound consequences for the shaping and sharing of community values. Let us move next to the consideration of *conscious* decisions, where choices are made by actors from a set of more or less explicitly delineated alternatives. The way in which this array is conceived is critical. Some, perhaps most, *possible* courses of action are never considered in community decision-making simply because they are inconceivable to the actors involved. No one seems ever to have seriously considered turning the privately owned New Haven Water Company over to the city, for example, although there seems to be no reason why this could not be done. The array of alterna-

32. Long, "Local Community as an Ecology of Games," p. 251.
33. See Vidich and Bensman, *Small Town in Mass Society*, e.g., pp. 81–82; Elin Anderson, *We Americans* (Cambridge, Harvard Univ. Press, 1938), passim; Walker, *Steeltown*, passim; Lynd, *MIT*, passim; Jones, *Life, Liberty and Property*, passim; and esp. Peter H. Rossi, "Community Decision-making," *Administrative Science Quarterly, 1* (March 1957), 415–43.

tives presented for community decision-making seems likely, then, to be determined by considerations very different from a rational canvassing of all technically feasible possibilities. What determines the agenda of alternatives within which community decision-making takes place?

There are several plausible answers to this question, but the current state of affairs seems to be centrally important in determining the future course of action.[34] Most of the American communities studied in any detail seem to be relatively healthy political organisms, which means that there is bound to be considerable conservatism, boundary maintenance and self-preservation rather than innovation and demand for change within the system. Sayre and Kaufman suggest two reasons why this is likely to be so: in the first place:

> every modification of the existing state of affairs—of the rules, of personnel, of governmental or administrative structure or procedure, or of public policies and programs—entails the fear of cost for some participants as well as hope of gain for the proponents. . . . In most instances the costs of change are more intensely perceived by participants close to the center of decisions than are the benefits of innovation. Those who perceive the costs of change in the city's going system have strategies and weapons with which to resist. They ordinarily have prizes to withhold, inducements to offer, sanctions to impose. . . . The prospects for any advocate of change are intense opposition: lengthy, costly, wearing maneuvering and negotiation, and uncertainty about results until the last battle is won. If the anticipation of such a struggle, with all its costs in money, time, energy, and the possible disruption of longstanding friendships and alliances, is not enough to discourage campaigns in support of many proposed innovations, the strain and the drain of the *actual* fight may well exhaust the supporters and induce them to abandon their causes before they have come near their goals.

In the second place, public officers and employees, whose action is required to make official the decisions reached by the participants in the specialized centers in which they operate, are ordinarily reluctant to move vigorously when there is extensive opposition within

34. Other plausible answers might be that the agenda of alternatives is determined by the ideologies of choosers; by the "real interests of choosers (The reality of the interests being stipulated by the investigator according to criteria that may or may not be explicit.); by accident; by certain underlying "structural" characteristics of the community (e.g., company town vs. dormitory suburb vs. metropolis). In presenting my own candidate for the best answer, I do not mean to exclude or for that matter to endorse these possibilities. A theory that claimed some measure of comprehensiveness would probably have to consider the extent to which each of these factors determined the course of community decision-making.

the constellation of interested individuals and groups. For they, as the formal authors of changes, are most likely to bear the brunt of enmities and retaliations provoked by adverse consequences of departure from established practice. They are the visible and vulnerable targets of blame for failure, though they must often share with others any credit for achievements. Indeed, officials are understandably wary even when there is a general consensus on the desirability of a particular novelty, for they must try to take into account consequences unanticipated by the assenters. They are doubly cautious when an important and highly vocal segment of their constituency stresses the dangers and costs. So the world of officialdom is often prudent when confronted by recommendations for innovation.[35]

Dahl has suggested as a general principle that: "If A's goal requires a slight change or weak response from B, and C's goals require a great change or a strong response, then with equal resources, rates and efficiencies [of resource employment], A is more likely to succeed than C. Or, to put it another way, A can attain his political goals with *less influence* than C can. Thus, if A's goals fall well within 'political consensus' he may have to do little beyond maintaining the consensus; whereas if C's goals fall well outside the 'political consensus,' then for him to achieve his goals may require access to enormous resources." [36]

The relevance of this hypothesis to the present discussion is to suggest conditions under which the "current state of affairs," or the "political consensus" does not rather drastically restrict the array of available alternatives in community decision-making. It is not enough, as the quotations above make clear, for an alternative to be technically feasible. It also must be politically palatable and relatively easy to accomplish; otherwise great amounts of influence have to be brought to bear with great skill and efficiency in order to secure its adoption. Conclusions that might be drawn from this are that the community agenda of alternatives is relatively insensitive to any but very great differences in the power of actors and that only influence differences of the greatest magnitude as between actors are likely to be reflected in changes in the alternatives presented to decision-makers.

Community agendas, then, are hard to change. But if insensitivities to power differences distinguish the array of alternatives presented to decision-makers, similar insensitivities mark the processes of choosing among

35. Sayre and Kaufman, *Governing New York City*, pp. 716–18.
36. Dahl, "Leadership in a Fragmented Political System," p. 18.

these alternatives. The uncertainties[37] of most real-world decision-making have been well enough documented and discussed elsewhere to obviate the necessity for going into the subject once more here.[38] Only one point needs to be reiterated: many community decisions distribute many values in unintended, unanticipated ways. Finally, as I have pointed out in previous chapters, the allegedly powerful often intend, and succeed in their intention, to distribute values to the nonpowerful. All of these circumstances suggest the unwisdom of depending upon knowledge of who gets what from community decisions for the purpose of determining who rules.

## WHO SUCCEEDS?

If the preceding analysis is correct, then the question "Who rules in American communities?" is in many ways devoid of meaning. Rulership, according to pluralist theory, is often characterized by (1) relatively wide sharing of powers among leaders specialized to one or a few issue-areas, calling upon many different resources and techniques for applying resources to influencing outcomes, (2) constraints upon decision-making applied by nonelites and by elites themselves, (3) conditions of all kinds imposed by impersonal outside forces, and (4) uncertainty about the distributions of payoffs of political actions. But given these conditions of modern American local life, some people attain their ends more frequently than others, and a theory of community power might reasonably be expected to explore "rulership" in this rather more limited sense of the term.

What distinguishes those who succeed from those who fail in gaining their preferences in community decision-making? Three kinds of events can be considered as, in some sense, indices of success: when an actor initiates some community policy, meets with no opposition, and it is enacted; when an actor prevents the policy of some other actor from being enacted; and when an actor initiates a policy, meets with opposition, and the policy is enacted.[39]

Success in these three situations evidently does not come automatically to possessors of great amounts of any one of the many possible resources available to actors in community life. This finding is significant not only

37. I.e., uncertainties with respect to the goals to be maximized, the best means for maximizing them, the likelihood that the best means is feasible, the possible disadvantageous by-products of various alternatives, the likelihood that these by-products will come into play if various alternatives are chosen, and so forth.

38. Robert A. Dahl and Charles E. Lindblom, *Politics, Economics and Welfare* (New York, Harper, 1953), pp. 161–68; Simon, *Administrative Behavior*, passim.

39. See Dahl, "Leadership in a Fragmented Political System."

as a statement about the real world, but for its bearing upon research strategy as well. Many resources in combination—time, knowledge, energy, esteem, money, legitimacy, and so on—must be applied with skill and diligence for actors to succeed in influencing community decisions in desired directions. This throws the focus of attention away from the sheer amount and distribution of resources available in the community to the rate and efficiency with which they are employed.

Resources and skill and diligence in exploiting them are three conditions which make for success in influencing community decisions. A fourth has been mentioned: ability to choose goals that do not strain the compliance of others in the system. A fifth condition of successful participation is closely related to the fourth: capacity to form coalitions with other participants in order to achieve one's goals. This entails choosing goals which do not preclude the possibility of joining with others; hence certain limits on the preferences of actors are implied in this condition as in the fourth. This condition for success also imposes a limitation on the strategies available to actors for achieving their goals. In order successfully to form coalitions with others, it is necessary to pursue courses of action which do not conflict with potential allies.

Certain hypotheses may be noted about coalitions.[40] They seem to come into existence in order to provide actors with the means for increasing the resources available to them in the pursuit of their own ends. We might hypothesize that *complementarity of resources* would be a powerful incentive for actors to form coalitions with one another, as, for example, an actor with popularity allying with one having wealth. A second prerequisite for the formation of coalitions would be *compatibility of goals and strategies*. Actors with different resources are not necessarily capable of pursuing compatible strategies. Furthermore, it seems likely that, given different bases of strength, their demands and expectations might diverge greatly even if their strategies were harmonized. From this hypothesis, one might deduce that the larger the coalition, the more fragile it is and the more limited its goals must be if it is to maintain itself intact and remain effective in its political environment. It seems plausible to suggest that successful coalitions are likely to be single-minded, and when coalitions take on new goals—perhaps as the result of bureaucratization—their membership may well be expected to fall away.[41]

40. Here, as elsewhere, I am drawing upon research memoranda which I wrote for the Hyde Park-Kenwood Demonstration Research Project, based on field work done in Chicago, and reported more fully in Rossi and Dentler, *Politics of Urban Renewal*.

41. The case of the Hyde Park-Kenwood Community Conference is in point. The

Perhaps the most important long-range task of a theory of community power is to distinguish among communities on the basis of their patterns of decision-making.[42] I hope such a theory would provide clues as to the characteristics of communities which are critically significant in determining the kinds of decision-making taking place. But before this problem can be addressed, it is necessary to reorient our expectations about the kinds of decision-making one typically finds in American communities. The literature we examined in previous chapters suggests an initial distinction between hierarchical and pluralistic decision-making patterns. However, no properly documented instances of communities where hierarchy predominates have come to light. Thus, for the moment, we are left with a plethora of independent variables, any or all of which may be sufficient conditions for the production of a single dependent variable— the pluralistic pattern of decision-making.

One might consequently expect, or hope, that the next steps in thinking about community power would be conducted along two broad lines. First, we might anticipate the differentiation of a few or several different forms of pluralistic decision-making whose course and effects could be observed in American communities.[43] Second, we might look forward to the identification of combinations of other features, of an economic, legal, demographic, social-structural, or cultural character, whose presence seemed to indicate the presence of one or another form of pluralistic decision-making. As studies in depth of individual communities accumulate, it will become necessary to seek devices such as this kind of comparative analysis for summarizing the information they contain. As students become increasingly concerned with satisfying the demands of scientific method and theoretical relevance in the conduct of their research, their results become more amenable to meaningful summary, and we may therefore reasonably expect the early formulation of provisional theories of community power which correspond more closely to the facts of the world around us.

Conference actually lost members over years when it was broadening its goals and increasing its staff. See Rossi and Dentler, *Politics of Urban Renewal.*

42. Harold D. Lasswell (*The Decision Process* [College Park, Md., Bureau of Governmental Research, College of Business and Public Administration, Univ. of Maryland, 1956]) gives seven categories which might be useful in developing a cross-community analysis. I have not employed them in drawing together information from a number of studies primarily because the data at hand were rather severely limited and seemed incapable of supplying sufficient information to make the introduction of this scheme worthwhile.

43. One study that makes progress in this area is Dahl's *Who Governs?*, especially in its discussion of the varieties of relationships among leaders possible in the modern American city.

# A Further Look at Problems of Evidence and Inference

To the true aquarium fan, dead fish are no drawback at all. One New Yorker who liked his aquarium simply threw out the dead fish and tossed a book full of beautiful fish photos in the aquarium along with a drawing of a fish that was his own creation. He says his "collection" inspires more comments than live fish ever did.

A New Jersey collector has taken it one step further. He bought a tank for his office and stocked it with the customary amenities: plants, rocks, decorations, and a filter. Then he pasted a sign on the aquarium worded: "Do Not Feed—Invisible Fish." Most of his co-workers caught the joke, but one didn't. After studying the aquarium at length, he said, "How do you know the fish are in there?"

"It's easy," answered the owner. "When the light reflects just right on the water's surface, you can see the water currents shift."

The other fellow peered back in the aquarium for a long while and then his face lit up. "Yeah, yeah, you know you're right!" he exclaimed. "Now I see them."

*Wall Street Journal,* July 8, 1971

# 8. Points of General Agreement

The chief goals of this book, as it was originally conceived, were as follows:

1. To describe a consensus about the locus of power in American communities.

2. To evaluate this consensus in the light of empirical evidence.

3. To diagnose the causes of discrepancies between this consensus and evidence failing to sustain it.

4. To indicate an alternative strategy for studying power in American communities, a program of research that seemed to escape the difficulties of the strategy that led to the evidently erroneous consensus.

5. To make recommendations about the course of future research, taking into consideration the foregoing, as well as other material.

How well these goals were accomplished is, of course, a matter of opinion. Judging from the reviews when *Community Power and Political Theory* first appeared and subsequent references to it in the literature, I would say that on the whole the accomplishment of the first three goals has been widely acknowledged, but my efforts with respect to the last two have not found general acceptance.

## The Critique of the Stratification Literature

As to the critique of the stratificationist literature, the verdict seems to be favorable. Considering that this book took a strong position against a substantial and respectable body of conventional wisdom, this ready acceptance seems, in retrospect, fairly remarkable. Nevertheless, the points I attempted to make in the early chapters appear to have been pretty much conceded. No one did so more graciously than Robert O. Schulze, author of the Ypsilanti study, who, despite great reservations on other matters, said:

> Although now and then strained, Polsby's guerilla foray into the very camp of the enemy is generally as perceptive and telling as it is sustained . . . [and] he astutely documents the pitfall of the self-fulfilling prophecy.[1]

1. Robert O. Schulze, "For a Brown Man's Bookshelf," *Brown Alumni Monthly* (Nov. 1963), 22.

Much the same sort of comment came from Phillips Cutright, writing in the *American Sociological Review:*

> Close examination of each source reveals that the research evidence in support of the stratification theory of community power is weak. Perhaps the most compelling aspect of Polsby's argument is his demonstration that the available evidence can be used either to support or to deny the theory.[2]

For some scholars these first chapters, far from disputing a consensus, as I thought I was doing, actually merely constituted a summary of the obvious, as Robert Wood's comment in the *American Political Science Review* illustrates:

> The task of the book is essentially to overturn the theory and conclusions of the stratification school . . . especially as this analysis is applied to community power structures. . . . Although Polsby executes his assignments skillfully, he adds little to what he has said before.[3]

And Warner Bloomberg, Jr., said:

> Polsby sometimes sounds as if he were the first to discover that the descriptions and analyses of Middletown, Yankee City and Elmtown-Jonesville provided us only with seminal beginnings, not final conclusions.[4]

More generously, Joseph LaPalombara said:

> Those who are not victims of the same snares that Polsby discusses will agree that the evidence provided by stratification studies can be used to draw diametrically opposed conclusions.[5]

Peter Bachrach and Morton Baratz wrote:

> Suffice it simply to observe that whatever the merits of their own approach to power, the pluralists have effectively exposed the main weaknesses of the elitist model.[6]

---

2. *Am. Soc. Rev., 29* (April 1964), 298.

3. *Am. Pol. Sci. Rev., 58* (June 1964), 415.

4. *Am. J. Soc., 70* (July 1964), 102–03.

5. *Annals of the American Academy of Political and Social Science, 355* (Sept. 1964), 171–72. Other reviews in more or less the same vein are Peter Rossi's in *Political Science Quarterly, 81* (March 1966), 170, and M. Kent Jennings's in *Journal of Politics, 26* (Nov. 1964), 939–40.

6. Peter Bachrach and Morton S. Baratz, "Two Faces of Power," *Am. Pol. Sci. Rev., 56* (Dec. 1962), 948.

And this is now what one says of this literature:

> In fact, it is quite easy, as Nelson Polsby has done, to show the lack
> of any empirical and theoretical foundation in Hunter's thesis.[7]

In the later judgment of two sociologists:

> The field of community power structure has matured considerably; it
> has lost its elite obsession. The older penchant to ferret out an elite
> composed of business leaders, who singlemindedly preserved in their
> own image the institutions of the community, has given way to a more
> complex and pluralistic view of communities.[8]

Perhaps the best indication of the general acceptance of early portions
of this book is the extent to which what were once hard-won insights are
now casually accepted as common knowledge. In 1975, an able British
student of community power, taking his inspiration, as it were, from the
air around him, could write the following extended passage summarizing
the general state of play in the literature:

> It was said that the reputational method is no more than a com-
> plicated way of asking local inside-dopesters for a quick rundown on
> the local big shots, an approach often used by newspapermen with
> just about the same validity and reliability of results. The main criticism
> was that the reputational method is appropriately named because it
> never gets beyond reputational or perceived power to real or actual
> power. Informants may know what is really going on, but they may
> not. They may base their opinions on idle gossip or the gospel truth,
> but there is no way of distinguishing gospellers from gossipers. Con-
> sequently the method may pick out the powerful but it may pick out
> those with nothing more than a reputation for power, and while it is
> true that what people do is affected by what they believe others have
> the power to do—the rule of anticipated reactions—the relationship
> between reputed power and actual power has never been examined at
> all closely.
>
>     There is also some ambiguity about the central terms "power" and
> "influence". It is argued that Hunter confuses the potential to do
> things, based on control of resources like money or political office, with
> actually doing them, as shown in political activity which influences the
> course of events. One man may have great potential for power, but

7. Manuel Castells, *The Urban Question: A Marxist Approach* (London, Arnold,
1977), p. 247.
    8. Michael Aiken and Paul E. Mott, *The Structure of Community Power* (New
York, Random House, 1970), p. 361.

not use it; another may have little potential but exploit it to the full. There is also the strong possibility that the informants may use the terms "power" and "influence" in a variety of different ways. Social scientists themselves find difficulty with closely related terms like "power", "influence", "control" and "authority", so there is no reason to believe that laymen, intelligent or otherwise, will use the words in any consistent way. It is all too easy to confuse power with status and, as a result, the reputational method may not pick out the most powerful, but simply the most visible and conspicuous. Lastly, there are problems about the scope of power. A man may be powerful in educational matters but relatively powerless on housing issues, so it may be misleading or entirely meaningless to produce general power rankings over all issue areas in the community, as the reputationalists tended to do.

It is also claimed that the reputational method produces self-fulfilling prophecies. Just to ask the question "Who is powerful?" is to assume that some people are powerful and others are not, and the term "power structure" implies a more or less stable pattern of power relations, as compared with a more fluid and impermanent pattern. Moreover, Hunter picks out the forty names mentioned most frequently by his informants, and then points to the small size of the elite. But why pick out forty? Why not four hundred, or four thousand, or just four? In addition, Hunter never really shows that the top forty operated as a more or less cohesive elite, something he must do if he is to demonstrate his case for the existence of a single power elite in the city.

In short, the reputationalists have been accused of assuming the answers to the questions they set out to investigate, of asking leading questions, or working with self-fulfilling prophecies, of using intolerably sloppy methods and concepts, and of systematically ignoring evidence they did not like. The obvious response to this onslaught is to verify the reputational results against the results yielded by other methods, something which quite a few people have tried to do, although with differing results. But this tactic makes little sense. The great strength of the reputational method is also its great weakness—its claim to give the inside story which cannot be uncovered in any other way short of years of participant observation. The need for an inside story will be felt as long as there are social scientists who believe that politics is a dirty game and that we can see only half of what goes on. According to this view of politics, some of the most important decisions may be taken in secret sessions held behind locked doors in smoke-filled rooms full of wheeler-dealer politicians who threaten and bluff and bribe and bargain as well as stab each other in the back and sell each other down the river. The only way of getting reliable evidence about this hidden part of the decision-making process is for the social scientist himself to become involved, either as a participant observer or as an influential politician. Since neither strategies are possible in most cases, and since both have their own drawback in producing hard evidence, the investigator has to rely on indirect information produced by people who he hopes are reliable. But the reputationalist is at the mercy of his informants. There is no way of checking their evidence against that produced by more "objective" methods.[9]

## WHY THE STRATIFICATION LITERATURE WENT WRONG: ALTERNATIVE EXPLANATIONS

On the basis of comments like these, I conclude that the argument of this book about the deficiencies of the stratification theory of community power is fairly well accepted.[10] On the third main point, the matter of diagnosis, there is what I would call a substantial explanation in the field that competes with the explanation I have offered. My view, based on a close reading of texts and an attempt to see the overarching logic of the position these texts espouse, was that the stratification theory of community power proceeds from general stratification theory, and that acceptance of the reasonableness or plausibility or usefulness of the general theory may well have predisposed investigators to adopt the special stratification theory (of community power) even in the face of inadequate or contradictory evidence.

A few scholars have come at the problem slightly differently, looking at large numbers of studies in the aggregate and offering correlations of

9. Kenneth Newton, "Community Politics and Decision-Making: The American Experience and Its Lessons," in Ken Young, ed., *Essays on the Study of Urban Politics* (Hamden, Conn., Archon Books, 1975), pp. 2–4.

10. One exception, a very minor one, occurs in the literature: Alan Rosenbaum, "Community Power and Political Theory: A Case of Misperception," *Berkeley Journal of Sociology*, 12 (Summer 1967), 91–116. Rosenbaum's argument that I misrepresent the literature analyzed in chapters 2 and 3 is based on a reading only of the illustrative footnotes in Chapter 1 and neglects both text and footnotes in the second and third chapters. Given Rosenbaum's refusal to look at evidence embarrassing—indeed fatal— to his conclusions, it is not altogether surprising that the argument he makes has found little support.

This book is in any event not alone in claiming that the stratification literature is defective. See, for example, Herbert Kaufman and Victor Jones, "The Mystery of Power," *Public Administration Review*, 14 (Summer 1954), 205–12; Robert A. Dahl, "A Critique of the Ruling Elite Model," *Am. Pol. Sci. Rev.*, 52 (June 1958), 463–69; and Raymond E. Wolfinger, "Reputation and Reality in the Study of 'Community Power'," *Am. Soc. Rev.*, 25 (Oct. 1960), 636–44.

some of their characteristics as explanations for their findings. Thus, by examining 33 studies of community power, John Walton is able to conclude:

> the disciplinary background of the investigator tends to determine the method of investigation he will adopt which, in turn, tends to determine the image of the power structure that results from the investigation.[11]

The relevant findings are as follows:[12]

WALTON FINDINGS

Discipline of Researcher

|  | | Sociology | Political Science |
|---|---|---|---|
| Type of Power Structure Found | Pyramidal | 12 | 7 |
|  | Other | 16 | 20 |
|  |  | 28 | 27 |

Correlations such as these presumably constitute not explanations but social facts which themselves need explaining. They still leave open the question of why sociologists tend disproportionately to adopt the reputational method and discover power elites, while non-sociologists do not, an issue to which my "internal" diagnosis purported to speak.

Thus, my inclination is to view findings of this sort as not constituting a refutation of the view I have expressed, since they may simply document the greater influence of a general theory of stratification among sociologists. This is a not altogether implausible state of affairs, given the far greater prominence of formal training in theories of social stratification in the graduate experience of sociologists.

A further inference has been made from these data, however, which seems to me to have generated an alternative explanation more vulnerable to criticism. It could be argued that what these data show is that it just so happens that sociologists tend to pick communities to study in which power is actually closely held, and political scientists tend to pick communities in which power is more dispersed. Clark et al. say, following a suggestion of Rossi's:

11. John Walton, "Discipline, Method, and Community Power: A Note on the Sociology of Knowledge," *Am. Soc. Rev., 31* (Oct. 1966), 688. Michael Aiken, "The Distribution of Community Power: Structural Bases and Social Consequences," in Aiken and Mott, *Structure of Community Power*, pp. 492–93, reports a similar pattern with a population of 57 studies.
12. The figures are from Walton, "Discipline, Method, and Community Power," Table 3, p. 687. The 33 studies providing his basic data codify information about 55 communities, as reflected in the table.

Is it not possible that researchers (often sociologists) who chose to use the reputational method also chose (perhaps consciously, perhaps not) to study communities that were characterized by relatively centralized decision-making structures? And correspondingly, might not other researchers, who chose to use a variety of research methods, also have tended to select for study (again consciously or unconsciously) communities with more decentralized decision-making structures?[13]

While this may be true, the proper basis from which to make such an argument ought not to be simple correlations of the sort presented in these studies, but rather should include a fairly conscientious evaluation of the adequacy of the empirical demonstrations that underpin assertions about the actual shape of the dependent variable. This is missing from secondary analyses which have so far reached print. The fact that we have available many primary studies does not dispose of the necessity for inquiring whether there is adequate empirical warrant for believing what each of them says about the concentration or dispersion of power in the local communities they discuss. We do know of at least one instance, that of Seattle, Washington, in which a sociologist found a concentrated and a political scientist a dispersed power structure within the same community.[14] This coincidence, which Walton codes, correctly, as supporting his basic correlation, undercuts an inference that the reason things sort out that way is because these two different disciplines tend to produce investigators who specialize in studying different sorts of communities. Rather, as this instance shows, it is more likely that different investigators bring different sorts of presuppositions to the same sorts of community, as my original argument maintained.

My view is that there is so much on the record that casts doubt on certain ways of studying community power—and for the moment I will restrict this charge to studies displaying difficulties of the sort discussed in early chapters of this book—that until the doubts that have been raised

13. Terry N. Clark, William Kornblum, Harold Bloom, and Susan Tobias, "Discipline, Method, Community Structure, and Decision-Making: The Role and Limitations of the Sociology of Knowledge," *The American Sociologist*, 3 (Aug. 1968), 215. Rossi's remark is in Peter H. Rossi, "Power and Community Structure," *Midwest Journal of Political Science*, 4 (Nov. 1960), 398.

14. See John Walton, "Substance and Artifact: The Current Status of Research on Community Power Structure," *Am. J. Soc.*, 71 (Jan. 1966), 430–38. Table 1 codes "Pacific City" as "pyramidal" and Seattle (the same city, but in a different study) as "coalitional." There are also sharp differences between Hunter and Jennings on Atlanta. See Hunter, *CPS*, and M. Kent Jennings, *Community Influentials: The Elites of Atlanta* (Glencoe, Free Press, 1964).

about these studies can be dispelled they ought not to be quoted, or enumerated, in support of general propositions purporting to say something about the actual power structures of local communities.

Once we get beyond the notion that because a study is in print whatever it says is true, what remains of these correlational studies? At the least, some correlations. These may conceivably yield, as I have suggested, to the explanation I have already offered, that is, to some sort of "internal" explanation that seeks to say what it is about being a member of one or another discipline that would tend to predispose a scholar to one or another point of view.

In my own opinion, the grip of disciplinary loyalties per se in matters of this kind is likely to be weak. There are, as we know, numerous instances of sociologists espousing a "pluralist" position—in some sense—with respect to community power, and of political scientists finding themselves in greater sympathy with the stratificationist position.[15] If cases deviating from a statistical regularity are frequent enough or interesting enough, as I believe they are here, the power of the alleged independent variable is open to question.

And, indeed, the very regularity of the statistics purporting to show differences along disciplinary lines is questionable as well. Walton's figures, given above, from his 33 studies (reporting distributions of power in 55 communities) can be compared with another study by Curtis and Petras, using a larger set of communities, including all those summarized in Walton's work plus 28 others:[16]

CURTIS AND PETRAS FINDINGS

Discipline of Researcher

| Type of Power Structure Found | Sociology | | Political Science |
|---|---|---|---|
| | Pyramidal | 22 | 4 |
| | Other | 28 | 14 |
| | | 50 | 18 |

An alert reader will note at least one anomaly. Although Curtis and Petras claim to have incorporated all the primary studies included in Walton's earlier work, they have somehow come up with nine fewer entries in the "political science" column. This raises the whole issue of coding

15. As I argue in n. 29, chap. 1. I claim below that identifying what a "pluralist" position is has been the occasion of no little confusion in this literature, but in any event numerous sociologists have held that in the communities they studied power was dispersed. See, for example, n. 5, chap. 9.

16. James E. Curtis and John W. Petras, "Community Power, Power Studies, and the Sociology of Knowledge," *Human Organization*, 29 (Fall 1970), 204–18; the figures are from Table 2, p. 207.

reliability, an issue given further point by a textual reference by Curtis and Petras (following Walton) to two political scientists as "sociologists."[17]

Thus these secondary studies display at least two problems with their basic data. First, there are difficulties in establishing an intelligible population of primary studies and, second, there are problems in making sure that primary studies have been correctly sorted into analytical categories. Are conclusions based on Walton's population of 33 primary studies more or less tenable than conclusions based on Curtis and Petras's 61? Or Michael Aiken's 57? Or Claire Gilbert's 166 cities (not studies)?[18]

Unfortunately, the answer is not perfectly straightforward. More rather than fewer primary studies presumably give a more complete, hence a better, picture of the relationship between discipline, methods, and conclusions. However, there is the problem of quality controls. Some primary studies in the larger population are not community power studies, and even when they are community power studies, what their findings actually show on key points are not always easy to establish. This vagueness is carried forward into secondary analysis. So it should come as no surprise that when a student took the step of asking the original authors of primary studies of 43 communities to classify the "power structure" they had allegedly discovered according to Walton's categories of secondary analysis, very large discrepancies appeared between what they thought they had found and what Walton, and Curtis and Petras, believed they had found: 30 cases of disagreement and 10 of agreement between Curtis and Petras and original authors; 15 disagreements and 8 agreements between Walton and original authors.[19]

Thus the correlations that give rise to the whole enterprise are themselves of dubious merit. An explanation of discrepancies between evidence and conclusions based upon the coincidence of an investigator's disciplinary loyalty and his consequent choice of method—which, as I have indicated, would constitute no explanation at all, even if it were correctly carried out—is unsatisfactory.

17. Ibid., p. 207. The investigators are George Belknap and Ralph Smuckler, miscoded by Walton in "Discipline, Method and Community Power," Table 1, p. 686.

18. Claire W. Gilbert, "Some Trends in Community Politics: A Secondary Analysis of Power Structure Data from 166 Communities," *Southwestern Social Science Quarterly*, 48 (Dec. 1967), 373–81; "The Study of Community Power: A Summary and a Test," in Scott Greer, Dennis L. McElrath, David W. Minar, Peter Orleans, eds., *The New Urbanization* (New York, St. Martin's Press, 1968), pp. 222–45; "Community Power and Decision-Making: A Quantitative Examination of Previous Research," in Terry N. Clark, ed., *Community Structure and Decision-Making*, pp. 139–56; "Communities, Power Structures and Research Bias," *Polity*, 4 (Winter 1971), 219–35; *Community Power Structure* (Gainesville, Univ. of Florida Press, 1972).

19. Michael D. Nelson, "The Validity of Secondary Analyses of Community Power Studies," *Social Forces*, 52 (June 1974), pp. 531–37.

Another candidate explanation for differences among findings, namely differences in the general ideological or political commitments of investigators, does have the disadvantage I pointed to earlier, namely that these differences fail to sort radicals like the Lynds or C. Wright Mills and conservatives like Digby Baltzell or Andrew Hacker into different categories: all these scholars in common appear to accept or produce stratificationist findings, yet their general political preferences evidently diverge sharply. I have not conducted a survey of political preferences among students of community power, and so have no systematic knowledge of their "positions" on a large number of issues. Casual knowledge suggests that, just as is the case on the stratificationist side, some scholars responsible for elements of the "pluralist" critique have espoused views in public that on a national political spectrum would be regarded as to the left; others would probably fall somewhere near the center. I do not personally know of any "pluralist" researchers—although they may well exist—who are so far right-wing in American politics as to consider themselves plain ordinary Republicans.[20] This suggests that insofar as the private—or, for that matter, public—loyalties of the persons who write in this field are concerned, most of the intellectual controversy is being generated from a relatively narrow band in the political spectrum, with much overlapping and criss-crossing in the extraneous sympathies of scholars. All this fortifies my view that diagnoses of differences in this field relying on the general political sympathies of scholars as an explanatory variable are likely to be mistaken or misleading, and that my "internal" explanation remains the most promising diagnosis of the factors responsible for differences among scholars in this area.

This more or less disposes of the issues in the field that are fairly easy to dispatch, and that are the source of relatively little disagreement. It was also a goal of my original study, however, to move beyond the identification of factors responsible for the discrepancies between empirical findings and conclusions in community power studies and, in a more constructive spirit, to explore an alternative strategy for studying community power that would escape the difficulties I had described. The recommendations I made, which more or less codify and rationalize large elements of the research strategy evolved by Robert Dahl in his study of New Haven, have themselves been strongly criticized. It is to elements of this critique that I now turn.

20. See the earlier discussion in this book, above, p. 107. Just as it is possible for scholars who agree politically to disagree about political science, the reverse also sometimes occurs. See, for example, Thomas R. Dye and L. Harmon Ziegler, *The Irony of Democracy* (Belmont, Cal., Wadsworth, 1970), p. vii.

# 9. A Symmetry of Error?

Perhaps the most pervasive criticism of the recommendations I have made about how to study community power, and of the New Haven study in general, is that the so-called pluralist alternative leads to mistakes exactly like those identified as crippling stratification studies.

As Robert O. Schulze put it:

> The pluralist alternative, no less than the social stratification model, is itself easily converted "into ideology, thus imprisoning rather than disciplining thought". And so I think that Polsby ... himself slips over the brink.[1]

The most famous and, if one can judge from the frequency with which it is cited, undoubtedly the most influential formulation of this criticism is Bachrach and Baratz's flat assertion:

> The pluralists' ... approach to and assumptions about power predetermine their findings and conclusions.[2]

Other statements of this kind abound in the literature.[3] They are not, however, entirely unambiguous in their meaning, since they allow for both a weak and a strong interpretation. One sort of allegation would assert

1. Schulze, "Brown Man's Bookshelf."
2. Bachrach and Baratz, "Two Faces of Power," p. 952.
3.      Our review of the areas of contention between Dahl and Mills and of the organization of their respective studies reveals, I believe, that their resulting analyses are in large part self-fulfilling. In each case the focal point of analysis (that is, the political arena vs. the interrelations of the identified elite) and the conceptual decisions made seem to foster the interpretation rather than to provide a test of it ... ; moreover, each reinforces his own position by making favorable assumptions about key (and for practical purposes, untestable) aspects of the system under investigation."
William E. Connolly, *Political Science and Ideology* (New York, Atherton Press, 1967), p. 30.

     [I]n examining the structure of pluralist theory, the critics have become impressed by the extent to which conceptual and operational decisions have prejudged the outcomes of inquiry. Conventional conceptualizations of

simply that pluralist investigators themselves entertain presumptions or, alternatively, that a set of presumptions can be imagined that are entirely or largely consistent with the findings of pluralist researchers. "Presumptions" in this context mean ideas about how the world is arranged that are for the purposes of a given research project themselves not open to investigation.

I believed, in the light of the argument I was making about stratification studies of community power, that it was desirable and proper to indicate (1) that presumptions different from those given in the general stratification theory could be stated and (2) what some of these presumptions might look like. One general lesson to be drawn from such an exercise should

---

"group" ... "interest" ... "power" ... "decision" and "politics," draw attention to those features of the system favorable to the pluralist interpretation while shoving unfavorable features to the background.
William E. Connolly, "The Challenge to Pluralist Theory," in Connolly, ed., *The Bias of Pluralism* (New York, Atherton Press, 1969), p. 21.

Polsby, in his understandable desire to refute the elitist claim that a connection invariably exists between high economic position and political power, appears not to recognize that power can arise from the use to which wealth is put. His over-sharp distinction between wealth and power appears to rule out the possible existence of a ruling elite of economic dominants by definition. Polsby, so alert to the errors of the earlier elitists in community power research, in this instance commits the mistake of which he accuses his adversaries. His pluralist conclusions are embedded in pluralist definitions.
Geraint Parry, *Political Elites* (New York, Praeger, 1969), p. 122.

Polsby's *Community Power and Political Theory* contains a formal justification for the pluralist model. The pluralist model is claimed to be superior to other alternatives for studying community power because it purports not to prejudge the issues. Yet, of course, it does prejudge them. The pluralists expect to discover shifting coalitions across a set of designated outcomes and needless to say, they find them. They do so because, (1) they do not investigate how the alternatives are structured; (2) they analyze decision-making only on those issues that are most controversial, and, hence, susceptible to widest public participation; and (3) they ignore the possibility that certain elites may maintain decisive roles over time on given issue dimensions. By failure to consider these matters, Polsby has prejudged the issue just as much as have the reputational theorists. The ideology that Polsby perceives the reputational theorists to be victimized by, victimized him, itself.
Bert A. Rockman, "A 'Behavioral' Evaluation of the Critique of Behavioralism," (paper delivered at the 1969 A.P.S.A. meeting, New York, Sept. 2–6, 1969), p. 15.

Polsby lays great stress on the self-fulfilling prophecy of stratification research, i.e., that the researcher will find what he sets out to find. But may not this same charge be levelled against all research, including his own?
William V. D'Antonio, review of *Community Power and Political Theory* in *Social Forces, 42,* (March 1964), p. 376.

have been that *all* researchers can be shown to produce results compatible with *some* set of presumptions, and that consequently it is not the existence of presumptions per se, no matter how peculiarly they might read, that causes research to be misguided, but rather the propensity of some researchers, some of the time, to be so influenced by their presumptions as to be deterred from giving an accurate account of their empirical findings.

It is this much stronger sort of allegation that I had sought to make about the stratification studies described early in this book; and it is this much stronger statement that critics of pluralist approaches seem to be making when they assert that pluralist assumptions predetermine their conclusions. This is the sort of allegation that ought to be sustainable by empirical evidence of internal contradiction, methodological error, and so on. Without such empirical evidence it is hard to see the scientific grounds upon which allegations can be sustained that presumptions are incorrectly substituting for findings. People may believe whatever they want to believe, of course, and may set for themselves as low a threshold of empirical demonstration as they like. For a proposition to be carried forward as a finding of social science, however, one may reasonably ask for a better warrant than fervent repetition alone.

Yet it appears to be a feature of the statements quoted and cited above that they are not fortified by empirical demonstrations showing that pluralists misreport or misrepresent their data. Nevertheless, these statements do appear to be widely believed. I think I can show, however, that not only are these and similar charges unsustained by empirical evidence, but also that a modest effort at gathering evidence will disclose them to be for the most part false.

In order to facilitate this task, I think it will be useful to make an attempt to rectify a pedagogical error of my own. In early articles on community power and in the first edition of this book I neglected to distinguish among several senses of the term "pluralism" as it is used in the literature. This may well have contributed to subsequent confusion in the use of the term.[4] In part as a measure of atonement, and in part to move the discussion

---

4. This confusion does not seem especially to have abated as the result of the publication in 1969 of my article, "'Pluralism' in the Study of Community Power: Or Erklärung Before Verklärung in *Wissenssoziologie*," *The American Sociologist*, 4 (May 1969), 118–22, wherein I first attempted to make the distinctions presently to be explained in the text. This suggests either that the article was published in too obscure a journal or that I am taking on too much responsibility and should not entertain the notion that anything I could have published, anywhere, on this subject would have made much difference.

forward, I propose a distinction among three uses of the term "pluralism" that seem to correspond to three different senses in which it is employed in the community power literature, though of course these are not the only uses to which it is put, in community power studies or elsewhere. Pluralism$_1$ then, refers to eclectic methods of gathering data. Pluralism$_2$ refers to propositions or sentences purporting to describe a certain state of affairs in one or more local communities. The Pluralist$_2$ state of affairs so described usually has one or more characteristics that will by now be familiar to readers: dispersion of power among many rather than a few participants in decision-making; competition or conflict among political leaders; specialization of leaders to relatively restricted sets of issue areas; bargaining rather than hierarchical decision-making; elections in which suffrage is relatively widespread as a major determinant of participation in key decisions; bases of influence over decisions relatively dispersed rather than closely held; and so on. The list is illustrative, not exhaustive.[5]

Pluralism$_3$ refers to an intellectual tradition that has had some strength in American political theory. I do not pretend to understand all, or even most, of its sources or ramifications. Moreover, Pluralism$_3$ is not always fully or coherently expressed in each work coming in some way or another under the influence of this tradition. But, in general, it has seemed to me helpful to group under this general heading works showing some indebtedness to writers as varied in their views as Madison, Tocqueville, Montesquieu, and Locke.

These writers in their distinctive ways concern themselves, for example, with the relations between human nature and political action, attribute varied motives (for example, greed, envy, ambition) to individuals, and argue that political organization and political action arise from the acting out of these motives according to the opportunities permitted by the differ-

---

5. Here are three quotations illustrating Pluralist$_2$ conclusions—all drawn, not incidentally, from the work of sociologists: "The policy-making activities of local government rest ultimately, if somewhat indirectly, on the consent of an electorate which periodically registers its preferences for candidates and parties in local elections." Peter H. Rossi and Phillips Cutright, "The Impact of Party Organization in an Industrial Setting," in Morris Janowitz, ed., *Community Political Systems* (Glencoe, Free Press, 1961), p. 81; "The answer to the question about concentration of leadership is that in Syracuse, a large number of persons and organizations were active in community decision-making and that 'experts' of one sort or another were key participants. No evidence for the presence of a ruling elite was found." Linton C. Freeman, *Patterns of Local Community Leadership* (Indianapolis, Bobbs Merrill, 1968), p. 79; "[T]here is no single locus of decision-making, but rather a number of loci, each differently structured." James B. McKee, "Status and Power in the Industrial Community: A Comment on Drucker's Thesis," *Am. J. Soc.*, 58 (Jan. 1953), p. 369.

ing resources of people and the customs and rules they enforce upon one another.

Pluralism$_1$ is not Pluralism$_2$ is not Pluralism$_3$. That is, eclectic research methods are not the same as statements like: "In New Haven, in 1960, the bases of influences over three issue areas were widely dispersed." And neither is the same as statements like: "People cluster in groups, not strata." A lack of clarity about this sort of distinction has caused many difficulties.[6]

One set of difficulties has to do with the characterization of certain students of community power as "pluralists." "Pluralists" have on occasion written articles advocating eclectic methods of research or pursued such methods, made claims that power is dispersed in one or more local communities and adopted views and research strategies compatible with Pluralist$_3$ assumptions. But these characteristics have not always run together. For example, early classic studies of community life, which formed the intellectual basis for much of the subsequent community power literature, such as Lynd and Lynd's Middletown studies and Warner's Yankee City study, were Pluralist$_1$, but not Pluralist$_2$ or Pluralist$_3$.

A second difficulty is that these different types of pluralism require entirely different arguments to sustain them. Arguments about research strategy, for example, about the appropriateness of means to ends, evidence to inference, go on all the time in the social sciences. Methodological argument in the community power literature occupies what, to be charitable, could be called a narrow band in this spectrum. It has been most heated over the merits of the so-called reputational approach to studying community power, in which Pluralists$_1$ have argued against reliance on the method while others—especially users of the method—have argued for its use.

Whether or not a given statement about the distribution of power in one or several local communities is true or false is sometimes contingent upon the outcome of an argument over the appropriateness of the methods used in collecting the evidence upon which the statement is based. So, in that sense, there may, from time to time, be an overlap between Pluralism$_1$

6. Among those evidently confused on this point are William V. D'Antonio and Eugene C. Erickson, "The Reputational Technique as a Measure of Community Power: An Evaluation Based on Comparative and Longitudinal Studies," *Am. Soc. Rev.*, 27 (June 1962), 362–76; Kenneth Newton, *Second City Politics* (Oxford, Clarendon Press, 1976), p. 228; and Newton, "A Critique of the Pluralist Model," *Acta Sociologica*, 12 no. 4, (1969), 209–10. See Nelson W. Polsby, "Community Power: Some Reflections on the Recent Literature," *Am. Soc. Rev.*, 27 (Dec. 1962), 838–41 for an early attempt to clarify matters.

and $Pluralism_2$. But this overlap cannot, I think, properly be generalized into a statement like the following: All those who advocate or use eclectic (or nonreputational) research methods in the community believe that power in one or more communities is widely dispersed. That is, $Pluralism_1$ is not $Pluralism_2$.

$Pluralism_2$ is, so far as I can tell, a set of beliefs highly contingent upon evidence, and subject to modification by empirical findings. There may, in fact, be categorical $Pluralists_2$ who believe that communities everywhere are alike in their dispersion of power; but, if so, they have not to my knowledge recently contributed to the community power literature.[7]

$Pluralism_2$ is not $Pluralism_3$. It is possible, in my view, to carry around a set of beliefs or axioms or rules of thumb or assumptions about "human nature" or society that are rarely subjected to empirical confrontation. In fact, it may be impossible not to. But these axioms may or may not hinder the process by which correct inferences are drawn from research and a further research program is established. It must be shown empirically in some way or other that they do: the mere announcement that researchers have assumptions will not suffice, because who has not? Obviously, the degree of hindrance may vary, as will the seriousness of the consequences of the hindrance. Both, once again, are empirical questions.

Finally, $Pluralism_3$ is not $Pluralism_1$. Although connections of various kinds may in practice exist between a propensity to favor eclectic methods and beliefs about an inertia-filled world, these do not seem to me to be necessary connections. This does not preclude the possibility that a more focused, less eclectic method of research might be more intimately related to certain basic assumptions or presuppositions.

Let us see whether these distinctions assist us in disentangling at least some of the difficulties into which the community power literature has been plunged. The structure of my original argument—which as I have indicated has had widespread acceptance—was:

> That *a priori* adherence to presumptions of a general stratification theory provided the best explanation for the widespread repetition of the stratification theory of community power in the face of empirical findings to the contrary.

---

7. Regrettably, $Pluralists_1$ and $Pluralists_3$ are sometimes incorrectly identified as categorical $Pluralists_2$. See, for example, D'Antonio and Erickson, "Reputational Technique"; Robert E. Agger, Daniel Goldrich, and Bert E. Swanson, *The Rulers and the Ruled* (New York, Wiley, 1964), pp. 93ff.; and Thomas J. Anton, "Power, Pluralism and Local Politics," *Administrative Science Quarterly*, 7 (March 1963), 425–57.

From this, does it follow

1. That all statements about individual communities alleging centralized power are therefore empirically false?
2. That all statements about individual communities alleging dispersed power are therefore empirically true?

My answer to both of these questions is no; yet it appears that scholars have either themselves inferred affirmative answers to one or both of these questions and become troubled by the results or have wrongly attributed affirmative answers to me or to "pluralists." As we shall see, however, negative answers are more consistent with what we have actually written.

## CAN PLURALISTS FIND CENTRALIZED POWER SYSTEMS?

Are all statements alleging centralized community power false? Statements about community power may be framed—as indeed they sometimes are in this literature—so that there is no way to tell if they are true or false. This comes about, as I think I have shown, when they are stated so as to be incapable of falsification.[8] But if they are properly framed, whether or not they are true depends upon empirical evidence. My point was, and is, that by means of the research procedures I deplored, it was apparent that researchers were disabling themselves from reporting accurately on the actual results of their research, but that the same disability did not lie against users of the research procedures I recommended.

As we have already seen, half of this argument has been widely accepted, but the latter half has been sharply disputed. Perhaps the most general statement of substance embodying this disagreement would be as follows: that a pluralist could not find a steeply stratified system of power even where one existed. This, I think, is substantively what is meant when it is alleged that pluralists' assumptions, "predetermine" their conclusions, that their conclusions are "embedded" in their assumptions. Yet nobody knows whether this charge is true or not because nobody has ever successfully caught a Pluralist$_2$ researcher in acts of misrepresentation similar to those I have documented in the second and third chapters of this book.[9]

The most ingenious statement of the issue has come from Andrew S. McFarland, who offers bona fide pluralist interpretations of such hierar-

8. A very helpful statement of many of the issues involved is that of Imre Lakatos in *The Methodology of Scientific Research Programs,* John Worrall and Gregory Currie, eds., (Cambridge, Cambridge Univ. Press, 1978), esp. pp. 8–101.

9. For this purpose, I do not count fictional illustrations as, for example, in Anton, "Power, Pluralism and Local Politics," p. 455.

chical enterprises as the industrial sector of the Soviet Russian economy
and the U.S. Forest Service.[10] If the Soviet steel industry is to be considered in some sense "pluralist," what is not in some sense "pluralist"? Does
this interpretation not utterly vitiate the utility of the distinction, so lov-
ingly preserved in the community power literature, between communities
dominated by power elites and "pluralist" communities? McFarland's own
answer is to say yes it does, by definition. He characterizes the pluralist
perspective as one which posits and seeks to discuss in all sorts of settings
the operation of greater causal complexity than the alternative stratification model. Therefore, according to McFarland's view, in the end, which
mode of explanation one chooses depends upon the level of complexity
that is wanted in statements purporting to explain how various social outcomes are caused.

This seems to me perfectly acceptable. It certainly does not assert of
Pluralist$_2$ researchers an incapacity to distinguish between a system of action that is steeply stratified and one that is not, or a blindness to the
organizational differences between a Soviet steel plant and the San Jose
Flea Market. It merely asserts that it is possible for researchers to exercise
their judgment on issues concerning the level or focus of inquiry, which
are normally not matters that in and of themselves require empirical
verification.

At the time of the original publication of this book relatively few studies
of "community power" had been completed. Those studies that had found
power elites, and which I reported on (there might have been others, still
unknown to me), seemed to me fatally contaminated. Could *any* study of
an American community escape a similar anathema if it reported a relatively centralized political system? Since in practice no such findings appeared to escape unscathed, how could an observer be sure that disclaimers
in principle were a true reflection of the purported intellectual openness
either of those who held Pluralist$_3$ assumptions or of those who reported
Pluralist$_2$ findings?

I can offer a few straws in the wind, suggesting that Pluralist$_3$ assumptions are in fact not so debilitating as to prevent students from differentiat-
ing at least grossly among local political systems possessing different
degrees of centralized direction. Indications to this effect are given in
*Who Governs?* The attentive reader of this volume will note that early New
Haven is characterized as a political system in which status and power

10. Andrew S. McFarland, *Power and Leadership in Pluralist Systems* (Stanford,
Stanford Univ. Press, 1969). See also Jerry F. Hough, *The Soviet Union and Social
Science Theory* (Cambridge, Mass., Harvard Univ. Press, 1977) esp. pp. 203–21.

are closely aligned, and that a somewhat later period in New Haven history is characterized as a time when economic prosperity is held to be a major prerequisite for power in the community. It is only in the modern years of New Haven's existence that a system of dispersed inequalities is held to prevail, and here, once again, a distinction is drawn between a relatively decentralized period preceding Richard C. Lee's time as Mayor and the centralization of city politics under Mayor Lee's leadership.[11]

This suggests that in a Pluralist$_2$ study it is possible to describe a reasonably rich and diverse set of community power systems, including three types of elite power: status elite dominance succeeded by economic elite dominance in earlier days, and dominance by an elected politician in Mayor Lee's time.

Seen from up close, to be sure, as Dahl cautions, nearly any political system takes on complexities invisible to the casual observer. So if Mc-Farland is right in suggesting that Pluralism$_2$ entails a more complex specification of the causes of social outcomes than the stratification theory of community power, it follows that any close examination of a phenomenon such as power in an American community of any size is bound to yield something close to Pluralist$_2$ conclusions; hence pluralist researchers are better able than researchers who adhere to the stratification theory to capture the complexity of what is really there. This is presumably true only so long as the political system being studied is in fact complex.

If complexity is not really there, and what is there is really a monolithic power elite, what will pluralist researchers report? It is to be regretted that no thorough studies have been done of company towns dominated by companies that are active in civic affairs, such as Hershey, Pennsylvania, Fremont, Michigan, or Kannapolis, North Carolina. Journalists, undoubtedly using methods very much akin to those described as Pluralism$_1$, have reported on politics in these communities in recent years and documented

11. Robert A. Dahl, *Who Governs? Democracy and Power in an American City* (New Haven, Yale Univ. Press, 1961), pp. 11–51, 200–14. Studies by historians come to conclusions roughly similar to Dahl's about late nineteenth-century politics in such varied settings as Stamford, Connecticut, Birmingham, Alabama, and New York City. In general these studies are more eclectic and wide-ranging in their search for historical evidence than the New Haven study and do not rely so heavily on information about the social backgrounds of high officeholders. See Carl V. Harris, *Political Power in Birmingham, 1871–1921* (Knoxville, Univ. of Tennessee Press, 1977), esp. pp. 270–85; Estelle F. Feinstein, *Stamford in the Gilded Age: The Political Life of a Connecticut Town, 1868–1893* (Stamford, Conn., Stamford Historical Society, 1973); and especially, David C. Hammack, "Problems in the Historical Study of Power in the Cities and Towns of the United States, 1800–1960," *American Historical Review*, 83 (April 1978), 323–49.

the dominance of company management in all manner of local activities.[12] Would Pluralist$_3$-influenced scholars, using Pluralist$_1$ methods, be too dense to see this and inexorably emerge with Pluralist$_2$ findings? We have no warrant to believe so, at least no warrant grounded in any sort of empirical demonstration. We have the evidence of Dahl's book, which strongly suggests otherwise.

## WHAT MAY WE INFER FROM THE EVIDENCE OF ONE COMMUNITY?

Are all statements alleging dispersed community power true? Here, once again, evidence must be allowed to speak to the question of what sort of power distribution prevails in a community. It is occasionally asserted in the literature that because Pluralism$_2$ was found in New Haven, the finders thereof assert that the New Haven pattern prevails in all American cities. "Some social scientists," a journalist has written, without, incidentally, mentioning any social scientists, "rather unscientifically jumped to the conclusion that if they couldn't find a power structure in, say, Central City or Midwestern Town, there was no such thing as a power structure, even in Regional City."[13]

My bases for disbelieving what Floyd Hunter reported about Regional City are given in Chapter 3, where readers will observe my inability to find a coherent or persuasive case in Hunter's own writings about the exercise of power in Regional City. The fact that we could not duplicate Hunter's incoherence in our account of New Haven has nothing to do with the acceptance or rejection of Hunter's case about Atlanta. Of course an independent and competent examination of politics in Atlanta, Georgia, might

12. For Hershey, see Cynthia Miller, "'Chocolate Camelot' Thirty Years Later: Somewhat Melted"; Eunice Telfer Juckett, "The Company Town"; and Rudy Maxa, "Remembering When," all printed in the Washington *Post* Style Section, 16 Sept. 1973; for Kannapolis, see Neil Maxwell, "Powerful C. A. Cannon Rules Kannapolis, N.C., But He Faces Challenge," *Wall Street Journal*, Apr. 29, 1969; for Fremont, see Leonard M. Apcar, "Says Fremont, Michigan to Gerber: Yes, Sir, You're My Baby," *Wall Street Journal*, July 27, 1977.

13. Fred Powledge, "Profiles: A New Politics in Atlanta," *The New Yorker* (Dec. 31, 1973), 28.

When this remarkable charge was first published, I wondered what Powledge could have had in mind, and, innocent of the supposedly marvelous *New Yorker* cadre of editorial checkers, wrote off an inquiry to the editor of *The New Yorker*. The letter, dated January 2, 1974, is still unanswered. A fundamental difference between journalism and scholarship is no doubt that the sense of accountability that scholars feel to a community of co-investigators is felt by journalists, and their editors, only toward people who make a public noise. See Clyde Haberman and Albin Krebs, "Tempest Over Turbot Stirred at Lutèce" *The New York Times* Feb. 23, 1979; Frank J. Prial, " 'Otto' Tracked Down in Pennsylvania" *The New York Times* Feb. 24, 1979.

or might not corroborate one or more of Hunter's claims. No matter how weak Professor X's case for a given proposition, in a free scholarly community Professor Y may come along later and do the job that X was unable to do. This, however, does not seem to have been Hunter's fate. At least one attempt, by Kent Jennings, to replicate Hunter's findings in Atlanta failed to do so.[14]

Hunter has recently had a defender in a journalist, Fred Powledge, who writes for a wider audience than academics customarily command. Powledge's defense, however, consists only of claims that Hunter was right, accompanied by copious evidence to the contrary. Here is a community, after all, where elected officials were held to be tools in the hands of "the power structure."[15] Yet consider the case of Atlanta's Mayor William B. Hartsfield, who was the elected mayor—except for two years in the 1940s—from 1937 until 1961, i.e. during the entire period of Hunter's research. Powledge, Hunter's defender, calls Hartsfield "a somewhat rambunctious, independent mayor but one who appreciated the importance of the power structure and *gladly accepted its assistance*" (italics supplied).[16]

What are we to make of this? If the rambunctious Mayor Hartsfield is a tool in the hands of "the power structure" how is it that the power structure is "assisting" him rather than the other way around? Are the two propositions simply interchangeable?[17] If they are not, then with defenders like Powledge, Hunter has no need of attackers.

The situation in Atlanta has since become even less congenial, if that is possible, to Hunter's view. "Four years ago," Powledge wrote in 1974, "the power structure suffered a severe setback. It lost its man [*sic*] in City Hall."[18] By now it is pretty clear that, contrary to the stratification interpretation of Atlanta politics, who sits in City Hall matters quite a bit, and the successive elections of Mayor Sam Massell and Mayor Maynard Jackson were meaningful events in the distribution of power in that community.

This, at any rate, rather than information about New Haven, is the sort of evidence we would have to consider in an evaluation of the state of

14. M. Kent Jennings, *Community Influentials* (Glencoe, Free Press, 1964), esp. pp. 155–64.

15. Floyd Hunter, CPS, pp. 82, 92–93, 100, 104.

16. Powledge, "Profiles." p. 29. Mayor Hartsfield's independence does not appear to be in doubt. See Douglass Cater, "Atlanta: Smart Politics and Good Race Relations," *The Reporter* (July 11, 1957), 18–21.

17. For an argument in defense of interchangeability, see Arthur Clun, "The Post-Behavioral Revolution in Community Power: A Brief Note from a Frontier of Research," *P.S.*, 5 (Summer 1972), 274–77. This article is thought by some readers to have been meant facetiously. I am not so sure.

18. Powledge, "Profiles," p. 29. The reference here is to Hartsfield's somewhat more liberal successor, Ivan Allen.

affairs in Atlanta. It is ridiculous to suppose that any amount of investigation in New Haven could dispose of empirical questions concerning Atlanta, or any other particular city, or even cities in general. And no student
of New Haven has made any such ridiculous claim. Yet such claims have
been made in behalf of the New Haven study.[19]

Dahl's study, manifestly, is not intended to illuminate the politics of New
Haven only. As he says:

> Though no city can claim to represent cities in general, and though
> certainly none can claim to display the full range of characteristics
> found in a national political system, New Haven is in many respects
> typical of other cities in the United States.[20]

This surely gives Dahl's readers ample warrant to consider other commu-

19. Matthew Crenson, for example, says:
> In any community, says Dahl, there will be a small minority of citizens who are
> much more highly involved in the town's political life than is the great bulk of the
> local population. Members of this small "political stratum" naturally exercise much
> greater direct influence over most local decisions than do ordinary citizens. Indirect
> influence is one of the things that prevents this minority rule from degenerating
> into oligarchy. Local political leaders, often taking their cues from the results of
> local elections, "keep the real or imagined preferences of constituents constantly in
> mind in deciding what policies to adopt or reject."

Crenson, *The Unpolitics of Air Pollution* (Baltimore, The Johns Hopkins Univ. Press,
1971), pp. 107–08.

The citation is to page 163 of *Who Governs?* where, far from discussing "any community," as Crenson claims, Dahl treats of New Haven exclusively and, even with
respect to New Haven, he is cautious not to overgeneralize. He says, in part, "If one
analyzes the way in which influence in these three issue-areas is distributed among
citizens of New Haven, one finds that only a small number of persons have much *direct*
influence, in the sense that they successfully initiate or veto proposals for policies. . . .
The choices made by constituents in critical elections, such as those in New Haven in
1945 and 1955, do have great *indirect* influence on the decisions of leaders, for results
of elections are frequently interpreted by leaders as indicating a preference for or
acquiescence in certain lines of policy."

There are further indications in the literature that the New Haven study is being read
as generally applicable. Harry M. Scoble says:
> No matter how good, i.e., valid and reliable, the study of a particular American
> community may be, it does not permit us to draw any inferences about the dis-
> tribution of political power in the national polity. Such inferences are impermis-
> sible despite Dahl's obvious desire in the latter portion of *Who Governs?* to
> generalize from New Haven to the entire national system.

Scoble, "Where the Pluralists Went Wrong," in Frederick M. Wirt, ed., *Future Directions*, p. 111.

Todd Gitlin says:
> Although Polsby and Dahl both indicate initially that they will be primarily
> concerned with New Haven decision-making, both end up generalizing.

Gitlin, "Local Pluralism as Theory and Ideology," *Studies on the Left*, 5 (Summer
1965), 24.

nities in the light of what he says about New Haven. But is there a sensible way to characterize those statements in *Who Governs?* that can be appropriately generalized and distinguish them from statements properly having a more restricted use?

Perhaps an example can help. Dahl says that in 1950 New Haven had a population of 164,443. Does anyone think that this, added to the quotation above, entitles us to claim that Dahl believes that all American cities have populations of 164,443? Obviously not. And the same is true of all other empirical statements about New Haven, including statements making empirical assertions about the shape and scope of power holding and power exercise in New Haven.

Embedded also in *Who Governs?* are other sorts of statements. Some are conceptual and definitional in character and constitute recommenda-

---

David Ricci says:

> Understanding of the deepest significance of the pluralist theory of democracy must begin with an appreciation of the fact that although the theory was initially expounded in terms of the situation found to exist in New Haven, it actually pertained to both national and local communities in the United States. Dahl asserted it as a general theory of community politics embracing and explaining the broad features of all American politics, and as such it was widely accepted by his political science colleagues.

David Ricci, *Community Power and Democratic Theory: The Logic of Political Analysis* (New York, Random House, 1971), p. 144;

Terry N. Clark says:

> In one of the most scrupulous studies, Dahl's *Who Governs?*, an appendix compared the position of New Haven with all American cities on many census-type variables. The purpose of this exercise, nevertheless, was not to analyze such variables per se but to suggest that New Haven was sufficiently similar to other American cities that the results could be legitimately generalized.

Clark, *Community Power and Policy Outputs* (Beverly Hills, Sage Publications, 1973), p. 13;

And

> Dahl has argued that political inequalities in the past were often cumulative, but today tend to be noncumulative or dispersed. In another context, distinguishing between direct and indirect influence, he has presented schematic diagrams of the distribution of influence suggesting that direct influence is largely stratified, but indirect influence is dispersed.
>
> Although the level of certainty with which it is possible to make such generalizations about a single city—such as New Haven—may be rather high, it would appear somewhat premature to generalize about the stratification of power.

Terry N. Clark: "The Concept of Power: Some Overemphasized and Underrecognized Dimensions," *Southwestern Social Science Quarterly, 48* (Dec. 1967), 284.

And Thomas Anton says:

> It is my feeling that Dahl's attempt to see New Haven as a microcosm of the over-all American political system is the root cause of many of his difficulties.

Anton, "Rejoinder," *Administrative Science Quarterly, 8* (Sept. 1963), 267.

20. Dahl, *Who Governs?*, p.v.

tions about how to use language, how to analyze things, and what distinctions are worth making. Here are three examples:

> In the political system of the patrician oligarchy, political resources were marked by a cumulative inequality: when one individual was much better off than another in one resource, such as wealth, he was usually better off in almost every other resource—social standing, legitimacy, control over religious and educational institutions, knowledge, office.[21]

> In New Haven, as in other political systems, a small stratum of individuals is much more highly involved in political thought, discussion, and action than the rest of the population. These citizens constitute the political stratum.[22]

> Political man, unlike civic man, deliberately allocates a very sizeable share of his resources to the process of gaining and maintaining control over the policies of government. Control over policies usually requires control over officials. And where, as in the United States, key officials are elected by voters, political man usually allocates an important share of his resources to the process of gaining and maintaining influence over voters.[23]

These sorts of statements seem to me eminently usable in other contexts, and moreover seem to me capable of encouraging other investigators to see in their data significant relationships that they might otherwise miss.

The same is true of statements asserting something about causes and effects in politics, even though they are frequently asserted only of New Haven politics. These propositions may or may not be true in New Haven, but in any event they assert relations between variables capable of receiving empirical interpretations with respect to more than one body of data. To say that such statements are true in New Haven is not to say they are true elsewhere. That remains an empirical question. Here is a paragraph containing several examples:

> Thus, although the executive-centered order of Mayor Lee had drastically curtailed the independence of the old petty sovereignties and had whittled down the relative influence of the various chieftains, that order was no monolith. The preferences of any group that could swing its weight at election time—teachers, citizens of the Hill,

21. Ibid., p. 85.
22. Ibid., p. 90.
23. Ibid., p. 225.

Negroes on Dixwell Avenue, or Notables—would weigh heavily in
the calculations of the Mayor, for the executive-centered coalition was
not the *only* important pattern of influence in New Haven. The un-
ending competition between the two political parties constituted another pattern of influence; thanks to the system of periodic elections,
the Mayor and his political opponents were constantly engaged in a
battle for votes at the next election, which was always just around
the corner.[24]

Although these sentences are about New Haven they can, I suggest, help
us to learn about other communities. One way is to convert these sentences
into more general, comparative statements in which the expressed relations
between variables are preserved.[25] An argument in favor of this procedure
would be as follows: A major goal of comparative study is the production
of general explanatory statements—preferably true and interesting statements. General explanatory statements are sentences whose nouns are not
proper names and which assert something about relations between variables. One strategy for producing such statements is to convert them from
descriptive statements—sentences in which some nouns are proper names.
The resulting general statement can then be tested against a wider body
of data. Thus inferences of general import that it would be possible to make
from the last quoted paragraph might be:

1. The tendency of elected officials to anticipate the reactions of elec-
torates in policy-making varies according to the frequency and competi-
tiveness of elections.

2. This tendency exists even when interest groups are uninfluential in
policy-making processes.

As I have indicated, three issues must be distinguished with respect to
these sentences. First, whether they exemplify a means by which descriptive statements about one community can validly be transformed into statements having a more general import. Second, whether they are generally
true. Third, whether they are true of New Haven. As to the first issue, I
think the answer is transparently in the affirmative. Much writing in the
social sciences is tacitly comparative even when it is not explicitly so.[26]
Some writers have a gift for couching their case studies in language that

24. Ibid., p. 214. Emphasis in original.
25. An admirable exposition of the principles involved, on which I draw, is Morris
Zelditch, Jr., "Intelligible Comparisons," in Ivan Vallier ed., *Comparative Methods in
Sociology* (Berkeley, Univ. of California Press, 1971), pp. 267–307.
26. See Harry Eckstein, "Case Study and Theory in Political Science," in Fred I.
Greenstein and Nelson W. Polsby, ed., *The Handbook of Political Science*, 8 vols.
(Reading, Mass., Addison-Wesley, 1975), 7:79–137.

invites conversion to comparative purposes, and it serves no useful purpose at all to impede this process of translation by insisting that something more literal-minded—and empirically unjustified—is intended by the expression of an author's entirely intelligible hope that a case study might carry some lessons into other contexts.

As to the second issue, I offer no argument at all, since such an issue can be settled only after an appropriate empirical investigation is concluded. As to whether the electorate loomed large in the calculations of Mayor Lee even though Lee virtually monopolized policy-making in urban renewal and "drastically curtailed" the influence of others who had earlier been important in policy-making, the answer is a clear yes, judging from what Lee said at the time and from the pattern of his behavior in such activities as negotiating for the sale of city-owned land.[27]

27. See Raymond E. Wolfinger, *The Politics of Progress* (Englewood Cliffs, N.J., Prentice Hall, 1974), e.g., pp. 290–94.

# 10. Reinterpretations of New Haven Politics

How believable is this conclusion about New Haven? Or other, similar conclusions of the New Haven study? It is possible to gain a measure of confidence in a general description of New Haven politics by reading in a synoptic fashion the small library of books about some aspect of the subject that have appeared from 1963 to 1977. Two are rewritten doctoral dissertations from former students of the Yale political science department.[1] Two are the work of professional journalists—one of whom lived for a time in New Haven.[2] Two are by former New Haven political activists, one an alderman, the other a city hall planning and public relations official.[3] And two books—one only slightly larger than a pamphlet, the other mainly about urban architecture—are the product of, respectively, a visiting city planner and a former New Haven Redevelopment Agency staff architect.[4] Together all these works present the fruit of many years of living and working in New Haven, and participating in and observing New Haven politics. While they do not agree in every last detail, and in some matters of historical interpretation, political analysis, and intellectual focus they vary, as befits the variety of perspectives and concerns of a varied group of authors, nevertheless there is striking agreement on the broad outlines of New Haven politics since 1950, and in only one case is the picture painted in *Who Governs?* called seriously into question.

This case concerns a disagreement over the interpretation of the develop-

1. Russell D. Murphy, *Political Entrepreneurs and Urban Poverty* (Lexington, Mass., Heath Lexington, 1971); Raymond E. Wolfinger, *The Politics of Progress* (Englewood Cliffs, N.J., Prentice Hall, 1974).

2. Jeanne R. Lowe, *Cities in a Race with Time*, (New York, Random House, 1967); Fred Powledge, *Model City* (New York, Simon and Schuster, 1970).

3. William Lee Miller, *The Fifteenth Ward and the Great Society* (Boston, Houghton Mifflin, 1966); Allan R. Talbot, *The Mayor's Game* (New York, Praeger, 1970).

4. Gregory R. Farrell, *A Climate of Change* (New Brunswick, N.J., Urban Studies Center, Rutgers, 1965); Harris Stone, *Workbook of an Unsuccessful Architect* (New York, Monthly Review Press, 1973).

ment and persistence of ethnic voting in New Haven in which Raymond Wolfinger's book, *The Politics of Progress,* offers a revision of the analysis given in *Who Governs?*[5] Since Wolfinger is normally lumped with Dahl as possessing the same incapacities that allegedly afflict all "pluralists" as they study community politics, a disagreement between them could hardly demonstrate their common source of error.

I have suggested that in order to give coherence to their critique of pluralists, critics must establish that pluralists actually commit the errors with which they are charged rather than merely claim that a symmetry of error exists. Occasionally, a hypothetical or fictional example is offered, such as the invented case of pluralists, blinded by their general presuppositions, wandering about Mississippi in the 1930s oblivious to the condition of Negroes in the south.[6] I suppose it is possible that they might have done so. After all, in the 1930s a fair number of Americans wandered about the Soviet Union oblivious to the Moscow trials. So we cannot rule out *a priori* even the grossest misapprehensions about the world. But it is worth noting that no actual instance of blatant misreporting or misconstruction by pluralists of data about the communities they have studied is as yet in the record.

If such mistakes began to turn up, it would of course be necessary to show that they fell into some sort of pattern that made a plausible connection with pluralist presuppositions, and that alternative sources of error were not more plausible. It can be stipulated that everyone makes mistakes, and so mistakes per se are not interesting. It is only after they can be shown to display some sort of traits in common, and these traits are accurately linked with other properties of the theory or the theorist, that they become interesting. These latter conditions lead me to reject the well-known argument that some sort of Pluralism₃ is responsible for the errors that several eminent social scientists made in diagnosing the sources of support in American society for the late Senator Joseph McCarthy.[7] There is undoubtedly something of substance to be explained when many talented social analysts go wrong, but the proffered explanation fails to account for the apparent ease with which other students of McCarthyism, no less evidently enmeshed in Pluralist₃ assumptions, escaped the errors that their

---

5. Dahl, *Who Governs?,* pp. 34–36, 48–60; Wolfinger, *Politics of Progress,* pp. 30–73.

6. As in Anton, "Power, Pluralism and Local Politics," p. 455: "Surely the historic passivity of the Southern Negro, for example, was due to something other than satisfaction with his position in Southern communities. Considerations of this kind suggest that one of the major problems of the pluralist method is that it assumes too much."

7. The charge is made in Michael P. Rogin, *The Intellectuals and McCarthy* (Cambridge, Mass., MIT Press, 1967).

presumptions ought to have led them to—if indeed these presumptions were at the root of error.[8]

## CRITICISMS BY PRICE AND MORRISS

Within the field of community power it is puzzling how little effort has been made to challenge the conclusions of pluralist studies on empirical grounds. For example, only three published works, to my knowledge, argue at any length and give some semblance of chapter and verse to the effect that in an important sense the New Haven study was mistaken about New Haven. The first of these is a brilliant review, by H. Douglas Price, of *Who Governs?*, the bulk of which consists of a highly creative sketch outlining how findings about New Haven might be integrated into an analysis comparing New Haven with other cities similarly—and differently—situated geographically, in terms of population composition, size, and stage of historical growth.[9]

None of this, of course, constitutes a quarrel with *Who Governs?* The only important disagreement Price has with Dahl is over the interpretation of the role of political leadership in New Haven. Perhaps the rich do not contest for power, Price says, because they have withdrawn to the Republican-controlled towns that surround New Haven, and therefore do not want to. For a mayor to meet Price's test of "municipal statesmanship," he must somehow seize control of the entire metropolitan area by creating a "metropolitan-wide jurisdiction" that then finds ways of taxing the suburb-dwelling rich. This is no mean feat in New England, where historic town boundaries are securely protected from the annexations that readily take place in other regions of the country. "From the local point of view," Price says, "federal or state aid may appear as 'free goods'." Indeed, he says, "the more emphasis one puts on the important and unusual resource base of federal funds, the less weight one need attach to the Mayor's particular talents."

This is off the mark. Federal funds, far from constituting a "free good," have to be schemed for, planned for, worked for, applied for, and qualified for. To gather these funds in, match them with local and state money, make them do work that turns them into local political as well as economic assets, all entails the exercise of political skills of a very high order.[10] Any

8. As, for example, Nelson W. Polsby, "Towards an Explanation of McCarthyism," *Political Studies,* 8 (Oct. 1960), 250–71, cited extensively by Rogin, *Intellectuals and McCarthy.*

9. Hugh Douglas Price, review of *Who Governs?* in *Yale Law Journal, 71* (July 1962), pp. 1589–96.

10. See Wolfinger, *Politics of Progress,* pp. 145–56.

number of run-down cities might equally well have served as the "Potem-kin Village" of the Washington bureaucrats whom Price describes as pro-viding "free goods" for New Haven. How New Haven and not the 149 other possible places roughly in New Haven's size class got to be that village is a story of political entrepreneurship that Price dismisses more quickly than he should. By doing so, he arrives at a reduced estimate of Mayor Lee's role in New Haven politics and at his principal disagreement with Dahl. Even giving full value to Price's reservations about Dahl's interpretation of the role of Mayor Lee, there are no grounds here to sus-tain the view that pluralists' axioms are contributing to a suppression or misreporting of findings or to erroneous conclusions. And Price makes no such allegation.

A second critique, by Peter Morriss, principally alleges two things: First, that data given in *Who Governs?* do not speak to the core concept of power as outlined by Dahl in earlier articles and, second, that Dahl fails to dem-onstrate that New Haven was not governed by a ruling elite of business-men.[11] I shall not further discuss the first charge because it is irrelevant to the empirical issue that presently concerns us.

Turning to his attack on *Who Governs?* Morriss makes several claims that even a quick reading of the book can easily refute: that there is "hardly any mention of what the decisions were" on which Dahl's analysis of power in New Haven rests, "who they affected, and by how much. Even in the issue area of urban redevelopment there is no mention of *how* the city center was being redeveloped, and who was likely to benefit from its redevelopment." "Because of this gap in the research, Dahl is unable to compare the importance of different decisions," says Morriss, "and so he has to assume that all decisions are equally important."

Of course Dahl does mention what the decisions were that he studied, and makes qualitative judgments throughout the book about the magnitude of their consequences. This, as Morriss presently observes, is how Dahl evidently settled upon nominations, urban redevelopment, and public education as issue-areas to be given intensive scrutiny. If public officials can be shown to be important, Morriss says, then "it is necessary to investigate who put them there; if they are not, there is no point . . . investigating them. So the relevance of this issue depends on the findings of the other two."

There then follows a truly baffling paragraph:

> The two other issues are both judged important because of their cost. Now if there were a ruling elite, it would have decided which

11. Peter Morriss, "Power in New Haven: A Reassessment of 'Who Governs?'" *British Journal of Political Science*, 2 (Oct., 1972), 457–65.

issues were important and would have spent money on them; it would also have decided that certain issues were unimportant, or did not serve the ruling elite's interest, and would not have spent much money on them. For an investigator to choose issues by the amount of money spent on them is, then, to accept the hypothesized ruling elite's criteria of relevance; it is, in effect, to ask the ruling elite which issues they think are most important and then only to investigate those that they suggest. Therefore a believer in the ruling elite would not accept that these two issues are necessarily the most important.[12]

One can only wonder why not, since it can be established by independent criteria that urban redevelopment and education were indeed by far the most expensive items on the New Haven agenda. It seems to me that if it can be shown that on such issues there is no ruling elite (as the term is commonly understood) then by Morriss's reasoning above it is established that there is no ruling elite in the community.

On one or two other points Morriss betrays an ignorance of New Haven politics that severely compromises his attempt to criticize Dahl. Evidently ignorant that the first major urban renewal project in New Haven, the Oak Street project, begun in 1955, was by New Haven standards a massive slum clearance scheme, he wonders why "a massive slum clearance scheme" was not initiated in New Haven in 1955. He jumps quickly to the conclusions—all incorrect—that there were "severe riots in the summer of 1968" in New Haven, that their cause was that "Negroes ... felt left out," and that this introduces difficulties for "the pluralist model."[13] He chooses to

12. Ibid., p. 461.
13. Ibid., The special problem that a riot creates for "the pluralist model" is presumably of the following sort. A pluralist researcher studies a community and neglects to mention unrest among the black population as a major problem. Later—in the case of New Haven, a full decade later—a riot breaks out in which black teenagers are major participants. This shows that ten years earlier dissatisfaction among black citizens was in fact a problem, although unnoticed by the pluralist researcher.

This interpretation, although offered as self-evident, seems to me vulnerable to the following objections: 1) Things may have changed in the ten years. In 1950 and 1960, the censuses that bracket the New Haven study, the percentage of nonwhite in the New Haven city population was 6.0% and 14.9% respectively. By the 1970 census, the percentage "Negro" in the city of New Haven was 26.3%. A twenty-year gain of this magnitude seems to me evidence of considerable change. 2) There is no pluralist doctrine that encourages researchers to neglect unrest among the black population if it exists; consequently if a pluralist does not mention it, it *may* be because it does not exist at the time of the study. 3) The relationship between a single outbreak of violence and the underlying structure of issues and problems in a community is by no means demonstrated. What causes riots in general is not terribly clear to anyone, the most durable hypothesis being that they occur during periods when the conditions of previously disadvantaged people are improved and their expectations run ahead of the capacity of

notice that Dahl takes account of the Mayor's anticipated reactions in his dealings with the Citizens Action Commission and concludes "the Mayor was a pawn of the CAC"; he chooses to ignore Dahl's account of the Mayor's anticipations of the reactions of the New Haven electorate. His fatal fascination with the CAC includes conspicuous notice of the over-representation of businessmen on the Commission and a belief in their consequent capacity to "control" others on the Commission or, if matters are carried unanimously, to get their way *ipso facto*. Evidently nothing can convince him that the CAC was almost entirely a public relations front group for the Mayor and his redevelopment program, and understood as such by virtually all concerned.

I think we must conclude that Morriss's attempt to set the world straight about New Haven is not a success, and the characterization of *Who Governs?* that emerges from it is tendentious and inaccurate.

## WHO REALLY RULES?

By far the most ambitious attempt to discredit *Who Governs?* and its account of New Haven is a book-length effort by G. William Domhoff entitled *Who Really Rules? New Haven and Community Power Re-examined.*[14] The title of the book admirably states its purpose. It is not, however, as so many books about New Haven are, the product of extensive

---

the political system to deliver. See James C. Davies, "Toward a Theory of Revolution," *Am. Soc. Rev.,* 27 (Feb. 1962), 5–19; and Hugh Davis Graham and Ted Robert Gurr, eds., *The History of Violence in America* (New York, Praeger, 1969), pp. 570–730. A current view is that susceptibility to violence is particularly great among people experiencing feelings of uncertainty about the future. See Abraham H. Miller, Louis H. Bolce, and Mark Halligan, "The J-Curve Theory and the Black Urban Riots," *Am. Pol. Sci. Rev.,* 71 (Sept. 1977), 964–82.

The New Haven riot took place for three nights in August 1967, not 1968. It began when a white lunchroom proprietor shot and wounded a Puerto Rican who allegedly had threatened him with a knife. Wolfinger, *Politics of Progress,* says, p. 201:

> The rioters, mostly black teenagers, threw rocks at windows and passing cars, set fires, and looted. No one was seriously hurt, no policeman fired a shot (Lee ordered them not to use their guns) and property damage was under $1 million.

Fred Powledge's account (in *Model City,* pp. 109–12), written by someone of quite different political sympathies from Wolfinger, is essentially the same, differing only in his willingness to give credence to "some residents of the black community" who disputed the claim that police did not fire a shot. He says:

> According to contemporary standards, the riot in New Haven was not an exceptionally destructive one. . . . According to the official compilation, no one was killed in New Haven, and only three persons were injured in the emergency period.

14. (Santa Monica, Cal., Goodyear, 1978).

research in the community. Professor Domhoff reports (in private correspondence) having spent only eleven days in New Haven, the bulk of that time immersed in the twenty-year-old files of Robert Dahl's project, and in other documentary materials.[15] Domhoff describes his effort as "based upon hundreds of hours of new research by myself and several research assistants, and by the historian A. Tappan Wilder. This research, by both myself and Wilder, includes a detailed searching of the minutes, memos and letters in numerous historical archives as well as personal and telephone interviews with people all over the country."[16]

On the face of it, one would think that eleven days is only a short time to do "hundreds of hours" of "new" research into New Haven politics,[17] but it rapidly becomes clear that Domhoff believes he possesses a superior methodology; it is Dahl's prolonged exposure to the community and that of his research group that makes it error prone.

> It may be that the most serious methodological criticism I can make of Dahl [Domhoff says] is that he never should have done this particular study in the first place, for it was doomed from the start to fall victim, for sociopsychological reasons, to the ambitions and plans of the politicians, planners, lawyers, and businessmen that he was interviewing.[18]

Evidently according to Domhoff's reconstruction, what happened was this: In November 1954 a national group to promote urban renewal programs was founded. It was called *Action*, and it had a "roster of officers and directors which made it clear that the heavyweights within the ruling class were squarely behind the program."[19] In 1957, *Action* hired reporter Jeanne Lowe to serve on its information staff. Lowe visited New Haven and subsequently wrote a favorable article for *Harper's* magazine about urban renewal and Mayor Lee.

15. Of course for some purposes it would not be necessary to have visited New Haven at all. I have never been in Atlanta, but can detect self-contradiction and incoherence in Hunter's study of Atlanta without difficulty. This is not the character of Domhoff's criticism, however. Domhoff claims that Dahl and his associates have read the historical record of New Haven politics incorrectly.

16. Domhoff, *Who Really Rules?*, p. 3. Wilder is a Yale-connected historian whose research is so far unpublished. Neither Domhoff nor Wilder makes the claim that their interpretations are in agreement.

17. It includes, however, library research and interviews on the telephone done from Domhoff's base in Santa Cruz, California (personal letter).

18. Ibid., p. 45.

19. Ibid., pp. 41ff.

That article was only one of many. . . . What Dahl recorded in his interviews in 1957 and 1958 . . . were the memories of the years 1949–55 as distilled through the ideological atmosphere created by *Action*, the Advertising Council, and popular magazines.[20]

In short, Dahl

> put himself at the mercy of the frailty of human memory and its tendency to personalize events. It is not safe to assume that what people say in 1957 and 1958 is an accurate description of events that took place several years earlier, even if there is considerable consensus among interviewees. This point about mistrusting even a consensus among interviewees is critical, for it alerts us to the fact that everyone interviewed may be a victim of the ideological consensus that has slowly formed over the intervening years and rearranged memories about what actually happened.[21]

Readers must judge for themselves the effects of this consensus among Dahl's informants not only about events of 1949–55 but also about events of the late 1950s, which were occurring while Dahl and his assistants were participant-observers in the community and had day-to-day contact over an extended period with people who were their informants about contemporary events as well as events in the recent past.[22] They must, like-

20. Ibid., p. 43.
21. Ibid., p. 40. In a later footnote, however, (n. 109, p. 119) Domhoff offers the following recommendations:

> In their book about the Watergate investigations . . . [Robert Woodward and Carl Bernstein wrote] that they never published a controversial claim unless they could verify it with at least two sources. Social scientists doing decisional analyses would do well to adopt the critical stance of investigative journalists and detectives, instinctively doubting everything told to them and constantly checking and cross-checking their findings against the claims of other interviewees and the written record.

Readers might be prompted to ask what conclusions we should draw if such a process produced "considerable consensus among interviewees."
22. For a description of the methods of the New Haven study, see Dahl, *Who Governs?*, Appendix B, and Wolfinger, *Politics of Progress*, pp. 3–5. Wolfinger says:

> From July 1957 through January 1958 I worked for Edward J. Logue, then in charge of all aspects of the city's urban renewal program and also the Mayor's closest adviser. I performed some assignments for Logue, in both urban renewal and the 1957 mayoralty campaign. Much of the time, however, I watched and listened. I attended meetings, talked with Logue and members of his staff, read his files and daily correspondence, and intruded into as many conversations as possible. . . . In February 1958 I moved next door to the Mayor's office and spent the next five months watching Lee do his job. Whenever Lee was in his office I sat in a corner.

wise, gauge the extent to which the other chroniclers of New Haven politics, with their own protracted access to informants and documentary materials, have also fallen victim to the problem Domhoff diagnoses.[23] Since these other works so frequently agree with Dahl we must conclude, I think, that the methodological disabilities that Domhoff outlines are very widespread.

Curiously, Domhoff's own methods come very close to those he deplores,[24] consisting of

> reading of organizational and committee minutes, position papers, letters written by important decision makers, secret memos, and other documents only recently available to researchers, and . . . interviews [Domhoff does not say how many or with whom] with people Dahl never interviewed or did not quiz closely.[25]

Evidently the main advantage of what Domhoff describes as his "more in-depth and holistic analysis"[26] is its relative remoteness in time from the events he describes. Cases of disagreement between an eyewitness and a scholar twenty years later must, presumably, be resolved in favor of the historian in order to avoid the "sociopsychological" contamination that rearranges the memories of contemporary observers of events. Yet it is not proven—and not easy to prove—that more distant observers may not

23. Powledge, for example, was an editor-writer in New Haven for the Associated Press from 1958–1960. William Lee Miller, a Yale Divinity School professor, was in 1963 elected Alderman from the 15th ward. Allan Talbot worked (for the city government) in New Haven from mid-1960 until 1965 and thus, he says,

> was close to most of the events which are described. I began preparation of the book in 1961 by keeping a personal record, and have supplemented it by interviews. . . . For background information I enjoyed full access to the Mayor's files, plus those of the Redevelopment Agency, Community Progress Inc., and Roger L. Stevens. (*The Mayor's Game*, p. x)

Russell Murphy spent the years 1963–1965 in "personal observation of top-level officials in New Haven's anti-poverty agency, Community Progress, Inc. . . . During the period I served with the agency I was given almost complete access to agency records: to files, financial reports, letters, memoranda, and working papers. . . . Time not spent examining agency records, observing staff behavior, or performing assigned chores was devoted to extensive informal interviews with agency personnel. . . . To supplement information I gathered through agency sources . . . I relied on interviews with individuals outside the agency . . . on an extensive file of newspaper clippings . . . as well as . . . reports of several federal agencies and congressional committees. (Murphy, *Political Entrepreneurs*, pp. 7–8)

24. See, for example, Domhoff, p. 67: "Rotival's outline of the objectives of the 1941–42 planning squares with the memories of Dudley, Mayer and Downe, the three people close to the study whom I was able to interview."

25. Ibid., p. 40. In personal correspondence, Domhoff identifies eighteen people with whom he talked who were "not on Professor Dahl's list of people interviewed."

26. Ibid., p. 49.

themselves fall victim to biases of various sorts. Moreover, they labor under
the disadvantage of not having many and varied tests readily to hand with
which to check their conceptions of reality—fellow eyewitnesses, for example, and the more copious documentary evidence of contemporary
events that is filtered out, lost, or destroyed in the course of time and is
never preserved in archives in the same profusion with which it exists in its
natural habitat. So at a minimum, we must regard Domhoff's methodological argument as novel if not eccentric; to me, it is unpersuasive. As
anthropologists argue, more rather than less exposure to a research site is,
barring the existence of physical hazards such as high levels of radioactivity,
greatly to be preferred. Eyewitnesses are better than "secret memos." Observing "important decision-makers" and reading their mail is better than
reading their mail alone.

This relatively abstract, methodological argument agrees with a position
that I hold with regard to substantive issues. I am not disposed to resolve
in Domhoff's favor cases where his interpretations of events conflict sharply
with those of people in a better position than he to interpret what was
going on. Nor, for the reasons already given, should any sane person.

The three substantive points to which *Who Really Rules?* is devoted are
(1) that, contrary to Dahl et al., economic and social notables in New
Haven substantially overlap, (2) that Yale University is not weak politically in New Haven, and (3) that the New Haven urban renewal program
was the product of New Haven's "active and organized business community" and not Mayor Richard C. Lee and his redevelopment staff.[27]

## The Overlap between Economic and Social Notables

Let us suppose we want to determine whether social and economic
notables are the same or different sets and, if not identical, the extent to
which the sets overlap. A strong test of identity will define "social" and
"economic" leaders by different criteria, and will keep the numbers of
potential members of both sets low, conceivably by defining the boundaries
of membership in a set strictly. Those who overlap in such circumstances
can be considered to have passed a rigorous test of inclusion.

It is possible to weaken these tests. The boundaries of membership in
each set can be expanded by definition, and the criteria by which the two
groups are defined can be made less distinct. Sooner or later, by such
means, the two groups can be made to merge toward one another.

In essence, this describes the different approaches employed by Dahl

27. Ibid., p. 3.

and Domhoff. Writing at a time when the top leadership of Atlanta, Georgia, was held to number 40 persons, and other, equally small groups of "key influentials" were regarded as exercising significant behind-the-scenes power in communities far larger than New Haven,[28] it could not have seemed unreasonable to Dahl to define economic and social notables in a town the size of New Haven rather narrowly. To define the relevant population broadly would have been to court criticism from stratification-ists that the New Haven study was inflating its economic and social elite and was not a fair replication of the methods that produced such small elites in much larger cities. Moreover, the larger the population of economic and social notables, the more of them were sure to be left out as uninfluential when the time came to tote up the ratio of economic and social notable participants to nonparticipants in key political decisions. This latter exercise is not one that Domhoff reports on; thus he does not disclose whether he has a far larger list of social notables who are political deadwood than Dahl, as I surmise.

Domhoff defines as New Haven's social notables not only members of the New Haven cotillion, as Dahl did, but also members of three local clubs: the Lawn Club, the Graduate Club, and the New Haven Country Club. When overlaps are struck off this gives a population of 1,350 families.

Domhoff's list of economic notables was compiled by taking the board of directors of New Haven's largest bank and adding to it the directors of any banks or corporations on whose boards of directors members of the first board also sat, plus law partners of lawyer members of the first board. Then, this larger population's fellow directors on still other boards was added to the list of economic notables, giving a total of 416 names. Dahl's method of identifying economic notables yielded 238 names. The list consisted of all directors of New Haven banks and three or more large local business firms, chief officers of local corporations above a certain threshold of wealth, plus heads of all banks and public utilities, and large individual taxpayers on New Haven land.[29]

Domhoff's grounds for not including as economic notables some of the people who turned up on Dahl's list but not his own illustrates how reliance upon only one—even an extended—social network can produce a tendency to blend the definitions of economic and social notability:

28. Seattle, for example. See Delbert C. Miller, "Decision-Making Cliques in Community Power Structures: A Comparative Study of an American and an English City," *Am. J. Soc.*, 64 (Nov. 1958), 299–310; and Delbert C. Miller, "Industry and Community Power Structure: A Comparative Study of an American and an English City," *Am. Soc. Rev.*, 23 (Feb. 1958), 9–15.

29. Dahl's criteria are given in *Who Governs?*, pp. 67–68; Domhoff's are described in *Who Really Rules?*, pp. 17–30.

Many of these men and women [on Dahl's list] are of Italian or Jewish background, which means they are likely to be excluded by the dominant group of economic notables. In any case, I do not think that car dealers, motel owners, and apartment house owners should be considered economic notables in an arbitrary fashion.[30]

And:

Eight people on Dahl's list are major executives with businesses whose headquarters are in other cities. They appeared on the list because their companies had real estate holdings, factories, or retail outlets in New Haven. . . . I do not think they belong on a list of local economic notables that is being compared with a list of local social notables.[31]

Domhoff removes roughly one quarter of the economic notables from his list because they are out-of-towners, and then he is ready to compare this reduced list with his expanded list of social notables. He finds that 58 per cent of this smaller list of economic notables achieves social notability in New Haven. There is indeed a discrepancy with Dahl's finding of a much smaller overlap but, as we have seen, Dahl's list of economic notables was encumbered with people meeting the economic, but not the social criteria of notability which Domhoff introduced into his economic listing. When the figures are run a little differently, we find that only 14 per cent of Domhoff's social notables are also economic notables; and if Domhoff's economic notable list is restored to its full strength and augmented by the 60 names on Dahl's list whom Domhoff did not include, the percentage of economic notables who are also social notables dips to 40 per cent. The accompanying table gives the numbers as they are given in Domhoff's book, along with Domhoff's qualifiers where it seems appropriate. The published figures do not seem to add up to 1,350 families; nonoverlapping cotillion subscribers evidently fill out the total to approximately 1,350.

As I have indicated, it is possible to gerrymander the definitions of economic and status notability in such a way as to produce greater or smaller degrees of overlap. A method of disciplining these proceedings is to require that the greatly enlarged population of status notables also form a basis for the discussion of the decision-making activity, political participation, and local political power of notables. It is safe to say that as the group of social notables is increased for purposes of establishing an over-

30. Domhoff, *Who Really Rules?*, pp. 29–30.
31. Ibid. It is unclear why it is inappropriate for economic notables of any description to appear on a list that is going to be "compared with" a presumably different list of social notables. If, on the other hand, the goal is not to compare the lists but to merge them, the grounds for Domhoff's objection become clearer.

lap with economic notables, the percentage of this group that is politically significant shrivels.[32] Thus by playing with the figures so as to establish a relatively high percentage of socially notable economic leaders, Domhoff undoubtedly diminishes the percentage—not large to begin with—of social and economic leaders who are politically active or important.

### DOMHOFF'S SOCIAL NOTABLES OF NEW HAVEN CA. 1959

| | Country Club | Lawn Club | Graduate Club | Total |
|---|---|---|---|---|
| Members | 650 local | "about" 500 | "a little over" 400 | 1,550 |

| Subtract overlaps: | | |
|---|---|---|
| | Lawn and Graduate | 113 |
| | Country and Lawn | 76 |
| | Country and Graduate | 56 |
| | "In addition" all three | 17 |
| | | 262 |

Total Social Notables 1,288

"these three clubs in conjunction with the cotillion attendance lists":

Total "about" 1,350

Source: G. William Domhoff, *Who Really Rules?*, p. 16.

### DOMHOFF'S OVERLAP BETWEEN SOCIAL AND ECONOMIC NOTABLES OF NEW HAVEN CA. 1959

| Economic Notable Members | Country Club | Lawn Club | Graduate Club | Total |
|---|---|---|---|---|
| | 93 | 83 | 77 | 253 |

| Subtract overlaps: | | |
|---|---|---|
| | Lawn and Graduate | 28 |
| | Country and Lawn | 15 |
| | Country and Graduate | 12 |
| | All three | 7 |
| | | 62 |

Total Overlap 191

| Overlap as a % of Social Notables | Overlap as a % of Economic Notables (Reduced) | Overlap as a % of Economic Notables (Augmented) |
|---|---|---|
| $\frac{191}{1,350} = 14\%$ | $\frac{191}{319} = 59\%$ | $\frac{191}{476} = 40\%$ |

Source: G. William Domhoff, *Who Really Rules?*, p. 30.

32. This percentage is not high using Dahl's definition, where the denominator is 231 socially notable families. See Dahl, *Who Governs?*, p. 64–65.

*The Political Power of Yale University*

The claim that Yale University's position in New Haven politics is weak arises from evidence such as the following: Yale is extremely unpopular with ordinary citizens of New Haven. There is continuous pressure from city officials to get Yale to pay substantial sums to the city in lieu of taxes, and the university's physical expansion has been largely blocked by the city over this issue. In urban redevelopment, where Yale ordinarily might have been considered an obvious redeveloper, the city dealt at arm's length with Yale, demanding—and receiving—a padded price—paid far in advance—for the city's dilapidated high schools (which were not part of any redevelopment plan), and once forcing Yale into an auction which Yale people believed was rigged against them. Most of the ten times Richard Lee ran for mayor he was sharply criticized for having once been an employee of the Yale News Bureau. Mayor Lee frequently referred to Yale's unpopularity with the rest of his constituents and, although he was personally friendly with many members of the Yale community, willingly enlisted Yale-connected people to support him in his various endeavors, and did not share the low opinion of Yale as an institution that was common currency in New Haven, he felt obliged to give very great weight to the general low opinion of Yale in the community in shaping public policy.[33]

Fred Powledge, no special friend of Yale, writes:

> Yale . . . was not able to decide until very late in the sixties whether it was proper for an Ivy League school to condescend to involve itself as an institution in the affairs of the city. . . . Political scientists might want to run for the board of alderman, city planners might want to devise new traffic patterns, and architects might want to accept commissions to design new buildings. . . . But beyond that, and beyond frequent scrapes between the students and the townspeople, Yale had little to do with the city around it. Town–gown relations were notoriously bad.[34]

As to most of this Domhoff has nothing to say. His one attempt to cope with the plain facts is an effort at reinterpreting Yale's loss of auctioned

---

33. See, in general, Wolfinger, *Politics of Progress*, pp. 25–28, 290–94.

34. Powledge, *Model City*, pp. 24–25. The most famous "scrape" was the 1959 St. Patrick's day riot, in which city police invaded Yale buildings and beat up students, many of them innocent and not even bystanders. Yale's only official response was to suspend two students for (verbally) insulting the Mayor. See Wolfinger, *Politics of Progress*, p. 26. Talbot, a Yale fan, emphasizes the friendship between Mayor Lee and President A. Whitney Griswold, *The Mayor's Game*, pp. 71–86.

development land as a "victory" for Yale because an official of Yale, after the event, told Dahl:

> I don't feel the least bit sorry that we're out of it. It was so complex, the arrangement was so complex, we were just involved in so much red tape of all kinds. . . . I don't care what the University Towers [the winning bidder] is or who it is if it gets some decent apartment houses over there. . . . In this I think we've won two thirds of the battle anyway and we don't have any of the headache and no responsibility and nobody can accuse us of taking more prime land off the tax roll.

Domhoff says: "His words are of considerable theoretical significance, for they show how major power centers get what they want even when they 'lose' a specific decision."[35] Actually, they show Yale's continued vulnerability on the tax issue and the exasperation of university leaders with the strings that Lee and his Development Administrator put on the project.

The remainder of Domhoff's observations about Yale in relation to New Haven are scattered through his book. They consist of such items as the fact that Connecticut's senior Senator, Prescott Bush, who was occasionally helpful to the redevelopment program, was a Yale alumnus and sometime trustee;[36] that Yale guaranteed a loan to the developers of the Church Street project at a time when it looked as if the project would fall apart;[37] that through a Yale connection Lee reestablished a lapsed contact with Macy's department store,[38] that many members of the Yale Corporation— that is, trustees of the university—are well-known national figures,[39] that Yale alumni work in law firms favored by local businessmen and by Yale itself, that Yale officials and Redevelopment Agency officials were in contact before 1955, and that a handful of Yale faculty and administrators sat on various boards of directors defined by Domhoff as economically elite.[40]

Undoubtedly, some of these are significant events, affiliations, acts, or activities. But in what sense are they properly attributable to "Yale"? There are, it is clear, many possible meanings when the word "Yale" is invoked. When we refer to Yale do we mean Yale trustees, Yale administrators, Yale students, Yale faculty, Yale nonacademic staff, Yale alumni? Does it not make sense to restrict the meaning of an expression like "Yale's influence" to circumstances where acts taken by Yale as an institution by persons

35. Domhoff, *Who Really Rules?*, pp. 106–07.
36. Ibid., pp. 45–47, 105.
37. Ibid., p. 112.
38. Ibid., p. 112.
39. Ibid., pp. 26–28.
40. Ibid., pp. 21, 26–27.

authorized to act and acting for it are involved? Or when the President of Yale buys bagels at a local delicatessen on Sunday morning is he exercising economic influence properly attributable to the university?

There is no sovereign answer to questions of this kind. For some purposes, we may wish to restrict the discussion of Yale influence to any formal act of the Yale Corporation and any act by others bearing upon the corporate plans or policies of the Yale Corporation. But for other purposes a wider net must be cast. As the net widens, however, it becomes harder to take a careful census of relevant acts and failures to act. Yale becomes one of many points of reference for individual actors. As Connecticut's senior Senator, for example, Prescott Bush might well have regarded New Haven redevelopment as worth encouraging even if he had never had a Yale connection. Yale alumni and Yale faculty may go off in a dozen different directions and if any or all of their activities are classified as the exercise of Yale influence, grossly misleading inferences might be drawn about the extent or direction of the influence of Yale as a corporate entity. This argues, I think, for a more restricted conception of Yale, one that attends to the institution as an organized body but which excludes the behavior of all others connected or partially connected, or formerly connected, with Yale as in the same sense reflecting the influence of the university in the community. Without some such narrowing of focus, intelligible classifications of acts become almost impossible. What are we to make of the Yale connections of people who opposed the university in the community on one or more issues? Although a small number of Yale faculty may have sat on the boards of New Haven companies, what about the overwhelming numbers of Yale faculty who did not, and who put their energies into other activities? How far must we track these activities to get an accurate portrait of "Yale" in the community? Presumably a measure of the Yale faculty's influence in New Haven on a per-capita basis would yield a result far different from the impression of Yale dominance that Domhoff wishes to convey. Yet the sort of evidence he mentions does seem to me to require a more thorough and a more broadly inclusive canvass of the activities and allegiances of Yale-related people—if any relation to Yale will suffice as evidence of Yale influence—than the sparse, casual, and one-sided anecdotes that Domhoff offers as evidence for his interpretation.

Domhoff's conception of politics relies heavily upon establishing networks of "connections" among various people, the underlying assumption being that to establish that people are "connected" is to establish that they have values, political interests, political goals, or political preferences in common. It is just as easy to believe that enmity, rivalry, distrust, or competition flow from the common membership on a board of directors or in a club or firm that constitutes a connection for the purposes of this sort of analysis. Further empirical inquiry must establish the extent to which the rather simpleminded bookkeeping involved in tabulating such items as the names on a letterhead has any concrete political meaning, and what meaning it has.

It is perhaps not widely appreciated that even in a society as large as the United States major segments of the population are closely knit into networks of acquaintance or association. A simple parlor game will make this clear: any reader can think of some far-off person and calculate how many steps in a chain of personal acquaintance it would take to link with that person. I, for example, am two steps away from the late Mao Zedong, since I am acquainted with people who know former President Nixon, who knew Mao. I have never met a President of the United States, but I have known someone who has met each President since my birth (one step each). Students of this phenomenon have calculated that the entire American population can be shown in principle to interlock with an average of fewer than three intervening steps.[41] Empirical investigation shows that interlocks established by actual searches (which are not necessarily maximally efficient) between ordinary citizens, strangers living in the middle west and New England, average five or six steps.[42]

This means that interlocking relationships between people in the same community, or in the same line of work, or from the same stratum of society, or who are reasonably well or widely known, are highly probable, and are not significant deviations from an entropy-filled, relationshipless world that a casual, unreflective address to the problem might suggest.

41. See Ithiel de Sola Pool, "Communication Systems," in Pool, Wilbur Schramm, Frederick Frey, Nathan Maccoby, Edwin B. Parker, eds. *Handbook of Communication* (Chicago, Rand McNally, 1973), pp. 3–26.

Equally impressive is the eminent physicist Elliott Montroll's demonstration that he is one cheek-pinch and four handshakes away from Benjamin Franklin. Franklin pinched the cheek of the boy John Quincy Adams. Adams shook hands with Joseph Henry in December 1837, during a Congressional session. Henry shook hands with Hubert Anson Newton at the 1864 meeting of the National Academy. Newton shook hands with Lynde Phelps Wheeler, who shook hands with Montroll in 1949. See Uzi Landman, *Statistical Mechanics and Statistical Methods in Theory and Application: A Tribute to Elliot W. Montroll* (New York, Plenum, 1977), p. 784. I should add that I have myself shaken hands with Montroll on many occasions and that all those who have shaken hands with me are only six handshakes and a cheek-pinch away from Franklin.

42. Stanley Milgram, "The Small-World Problem," *Psychology Today, 1* (May 1967), 61–67; Jeffrey Travers and Stanley Milgram, "An Experimental Study of the Small World Problem," *Sociometry, 32* (Dec. 1969), 425–43; Charles Korte and Stanley Milgram, "Acquaintance Networks Between Racial Groups: Application of the Small World Method," *Journal of Personality and Social Psychology, 15* (June 1970), 101–08.

This does not mean, however, that *ipso facto* all relationships are meaningless or without political import. What it means is that to establish a "relationship" or "connection" does not establish what its meaning and political import are.

None of this adds up to an argument that Yale, undoubtedly a national institution of great visibility and some influence, at least in matters of higher education, was locally politically influential. Indeed, if we can argue with Sherlock Holmes that it is significant when the dog does not bark in the night, then we would have to conclude that Domhoff's very failure to make a case is eloquent additional testimony to Yale's marginal political influence as an institution in New Haven politics.

### Urban Redevelopment: Lee or the Business Community?

I have shown, I think, that while Domhoff casts aspersions on the methods of the New Haven study, these are for the most part the methods that he himself uses. Moreover, he is handicapped by his lack of experience in New Haven as a firsthand observer, and his very brief acquaintance with the city itself renders him almost entirely dependent upon whatever materials others have collected or can (in the case of documents and archives) point out to him. Nevertheless, he concludes:

> Ruling-class power at the national and state levels created the crucial ideological context and governmental structures which encased local decision making, and ... big businessmen and Yale officials were the major connections to those levels.

And

> Ruling-class leaders were central to urban renewal in New Haven.

And

> Whether we look at the origins of the local urban renewal program (in the Chamber of Commerce and Yale) or its eventual outcome (land for the expansion of Yale, the hospital, and the downtown business community) we must conclude, contrary to *Who Governs?* that there is a power structure in New Haven, with Yale, the First New Haven National Bank, and the Chamber of Commerce at its heart.[43]

Domhoff's case for these propositions is neither orderly nor even coherent and entails very little in the way of positive demonstration. Rather,

43. Domhoff, *Who Really Rules?*, p. 113. In fact, Yale got no land from the urban renewal program.

it consists principally of three elements: (1) many statements alleging that Dahl and his associates neglect, ignore, or misunderstand crucial evidence which is either not produced or, when produced, will not bear the weight Domhoff puts on it, (2) simple repetitions of observations already made by Dahl and his associates, and (3) new information, almost all of it irrelevant to the question of whether or not there is a "power structure" in New Haven.

Only a few examples of each of these elements should satiate readers of normal appetites. Pages 45–48 of Domhoff's book are devoted to what a subhead calls "Dahl's Limited Theoretical Focus," in which it is charged that Dahl neglects the importance of the state and national government. This is shown because one of Dahl's informants, quoted by Domhoff at length,[44] mentions that Senator Prescott Bush was "helpful," but Dahl did not make much of this at the time of the interview; and another informant of Dahl's, also quoted at length, says the CAC had a "fruitful discussion" on the relocation of Route 5 by the State Highway Department, and (as a participant in the interview) I asked whether something similar ever happened with respect to a purely local decision.

On the face of it, these examples show nothing, certainly not "Dahl's limited theoretical focus," and, as a matter of fact, not even much about the connections between New Haven decision-making and relevant activity elsewhere.

This problem also plagues Domhoff's discussion of the New Haven Chamber of Commerce, which, he says, did things like sending letters and forming committees between 1949 and 1953, and definitely favored urban renewal; indeed, by June of 1953, the Chamber had a "ten point program" that included such desiderata as downtown parking and recommendations drawn in part from a city plan drawn up in 1941 by the well-known planner (then at Yale) Maurice Rotival for an official body, the City Plan Commission. None of this, nor any of the rest of Domhoff's very elaborate account of the largely ineffectual activity in New Haven on urban renewal before 1953, contradicts Dahl or Wolfinger, although Domhoff says it does. But in fact both Dahl and Wolfinger say that in New Haven, as in many American cities, plans, proposals, committees, wishes, and ambitions for civic improvement existed.[45] What needed explaining surely, was why in New Haven, uniquely in terms of actual results, so many plans were put into effect.

44. Dahl made available to Domhoff transcripts of all 49 transcribed interviews of the New Haven study and other working papers of the study. Domhoff makes sparing use of this material.

45. See, for example, Dahl, *Who Governs?*, pp. 116, 128.

This reveals the essential defect of an argument that insists on the critical importance of "national and state level ideological context and governmental structures." If they are crucial, and local political leadership negligible, then why did a massive urban renewal take place in New Haven, and not in Worcester or New Britain or Wilkes-Barre or Bridgeport? Why was New Haven's renewal so much bigger than any program anywhere in the country? And why, if Mayor Lee and other city officials were so unimportant, was there a four-year hiatus—before Lee's election—between the creation of a national context and the commencement of the New Haven program? Domhoff has no satisfactory answers to any of these questions; rather, he merely insists on the importance of Yale and the New Haven business community.

At certain places in Domhoff's book, glimmers of light appear. Domhoff drops into a footnote the fact that the "chief aide" to Lee's predecessor, Mayor Celentano, "recalls that Celentano was basically sympathetic to urban redevelopment, but not notably active in the matter," just as Dahl and Wolfinger report.[46] He puts into a subordinate clause the news that "interviewees" recall "that Yale leaders took virtually no interest in the program in its early stages."[47] He indicates that the Chamber of Commerce was handicapped in community affairs and could not take the lead because it was saddled with a "right wing image . . . with its penchant for alienating labor and liberals."[48]

All these tidbits testify to the proposition that neither Yale nor the Chamber of Commerce nor Mayor Lee's predecessor was a significant originator of New Haven urban renewal. They are, however, tidbits. They and all the other bits and pieces of information a reconstruction of historical events entails have to be read carefully and circumspectly and in the light of as many other relevant facts as it is possible for devoted researchers to assimilate.

For example, a serious canvass of "big business" relations with the urban renewal program would include—at a minimum—the following observations:

1. "Big business" in New Haven is not very big. The only Fortune 500 company in town was the Winchester branch of Olin Industries, located outside the urban renewal areas, uninvolved and, despite Domhoff's view that local power structures are dominated by national concentrations of money and power, unmentioned by Domhoff. Even the largest local banks were small by national standards. As Dahl says:

46. Domhoff, *Who Really Rules?*, p. 117, n. 79.
47. Ibid., p. 78.
48. Ibid., p. 101.

REINTERPRETATIONS OF NEW HAVEN POLITICS

The city's borrowing is not even handled by local banks; New Haven is not a large financial center and its facilities are inadequate for marketing the city's bonds, which until 1958 were mainly handled by a Boston firm and since then by a Hartford bank.[49]

There is other evidence of the inability of New Haven banks to monopolize local credit. The successor to the founder of an innovative New Haven manufacturing firm told us:

In the beginning New Haven gave him a hard time . . . He could only find credit from one bank in town and that was the Mechanic's Bank which folded in '33. That was the only local bank that would even sit down and talk with him about his problems. . . . Being in a seasonal business, he had to have short term credit and he could only get it in New York and Boston. They gave it to him and they still give it to us.[50]

2. The Lee administration gerrymandered the Wooster Square project so that the city could buy the run-down Sargent lock company building. Sargent was threatening to move away from the city. Instead, it bought a 20-acre parcel in the Long Wharf redevelopment area and erected a new building there. Domhoff does not mention this.

The Lee administration made varying sorts of land deals with a number of other large economic entities: The First New Haven National Bank, the Southern New England Telephone Company, Macy's, the Bahr Corporation, Malley's Department Store, the Knights of Columbus, Yale, College Plaza Inc., University Towers, Inc., Roger Stevens, and G. Harold Welch. Each of these economic entities had its own problems and goals, and on the whole they did not coordinate with one another in their dealings with the city administration. Indeed, some of them were competitors. Some favored the renewal plans, some did not. Some lost money as a result of their dealings with the city.[51] The idea that cooperating with a city administration in an urban redevelopment program is a risk-free venture is nonsense. For example, Roger Stevens, the New York financier who was the main redeveloper for the biggest block of land created by the Church Street Development in the middle of town, had reason to know this. The history of his dealings with the city and with the large department stores and hotel that finally occupied this site shows the complexities and difficulties involved and helps to give reality to any discussion of the relations between politics and economics in urban renewal. Yet Domhoff gives Stevens only one quick mention. I quote in full:

49. Dahl, *Who Governs?*, p. 241.
50. Interview transcript.
51. Almost certainly, at a minimum, Stevens and Welch did. See passim Lowe, Talbot, Wolfinger.

The first thoughts on downtown urban renewal involved a completely private project by a multimillionaire developer, Roger Stevens, known to Logue and Lee because he was a major Democratic party fund-raiser and contributor.[52]

It would presumably have strengthened Domhoff's case for the proposition that big business was significant in New Haven urban renewal if he had known enough about the program to be able to say, for example, with Wolfinger that:

> Stevens's most important impact on the project came during its conception, for he rather than city officials first thought that the project had to be ... sweeping.[53]

It would have complicated his account and weakened his case to have reported that Stevens evidently lost money on his New Haven venture, and publicly vowed never again to get involved with any urban redevelopment program which allegedly showers riches on "big businessmen."

3. Many aspects of the physical plan for urban redevelopment indeed followed the master plan drawn up by Maurice Rotival in 1941 for the City Plan Commission. Dahl says:

> In so far as one can ever locate a source of ideas, probably Maurice Rotival was as much the ultimate fount as any living person. . . . But none of Rotival's proposals, nor those of anyone else, were self-enacting.[54]

This explains succinctly why going on at length about Rotival's plan, as Domhoff does, fails to explain why and how it was finally enacted as it was.

It is not germane to our discussion to describe what happened in detail. That has been done elsewhere, and serious students of the relations in New Haven between large economic entities and the politics of urban renewal can find what they need in the literature. Only a very partial, garbled, frequently inaccurate, and unclear version can be found in Domhoff's book. Instead of describing what happened, he dwells upon what one or more committees of the Chamber of Commerce wished would happen. His conclusions are certainly not sustained by the available historical evidence, of which his book gives what can charitably be called a skewed sample. And even within the pages of his own book, there are strong indications that such data as he discloses will not bear the interpretations he forces upon them.

52. Domhoff, *Who Really Rules?*, p. 108.
53. Wolfinger, *Politics of Progress*, p. 345.
54. Dahl, *Who Governs?*, p. 128.

# 11. The Mobilization of Bias

I have so far dealt with a number of criticisms of Pluralist$_2$ community power studies, including those alleging that presuppositions of researchers —presumably something like Pluralist$_3$ axioms—prevented them from finding centralized power systems in much the same manner that the axioms of general stratification theory (according to my earlier claim)—combined with certain methodological errors—predetermined the outcomes of stratification studies of community power. And I have argued that no comparable methodological errors have been demonstrated to have been committed by Pluralist$_2$ researchers, despite some effort to show otherwise, at least with respect to the New Haven study.

I now move to a different sort of criticism, one which alleges that Pluralist$_2$ researchers may well have looked at the wrong sort of data. The most famous source of this charge is Peter Bachrach and Morton Baratz's article "Two Faces of Power," which has achieved a great importance in the community power literature.[1] Bachrach and Baratz ask:

> Can a sound concept of power be predicated on the assumption that power is totally embodied and fully reflected in "concrete decisions" or in activity bearing directly upon their making?

And they answer:

> We think not.

They raise

> The possibility, for instance, that an individual or a group in a community participates more vigorously in supporting the *nondecision-making* process than . . . in actual decisions within the process. . . . [C]an the researcher overlook the chance that some person or association could limit decision-making to relatively noncontroversial matters,

---

1. The original article was Peter Bachrach and Morton S. Baratz, "Two Faces of Power," *Am. Pol. Sci. Rev.*, 56 (Dec. 1962) 947–52. It is reprinted with only slight changes in Bachrach and Baratz, *Power and Poverty* (New York, Oxford University Press, 1970), pp. 3–16, from which I draw my citations.

by influencing community values and political procedures and rituals, notwithstanding that there are in the community serious but latent power conflicts? To do so is, in our judgment, to overlook the less apparent, but nonetheless extremely important, face of power.[2]

This "second face" of power is also referred to as "the mobilization of bias", the phenomenon described by E. E. Schattschneider as follows:

All forms of political organization have a bias in favor of the exploitation of some kinds of conflict and the suppression of others because organization is the mobilization of bias. Some issues are organized into politics while others are organized out.[3]

Thus, the argument goes, an integral property of any political system worthy of the name "system" is the capacity to limit the type and number of issues that at any time are available for consideration and/or resolution by its decision-making machinery.[4] Moreover, it is suggested, the means by which limitation is achieved are not necessarily similar in any significant respect to the means by which ordinary decisions within the system are considered or resolved; and so claims about the distributions of power within political systems relying only on data having to do with normal processes of decision-making are at the least incomplete, and perhaps utterly misleading.

This, presumably, is the rationale for dismissing or questioning claims about power distributions in local communities made by students who can supply information only about the course of actual decision-making as evidence in support of their conclusions.

How to study this second face of power? To what manifestations of social reality might the mobilization of bias refer? Are phenomena of this sort in principle amenable to empirical investigation? If so, presumably evidence about how the biases of the system are actually mobilized, and by whom, can be added to whatever account of power in a given system is already available, and these sorts of evidence can affirm or weaken or modify conclusions about the distribution of power in a community based on a discussion of those issues that are organized into politics. If not, then assertions about this second face of power cannot in principle be agreed to or disagreed with on empirical grounds, and whether or not one chooses

2. Ibid., pp. 7, 8–9. Emphasis in original.

3. E. E. Schattschneider, The Semi-Sovereign People (New York, Holt, Rinehart & Winston, 1960), p. 71.

4. I believe so myself. See above, pp. 134–36 on the conservatism of political agendas.

to believe them, or contrary assertions, becomes entirely a matter of taste, ideological preference, or prejudice. The patent undesirability of establishing conclusions purportedly about the world at large in this latter fashion seems so obvious as to require little argument. And so efforts to move assertions about the mobilization of bias from the realm of the *a priori* and toward the realm of the empirically confirmable seem obviously worthwhile.

## CONTEXT

The literature gives some support to at least five different interpretations of what it means to study the second face of power. For example, perhaps what Bachrach and Baratz are suggesting is that researchers should attend to the context of decision-making. This might entail discovering whether or not decisions are taken under threat of coercion, or whether the political system under examination is one in which votes are counted honestly, in which there is ready access to political information, and in which opposition to current officeholders may safely be organized.[5] Closer examination of their views, however, suggests that this is not what Bachrach and Baratz have in mind. The pluralist targets of their criticism frequently do provide narrative reports of laws, customs, political traditions, and institutionalized practices that prevail in the communities they study.[6] Moreover, the ways in which these practices operate are in principle highly observable and reportable and evidently do not require extraordinary measures to be adequately studied.

The fact that so many pluralists do discuss political context, sometimes in very copious detail, has led students to the assumption that when Bachrach and Baratz recommend observation of "[T]he dominant values and the political myths, rituals, and institutional practices which tend to favor the vested interests of one or more groups, relative to others," and warn students against neglecting "prior study of the political and social views of all concerned"[7] in decision-making they are asking for an even greater level of detail than the literature already provides.

There is, of course, another possibility, namely that Bachrach and Baratz have simply not noticed the rather ample extent to which the work they

5. In *A Preface to Democratic Theory* (Chicago, Univ. of Chicago Press, 1956), pp. 63–85, Robert A. Dahl refers to items such as these as characteristics of polyarchy.

6. A famous example of contextual description by a political scientist whose work is generally congenial to the pluralist perspective is V. O. Key's discussion of "Restrictions on Voting," chaps. 25–30 (pp. 531–663) and "The One-Party System—Mechanisms and Procedures," chaps. 18–22 (pp. 384–488) in *Southern Politics* (New York, Knopf, 1950).

7. Bachrach and Baratz, *Power and Poverty*, pp. 11, 15.

principally criticize has already fulfilled their requirement. There is some evidence to support this view. Consider their reading of pluralists on "issues": Pluralists, they say, in fact,

> Polsby is guilty . . . of the same fault he himself has found with elitist methodology: by presupposing that in any community there are significant issues in the political arena, he takes for granted the very question which is in doubt. He accepts as issues what are reputed to be issues. As a result, his findings are foreordained. For even if there is no "truly" significant issue in the community under study, there is every likelihood that Polsby (or any like-minded researcher) will find one or some and, after careful study, reach the appropriate pluralistic conclusions.[8]

Are pluralist researchers capable of seeing when the exercise of power in a community is so dispersed that nothing aggregates into an issue-area large enough to be termed "significant" by one or another obvious criteria? Bachrach and Baratz assure us that the answer to this question is no. But absolutely nothing in the way of empirical demonstration backs this claim. It is merely assertion. It is, moreover, mere assertion that warrants the claim that if pluralists invented issue-areas out of whole cloth, they would then reach pluralistic conclusions with respect to them. How do Bachrach and Baratz come to know so much about the sources of pluralist error, when they can point to no actual error in the real world of research that supports their diagnosis, that is, no erroneous description of a community, no invention of an issue, no misrepresentation of a finding?

Part of the difficulty Bachrach and Baratz seem to have in reading pluralist studies is their inattention to a distinction between "issues" and "issue-areas." "Issues" in Bachrach and Baratz's lexicon appear to be matters of controversy in a community. They correctly quote Dahl as claiming that matters of controversy—"issues"—provide excellent data about the comparative abilities of actors differently situated to affect outcomes. There is nothing implausible in this. Do Bachrach and Baratz doubt that a good way to settle a difference of opinion about the relative strengths of the Yankees and the Red Sox is to observe the results of a match between them?

It is, however, incorrect to say or to imply that Dahl restricted his study of New Haven to the study only of controverted matters. "Issue-areas," that is, subject matter domains encompassing both routine and nonroutine decisions, conflict and innovation, with a rather heavy emphasis on innova-

8. Ibid., p. 10.

tion, were in fact the main object of study in New Haven, as even a cursory reading of *Who Governs?* discloses.[9]

There is reason to suspect, therefore, that Bachrach and Baratz do not appreciate the extent to which contextual information of all sorts is already available in the studies they criticize. If, however, even more contextual information is genuinely wanted, for whatever reason—if, for example, the study of "all" concerned and their "political and social views" prior to the study of actual decision-making is literally meant—certain practical problems are bound to arise, of which I will mention two.

The first of these concerns the term "all." It is reasonable enough to suppose that a canvass of "some" or "many" groups or citizens constitutes a feasible research agenda. Presumably one would find that with respect to most issue-areas, most respondents selected in a broad and undiscriminating sweep through the population would be indifferent and uninformed.[10] If the *expression* of concern is what is meant by concern when Bachrach and Baratz speak of "all concerned," it is quite likely that for most community political activity the study of the opinions and views of all concerned would not be terribly onerous. Indeed, one might argue that in general this is precisely what the pluralist researchers whom Bachrach and Baratz criticize actually did.

In order, therefore, to preserve some core of coherence in their criticisms, one must reject the notion that this is what they had in mind by recommending the study of the political and social views of "all concerned." Bachrach and Baratz supply no independent criterion by which concern can be measured; but in general we can say that, whatever criterion is used, if it is meant to apply very broadly, then the population constituting "all" grows apace, and it is conceivably beyond the capacity of any serious researcher deploying finite resources to study adequately.[11]

Once or twice in community power studies very large proportions of—conceivably by some standard "all"—local *interest groups* have been studied. The conclusions of these studies have, contrary to the expectation implied by Bachrach and Baratz, offered no embarrassment and much

9. See *Who Governs?*, Appendix B, pp. 340–40. On pp. 332–37 there is a discussion of "decisions in different issue-areas." Included among the decisions studied are such items as "Redeveloping the Church Street area" and "The Long Wharf project," which mostly involved not conflict but organizing to do something that had not been done before, and school budgets, which involved recurring activities.

10. The massed findings of survey research on this topic seem to me quite unequivocal. For a classic study, see, for example, Samuel Stouffer, *Communism, Conformity and Civil Liberties* (Garden City, Doubleday, 1955).

11. This point, among others, is made by Raymond E. Wolfinger in, "Nondecisions and the Study of Local Politics," *Am. Pol. Sci. Rev.*, 65 (Dec. 1971), 1063–80.

support to pluralist conclusions.[12] That is, by increasing markedly the population of community groups studied, patterns of power fundamentally discontinuous with those patterns disclosed by studying important concrete decisions have *not* been discovered. This suggests that there are useful things to be said about community power short of studying the views of "all"; and the fact that even specifying a population sufficiently inclusive to encompass "all" may prove too difficult in many communities— especially sizeable ones—should not act as a deterrent to more modestly conceived research.

The second problem has to do with ambiguities in the notion of "prior study" of "political and social" views. Here I think a fair reading of

12. See Kenneth Newton, *Second City Politics* (Oxford, Clarendon Press, 1976) for a study that discusses a very large number of groups. Newton characterizes the Birmingham (England) political system (pp. 242, 244), with important qualifications, as "a pluralist democracy" and "a pluralist system." These accurately reflect his main findings. I am grateful to John Dearlove for reminding me that the text has some contradictions of these straightforward conclusions, but I believe the contradictions are not damaging to my point. To illustrate: on p. 62, Newton "takes some propositions from pluralist theory and compares them with the Birmingham data," and concludes: "Pluralism . . . fares poorly against the empirical evidence." My view is that this assertion of Newton's is in error and results from a misreading of what pluralists actually say.

Newton says his evidence

> shows, contrary to pluralist arguments, [1] that group resources are distributed with cumulative inequalities; [2] that groups generally operate unilaterally within their own sphere of interests, with little or no organized opposition; [3] that coalition-building and the escalation of group politics are the exception rather than the rule; [4] that the great number and diversity of groups (social pluralism) should not be equated with political pluralism if only because the breadth of group activities may conceal a narrow range of activists, most of whom appear to be middle- and upper-class.

None of these findings is squarely contrary to pluralist arguments. Consider, for example, a few excerpts from the summary of findings—mostly from "pluralist" research—that is contained on pages 122ff of this book:

> One of the most common patterns of behavior to be observed in American community life is that participation in the making of decisions is concentrated in the hands of a few. Ibid., p. 123.

> Different small groups normally make decisions on different community problems. Ibid., p. 124.

> Decisions made by small groups are almost always considered routine or otherwise insignificant by most other members of the community . . . Ibid., p. 124.

Even with respect to "cumulative inequalities" Newton's claim to have found something "contrary" to pluralist arguments is suspect. On page 76 he tortures a quotation from Robert Dahl as follows:

> Robert Dahl has argued that "a citizen who has less of one resource than another citizen may nonetheless gain greater influence because he has other resources. Though he may have less money, he may have more time, more energy, greater

Bachrach and Baratz's intention is as follows: They believe that no account of the distribution of power in a community is satisfactory without allowing for the possibility that large segments of the population lack an understanding of what political activities would be appropriate to effectuate ends they already privately espouse. And this lack of instrumental rationality keeps them from participating in decision-making that otherwise would, or might, engage their participation. A quick check of the privately held political and social views of such potential participants would, presumably, meet this problem, especially if there were a clearly discernible relationship between privately held views and actual or probable or likely public actions.

---

popularity, stronger ethnic ties." Consequently [Newton continues on his own], while political groups are not all equally matched, all have some resources which give them weight and leverage in the political system. As a result nobody is likely to lose out completely, and every group can get something out of the system, even if it cannot get most of what it wants. As Dahl puts it, "few groups in the United States who are determined to influence the government—certainly few if any groups of citizens who are organized, active, and persistent—lack the capacity and opportunity to influence some officials somewhere in the political system in order to obtain at least some of their goals."

Newton's interpolation seeks to deprive Dahl of the qualifications integral to his definition of noncumulative inequality and his empirical statement about American politics. "May" and "few" become "is" and "nobody." "Determined" groups of "citizens" who are "organized," "active," and "persistent" are transformed into "every" and "all." But "every" and "all" and "nobody" are not what Dahl, whom Newton chooses to make the pluralist case, says. They are what Newton puts in Dahl's mouth.

If Dahl is read as saying that *all* groups have adequate resources to enter successfully into politics, and *no* groups have more than one resource, then Newton's demonstration that some groups in Birmingham have more resources than others can be held to refute this reading of pluralist theory. However, Dahl does not say this, except about New Haven, in certain limited circumstances (*Who Governs?* p. 228). Rather, he starts with a presumption of inequality—"extensive inequalities in the resources different citizens can use to influence one another" is the way he puts it on page 1 of *Who Governs?*—and asks in light of this how something approximating pluralist democracy can exist.

It can exist if resources are spread. Dahl's argument, in short, entails not perfect equality of resources and not that everyone or every group has some resources but only that political resources not be monopolized by one group or closely held by a few. What does Newton find in Birmingham? That on four measures of group resourcefulness one group in eight stands high on all measures, and another one eighth on three out of four (p. 77). This means that roughly 1,000 formally organized voluntary organizations (out of the population of 4,250 studied by Newton) possessed significant political resources (p. 61). This seems to me entirely consistent with what pluralists generally find.

A study reaching pluralist₂ conclusions that covers virtually every sort of political activity in a small town (Oberlin, Ohio) for a period of three and a half years (1957–61) is Aaron Wildavsky's, *Leadership in a Small Town* (Totowa, N.J., Bedminster Press, 1964).

That this relationship very frequently does not exist constitutes a major empirical difficulty. In part it does not exist because people often do not have well-formed private views of public questions. Even sophisticated analysts who have such views may find themselves in disagreement about what constitutes an instrumentally rational course of action in politics;[13] and so it must not come altogether as a surprise to find people who are relatively inactive politically lacking in resolution about what, if anything, to do politically. Analysts must use circumspection in substituting their judgment for that of community citizens as a means of arriving at conclusions about what people would do if they were instrumentally rational by observers' standards.

There is the danger that an analyst will refuse to take no for an answer and insist on a regress that could, suitably manipulated, easily become infinite. Such an argument would proceed in this fashion: If citizens do not display the requisite political and social attitudes to cause them to see the "connections" between their private troubles and possible public actions, and hence to raise issues, participate, or change the local configuration of power, may it not be that in some earlier period they were rewarded or punished, brainwashed or educated, coerced or persuaded, voluntarily or involuntarily socialized into attitudes toward politics that are the precursors of the instrumental irrationality now observable?

Such an allegation enjoys the symmetrical beauty of being both hard to establish and hard to refute. The fact is, no student of community power has made the slightest effort to establish such a proposition, although the study of political socialization is occasionally brought forward as a serious strategy for students of community power to pursue.[14] Certainly before political socialization studies become *de rigueur* for students of community power one or two elementary plausibility checks might be employed. For example, it might be fairly inexpensive to ascertain whether people were being intimidated from raising issues, as people occasionally are in various settings.[15] If we must search all the way back to the formative stages of a

13. A classic example is the voting behavior of the rich in the 1932 U.S. presidential election. On one hand, a vote for Roosevelt was regarded as instrumentally irrational on grounds that Roosevelt would seek to tax the rich more heavily than Herbert Hoover. On the other hand, it could be argued that Rooseveltian reforms preserved the American economy and thereby the privileges of the rich. By more or less equally plausible chains of reasoning (depending, among other things, on whether a given actor valued short- or long-run consequences and on estimates of the probability of valued outcomes actually taking place) rational rich voters might have arrived at opposite conclusions.

14. See, for example, Frederick Frey, "Issues and Nonissues," p. 1094.

15. See, for example, Lester M. Salamon and Stephen Van Evera, "Fear, Apathy and Discrimination: A Test of Three Explanations of Political Participation," *Am. Pol. Sci. Rev.*, 67 (Dec. 1973), 1288–1306.

population's attitudes toward political participation, it might be possible to inquire whether the socialization experiences of large groups of nonparticipants were in gross structural ways divergent from those of participants and, if so, whether the manifest content of their different experiences impinges materially upon the sorts of decisions that arise or fail to arise on community agendas.

In the American context, for example, it seems overwhelmingly probable that community participants will have had more formal education than most community members, and hence more exposure to such civic training as is widely available in American secondary schools.[16] It is plausible to think that if anything characterizes nonparticipants as a class it is not how much but rather how little has been demanded of them in the way of civic or political attentiveness. This lack of brainwashing may well result in precisely the sort of political and even social incompetence that observers deplore in nonparticipants, and it may suffice to explain their nonparticipation, in at least some instances.[17] Such an explanation would neither confirm nor undermine propositions purporting to describe the configuration of power in a local community, although it might well contribute to an understanding of why that configuration exists. It is unlikely, however, that it could be shown that the same people who governed the local community in contemporary times were in some way at an earlier time responsible for the manifold of lost opportunities, failures, mischances, or ignorances in the life histories of nonparticipants that sustains their nonparticipation today,[18] and therefore it is doubtful that a socialization study will disclose that contemporary decision-makers are the cause of the nonparticipation of nonparticipants.

It is likely, as I have suggested, that if such a demonstration were attempted in an American context, roughly the reverse of the structural

16. See Stouffer, *Communism, Conformity,* passim.

17. For illumination of some of the empirical issues surrounding this point, see Paul M. Sniderman, *Personality and Democratic Politics* (Berkeley, Univ. of California Press, 1975). From an entirely different perspective, Nicholas Abercrombie and Bryan S. Turner offer confirmation in, "The Dominant Ideology Thesis," *British Journal of Sociology,* 29 (June 1978), 149–70. The abstract of this article says, among other things, "There is good evidence that the subordinate classes are not incorporated into the dominant ideology and that, by contrast, the dominant classes are deeply penetrated by and incorporated within the dominant belief system. In most societies the apparatus of transmission of the dominant ideology is not very efficient, and, in any event, is typically directed at the dominant rather than the subordinate class."

A good discussion of logical problems attending research on some of these and related issues is Richard M. Merelman, "On the Neo-Elitist Critique of Community Power," *Am. Pol. Sci. Rev.,* 62 (June 1968), 451–60.

18. Frey, "Issues and Nonissues," p. 1098, also makes this stipulation. See, in addition, Terence Ball, "Power, Causation and Explanation," *Polity,* 8 (Winter 1975), 202.

relationship usually posited would be discovered. That is, nonparticipants would not be those subjected to the greatest amount of civic indoctrination, but rather to the least. I do not know if this poses a severe problem to "structural" theories or not. In any event, I do not think it would be impossible to show something approximating structural differences in the overall social characteristics of civic participants as compared with non-participants. Whether we can demonstrate that nonparticipation is irrational,[19] or that if nonparticipation were reduced it would materially change most civic outcomes or reorient the community political agenda, is another matter.[20] Moreover, if some—even though not a majority of—civic participants *do* share various social characteristics with chronic nonparticipants —in short if the social mechanisms that allegedly prevent civic participation appear to work inefficiently—then their causal efficacy must be doubted and other, supplementary causes must be sought.

Perhaps the most obvious formulation of this problem is as follows: As

19. For an entertaining argument to the contrary, with respect, at least, to voting, see Paul E. Meehl, "The Selfish Voter Paradox and the Thrown-Away Vote Argument," *Am. Pol. Sci. Rev.*, 71 (March 1977), 11–30. The great American ethnographer of "alternative" life-styles, Tom Wolfe, describes in detail the joys of withdrawal from participation in the central status-conferring institutions of modern society: "After all," he says, "the community has never been one great happy family for all men. In fact, I would say the opposite has been true. Community status systems have been games with few winners and many feel like losers. What an intriguing thought—for a man to take his new riches and free time and his machines and *split* from *communitas* and start his own league . . . The intriguing thing today . . . is that so many Americans and Englishmen of middle and lower incomes are now doing the same thing. Not out of 'rebellion' or 'alienation'—they just want to be happy winners for a change." Tom Wolfe, *The Pump House Gang* (New York, Farrar, Straus & Giroux, 1968), p. 6. See also Wolfe's, *The Kandy-Kolored Tangerine-Flake Streamline Baby* (New York, Farrar, Straus & Giroux, 1965). I should emphasize that I do not think these examples settle the matter; they should merely indicate that the assumption that political participation is a rational strategy for everyone under all conditions is not, as many writers suggest, self-evidently true.

20. Perhaps still another word of caution is in order, concerning the benefits of political mobilization and the raising of issues. It is possible to imagine circumstances in which the wilful suppression of items on a potential agenda is not held by observers to be entirely deplorable. Frequently in democratic societies the differential commitment of political leaders to underlying democratic values provides a framework for a refusal to raise issues. An example might be the tendency of many politicians in situations where intense racial or ethnic or religious conflicts are latent to refuse to be drawn into the exploitation of these strong and destructive underlying feelings. Conversely, the willingness of political leaders—recent examples might be George Wallace, Enoch Powell, or even Margaret Thatcher—to raise issues of this kind and to mobilize underlying attitudes that undeniably exist in the population at large is not necessarily indicative of the sort of responsiveness one associates with the long-run maintenance of a democratic community. This suggests that we would need to know much more before endorsing "responsiveness" per se, even "participation" per se, as adequate indices of the goodness of a polity.

we all know, slums breed delinquency, but not all slum children, perhaps not even a majority, grow up delinquent. It thus seems inappropriate to deny to all denizens of the slums a provisional status as moral persons, as at least in part responsible for the disposition of their own fate. To grant them this recognition, however, sorts badly with structural propositions that seek to allocate responsibility for their social behavior to conditions beyond their control.

I do not know of any findings of research that can resolve this disagreement. For our narrow purposes, the issue frequently posed is whether a given description of community decision-making would or would not be materially altered if different sorts of decisions were on the community agenda. A theory of structural bias gives unclear predictions: pessimistically, on the one hand, if indoctrination is truly efficient, nonparticipants are permanently incapable of altering the community agenda and no alteration in the agenda will activate them. On the optimistic hand, nonparticipants are not permanently brain damaged but only slumbering, and given the right stimulus—a stimulus that might be denied them because of the way issues are defined but which might appear for other reasons— they would activate themselves, participate, and change the structure of community power.

Uncertainties about what a "right" stimulus might be plague this literature, although some effort has been expended in the direction of giving this notion some sort of empirical meaning.[21] It is unsurprising, however, given all the complexities of the relevant research program and given also the tenuousness of the causal connections that must be posited to justify research of this sort, that structural and socialization research has remained unexploited as a strategy for studying community power.

## ANTICIPATED REACTIONS

A second inference we might make from the "two faces" argument is that an appropriate object of study would be the anticipated reactions of political actors, on the grounds that these sorts of data would be likely to supply clues to the underlying structure of community power. It may be

21. See, for example, Robert E. Dowse and John A. Hughes, "Sporadic Interventionists," *Political Studies*, 25 (March 1977, 90. Curiously, Dowse and Hughes appear to think that they are attacking the Pluralist[2] literature, when in fact they are illustrating some of its findings. See, for example, Dahl, *Who Governs?*, pp. 190–99, discussing William K. Muir, Jr., *Defending "The Hill" Against Metal Houses*, ICP Case Series, No. 26 (Univ., Ala., Univ. of Alabama Press, 1955); Nelson W. Polsby, "Victor Towns: Portrait of an Activist," in *American Governmental Institutions*, Aaron Wildavsky and Nelson W. Polsby, eds., (Chicago, Rand McNally, 1968), pp. 489–91; Aaron Wildavsky, "Bill Long: Portrait of an Activist," in ibid., pp. 492–500.

well in this connection to pick up the thread of Bachrach and Baratz's own discussion in some detail.

As I have mentioned, Bachrach and Baratz concede the critique of stratification studies. They say there are, however, two "defects" in the pluralist position

> which seem to us to be of fundamental importance. One is that the model takes no account of the fact that power may be, and often is, exercised by confining the scope of decision-making to relatively "safe" issues. The other is that the model provides no *objective* criteria for distinguishing between "important" and "unimportant" issues arising in the political arena.[22]

The second objection is easiest dealt with. On page 96 of this book the reader will find sample specifications for ascertaining whether an issue-area is "important" in the political arena. Since this book's original publication roughly coincides with the publication of Bachrach and Baratz's article, Bachrach and Baratz cannot be taxed with failing to consult it before publishing their critique. Somewhat more difficult to understand, however, is their repetition of the charge, word for word, in a book published in 1970, seven years after their complaint was answered. Even if I had not taken the trouble to do so, however, the answer is entirely obvious.

Although Dahl explained the significance of the issue-areas in New Haven that he chose to study,[23] it might have occurred to nearly anyone that a series of activities entailing the demolition, relocation, and rebuilding of most of the downtown business district in a medium-sized city would be "significant" by some sort of "objective criteria" capable of formulation by social scientists of average ingenuity. Likewise the disposition of outcomes in the single issue-area soaking up half the city's annual budget. And what about political nominations? If it became clear through empirical study that elected politicians and their appointees were important actors in the first two issue-areas, there might understandably arise on the part of observers a desire to know where elected officials came from, to trace their routes to power, precisely so that it would be possible to gauge the operation of norms of recruitment at a remove from the actual exercise of power. This presumably would take direct account of what otherwise might be a criticism that the study failed to note the influence of covert elites who put politicians in office.

Contrary to their claim that the issue-areas studied in New Haven were not justified by objective criteria, Bachrach and Baratz themselves note

22. Emphasis in original. Bachrach and Baratz, *Power and Poverty*, p. 6.
23. Dahl, *Who Governs?*, esp. p. 333.

what these justifications were: their cost and size and the centrality of the values being disposed of for the future of the community political system.[24] Yet Bachrach and Baratz profess to see a difficulty in this. Why? "... [T]he Notables are in fact uninterested in two of the three 'key' decisions."[25]

Why would this finding vitiate the importance—by criteria already described—of issue-areas for study? It would do so only if a scholar believed that the true measure of importance was what "notables" cared about, regardless of other criteria. We have met with this presumption before, the tendency to organize a community study around the perspectives of putative big shots, defined as such in advance of empirical investigation.[26]

Bachrach and Baratz are selectively blind to the actual scope of the New Haven study. This can be discerned in their accusations about what the study "ignores." Bachrach and Baratz claim, for example, that Dahl is "silent" on the question of whether social and economic notables influence the public education budget through the New Haven Board of Finance. Dahl "ignores ... the possible exercise of influence or power in limiting the scope of initiation" that the CAC might have exercised over Mayor Lee. "How, that is to say, can a judgment be made as to the relative influence of Mayor Lee and the CAC without knowing (through prior study of the political and social views of all concerned) the proposals that Lee did *not* make because he anticipated that they would provoke strenuous opposition and sanctions on the part of the CAC?[27]

An even more sweeping indictment along the same lines comes from a Yale law professor, Jan Deutsch. It is so similar in its shape and content to the complaints of Bachrach and Baratz that one suspects Deutsch of reading the few pages of Bachrach and Baratz, whom he emulates, with greater attention than he has devoted to the works he criticizes. Since the criticisms Deutsch makes are an elaborated version of Bachrach and Baratz, an address to Deutsch's objections can perform the dual service of illustrating the considerable, and harmful, influence "Two Faces of Power" has had on the literature, and also can illustrate how ill-founded are the criticisms raised by this article and its imitators.

24. "The Notables do recognize that public school expenditures have a direct bearing upon their own tax liabilities. This being so, and given their strong representation on the New Haven Board of Finance, the expectation must be that it is in their direct interest to play an active role in fiscal policy-making, in the establishment of the educational budget in particular.... [Redevelopment] is by any reasonable standard important for purposes of determining whether New Haven is ruled by 'the hidden hand of an economic elite.'" Bachrach and Baratz, *Power and Poverty*, pp. 13–14, 15.

25. Ibid., p. 12.

26. For example, see pp. 56–58 above.

27. Bachrach and Baratz, *Power and Poverty*, p. 15.

Deutsch states his "primary" complaint in words nearly identical to those of Bachrach and Baratz quoted above with respect to the "first defect" of the New Haven study:

> The primary difficulty with *Who Governs?* as an analysis of the existing distribution of power is its assumption that the decisions canvassed represented conflicts sufficiently serious to force all potentially affected powerholders to mobilize their resources in the hopes of obtaining a favorable outcome.[28]

Deutsch goes on to make a prima facie case: Many of the economic and social elite lived in New Haven's suburbs; therefore, why should they have cared about public education or political nominations? And perhaps they did not feel threatened by urban renewal.

> The important question, then, the question that Dahl never asks in connection with, for example, the power of the citizens' action commission, is whether that commission failed to assert itself because it was powerless or because, given the program as proposed by the mayor, it was indifferent to further modifications. The inquiry is whether the commission's failure to oppose the mayor's proposals represents an index of powerlessness or can be explained, rather, by the hypothesis that the mayor never proposed to the commission anything that he thought that body might reject. If the latter hypothesis is true, and the mayor would in fact have formulated different proposals had he thought the commission would accept them, who then holds power in New Haven?[29]

Deutsch then argues this position at length, making essentially two points. First, invoking the "rule of anticipated reactions,"[30] Deutsch asserts that Dahl never really demonstrates that an economic or social elite is relatively powerless in New Haven. This can only be done, Deutsch says, by studying issues which are important to such an elite. Second, Deutsch asserts that there is some reason to believe that in fact such an elite exists because of the existence of a political status quo in the community, of which the elite is the "passive beneficiary."

28. Jan G. Deutsch, "Neutrality, Legitimacy, and the Supreme Court: Some Intersections Between Law and Political Science," *Stanford Law Review, 20* (Jan. 1968), 169–261, p. 251.

29. Ibid.

30. The coinage is, of course, Carl Friedrich's See *Constitutional Government and Democracy* (Boston, Ginn and Co., 1946), pp. 589–91.

As long as that agenda [the status quo] continues to benefit the elite, therefore—and if an elite exists at all it is presumably because the agenda *does* favor it—it seems reasonable to expect that the elite will remain largely indifferent to the outcomes of community decisions.[31]

Dahl "resolutely refuses to address the difference between those conflicts that an elite would perceive as both significant and threatening and those to which it would remain relatively indifferent,"[32] Deutsch says, concluding that "any study of the distribution of political power that does not include a detailed analysis of the origins and content of the community agenda must be adjudged incomplete."[33]

In advancing this argument, Deutsch is making the following asymmetrical inferences: Inactivity by the mayor—that is, his presumed failure to do some unspecified things that he might otherwise do—shows his lack of power, since he is controlled by anticipated reactions. Inactivity by social and economic leaders—that is, their actual failure significantly to influence decision-making—shows that they are powerful because the existence of any community agenda "presumably" benefits them. This reasoning is not appealing. On what grounds are we to infer that anticipated reactions apply only to the mayor? And why must we "presume" that the (undemonstrated) receipt by one group of some (unspecified) benefit from the status quo thereby invests them uniquely with political power?

As we have seen, it is claimed that Dahl ignores, dismisses, neglects, "resolutely refuses to study" anticipated reactions. Presumably if he does, then his account of New Haven politics neglects the important possibility that political actors in New Haven are responding not straightforwardly to political goals they have set themselves but to their perceptions of limitations on their own behavior. It is sometimes asserted as a blanket proposition that insensitivity to this dimension of political behavior is a necessary feature of the pluralist approach to the study of community power, and so it follows that Dahl never treats of it.

But of course, as any reader of *Who Governs?* can easily ascertain, the topic is by no means neglected in Dahl's discussion of New Haven politics. Three examples ought to suffice to illustrate the point:

> Most citizens . . . possess a moderate degree of indirect influence, for elected leaders keep the real or imagined preferences of constituents constantly in mind in deciding what policies to adopt or reject. Subleaders have greater indirect influence than most other citizens, since

leaders ordinarily are concerned more about the response of an individual subleader than an individual citizen. Finally, leaders exert a great amount of indirect influence on one another, for each is guided to some extent by what he believes is acceptable to some or all of the other leaders.[34]

Despite their incredible opportunity, one cannot say with confidence exactly what or how much effect the newspapers have. . . . The political goals of the newspapers have usually been negative rather than positive. A more progressive and adventurous publisher might have sought ways and means of mobilizing public opinion; Jackson was more interested in immobilizing it.[35]

Thus, properly used, the CAC was a mechanism not for *settling* disputes but for *avoiding* them altogether. The Mayor and the Development Administrator believed that whatever received the full assent of the CAC would not be strongly opposed by other elements in the community. Their estimate proved to be correct. And the reason was probably not so much the direct influence over public opinion of the CAC collectively or its members individually, as it was that the CAC *was* public opinion; that is, its members represented and reflected the main sources of articulate opinion in the political stratum of New Haven. The Mayor and the Development Administrator used the CAC to test the acceptability of their proposals to the political stratum; in fact, the very existence of the CAC and the seemingly ritualistic process of justifying all proposals to its members meant that members of the administration shaped their proposals according to what they expected would receive the full support of the CAC and therefore of the political stratum. The Mayor, who once described himself as an "expert in group dynamics," was particularly skillful in estimating what the CAC could be expected to support or reject. If none of the administration's proposals on redevelopment and renewal were ever opposed by the CAC, the explanation probably lies less in the Mayor's skills in the arts of persuasion than in his capacity for judging with considerable precision what the existing beliefs and commitments of the men on the CAC would compel them to agree to if a proposal were presented in the proper way, time, and place.[36]

These examples give us ample warrant to say that Dahl's conclusions about the distribution of power in New Haven were not arrived at in ignor-

34. Dahl, *Who Governs?*, p. 164.
35. Ibid., p. 257.
36. Ibid., 136–37. Emphasis in original.

ance of the phenomenon of anticipated reactions or without paying due regard to its actual impact on the behavior of politically significant persons and institutions in New Haven. The charge that Pluralist₂ conclusions must of necessity neglect anticipated reactions is clearly false. Insofar as studying the mobilization of bias entails studying the anticipated reactions of significant community actors, familiar methods—interviews and observations —are available to cope with the problem, and there is no reason to suppose that pluralists are any less able to deal with it than anyone else.

Dahl studied the Mayor's relations with the Citizens Action Commission carefully in a variety of ways and could find no direct evidence of the limitations upon the Mayor's power that Deutsch suggests. But were there in fact such limitations, unnoticed by Dahl? Dahl took every reasonable step to investigate this possibility. Did Deutsch, for his part, take reasonable steps in his bid to discredit Dahl's explanation?

To a scholar with the impressive evidence of New Haven residence to which Professor Deutsch's string of Yale degrees and current Yale employment attest,[37] it might have been worth a few minutes on the telephone, or a few days downtown, to find out how accurately Dahl had described the political roles of the economic leaders of New Haven. The innuendos Deutsch substitutes for such an investigation, having to do with anticipated reactions, would, of course, vex a nonexperimental, empirical study of any kind; they lie with equal force against all methods presently known for studying nonmanipulable phenomena.[38] The essential form of Deutsch's methodological objection is the charge that Dahl fails to exclude hidden

37. A.B., 1955; LL.B., 1962; Ph.D. (in political science), 1962; all from Yale University. Associate Professor of Law, Yale University, at the time his article was published, and now Professor of Law at Yale.

38. The same is true of what Deutsch refers to as his "more important" objection to Dahl's conclusions: the problem of the time scale. "The absence of conflict concerning the community agenda during any reasonably limited period of time does not . . . imply that such a conflict is not likely in the future. This question . . . is always whether the time scale chosen was a sufficiently long one." Deutsch, "Neutrality, Legitimacy, and the Supreme Court," p. 255. One may inquire: sufficient to explain what? Clearly not to explain everything about "the future." The time scale of Dahl's inquiry did reach as far back as the incorporation of New Haven in 1784; it included an interpretation—with evidence—of changes in patterns of local leadership over the late eighteenth, nineteenth, and early twentieth centuries; and it included an intensive discussion of the evolution of local politics in the fifties. Even so, I know of no claim by Dahl or his associates that they could thereby predict the future. In this connection, see p. 97 above.

In light of this, one would have to say Deutsch's diagnosis is faulty. It is not the time scale of the New Haven study, which for some purposes stretched from 1784 to 1958, that renders prediction difficult; it is the lack of relevant theory. Readers may decide for themselves whether Deutsch's own attempts to fashion such a theory in the second paragraph of page 255 his article seem worthwhile. To me they seem jejune.

causes of the effects he observes in community policy-making. That Dahl is aware of the problem is plain from much of his writing, some of which Deutsch cites.[39] The problem is, by strict standards, intractable. Reasonable ground rules, explicitly stated, have to be established—a responsibility Dahl discharged. That is, Dahl went to great lengths to determine whether, on empirical grounds, a case could be made for the proposition that New Haven was governed by means or persons other than those he describes as governing New Haven.[40] As I think I have indicated, this description has not been competently challenged, except in minor ways, by anyone who bothered to find out about New Haven politics. That Deutsch did not so trouble himself is painfully apparent: He offers not a shred of evidence of any kind in support of his critique of Dahl's interpretation. Further, he ignores much relevant material that Dahl presents on relations between New Haven economic and political leaders.

## WHO GOVERNS VS. WHO BENEFITS

Ultimately, Deutsch concedes that *Who Governs?* supplies "a correct answer to an often irrelevant question." I take him to mean by this that, on the whole, he has no quarrel with Dahl's account of how New Haven is actually governed. Deutsch says:

> Dahl's insistence on attacking only a model of an elite that actively manipulates the community consensus, rather than considering the possibility of an elite that is the passive beneficiary of the consensus, once again runs the risk of supplying a correct answer to an irrelevant question.[41]

The "relevant" question, it appears, is not "who governs?" (to which Dahl has apparently supplied a correct answer), but "who benefits?" It is not clear how Deutsch wishes to regard the relationship of these two questions. I think his position is that "who governs?" is in some sense dependent upon, subsidiary to, or epiphenomenal to the answer to "who benefits?" And, no doubt, in some sense, it is (as is also true of the reverse). The reasoning here seems to go as follows: It is assumed that any given status quo benefits some people disproportionately, and that these people, the beneficiaries of the normal everyday operations of a community political system, ought to be described as the rulers of that system—even if they are not visibly

39. Deutsch, "Neutrality, Legitimacy, and the Supreme Court," pp. 253 (n. 281), 254 (n. 283).
40. Dahl, *Who Governs?*, pp. 63–84.
41. Deutsch, "Neutrality, Legitimacy, and the Supreme Court," pp. 252, 255.

in charge of decision-making. Consequently, in order to discover who governs we must ask who benefits, and the answer to the latter question becomes the answer to the former.

This view can be found in a number of places. In *Power and Poverty*, for example, Bachrach and Baratz conclude:

> We ask neither "Who runs things here?" nor "Does anyone run things here?" but rather "Is the distribution of benefits and privileges highly unequal, and if so, why?"[42]

And Frank Parkin says:

> To speak of the distribution of power could be understood as another way of describing the flow of rewards; the very fact that the dominant class can successfully claim a disproportionate share of rewards *vis à vis* the subordinate class, is in a sense a *measure* of the former's power over the latter.[43]

To adopt this view entails a number of difficulties. It assumes, first of all, that none of the following possibilities has empirical reality:

1. That no explicit decision-making took place at all, and that beneficiaries, far from actually governing, are simply reaping windfall benefits (e.g. largely powerless Black Panthers, who oppose gun control, are beneficiaries of the fact that there are no gun control laws).
2. That beneficiaries are receiving benefits from decisions made outside the community and over which they have no control (e.g. shopkeepers in a community prosper from a decision made in a far-off corporate headquarters to operate a local plant on overtime).
3. That beneficiaries are the unintended recipients of benefits resulting from decisions made by others within the community (e.g. apolitical, absentee, or deceased owners of adjacent real estate prosper because of decisions made in a bureaucracy to site a public facility).
4. That the powerful are intentionally conferring benefits on the non-powerful (e.g. in at least some welfare systems).[44]

At a bare minimum, one would think that the prudent analyst of power would want reasonable assurances that none of these possibilities contaminated the hypothesized one-to-one relation between answers to the

42. Bachrach and Baratz, *Power and Poverty*, p. 106.
43. Frank Parkin, *Class Inequality and Political Order* (London, MacGibbon and Kee, 1971), p. 46. Emphasis in original.
44. The preceding four points paraphrase and augment the points I have already made above, p. 132. Some of the new material is drawn from Raymond E. Wolfinger, "Nondecisions and the Study of Local Politics," *Am. Pol. Sci. Rev.*, 65 (June 1971), 1063–80.

questions who benefits and who governs. To launch into the sort of empirical inquiry that the disposal of these alternatives would require might well vitiate the advantages of economy and efficiency entailed in substituting the answer to one question for the answer to the other.

More to the point, however, is the strong possibility that the equation of the two questions leads to answers that are simply wrong. What is required to test such a possibility is inquiry of quite a different kind, as the following illustration suggests:

> Suppose ... we notice that it rains in Seattle. We speculate that taxi drivers make more money on rainy days. Therefore ... taxi drivers cause it to rain in Seattle. This conclusion will still be defective even if we are energetic in buttressing some empirical points: we can test the theory that taxi drivers do indeed benefit from rain; we can learn if they know they benefit from rain; we can find out if they actually favor rain. But it is still impossible to conclude that they cause it to rain since we do not show *what they did* to bring about rain and how these actions fit into existing knowledge about the phenomenon.[45]

The central empirical problem is this: Even if we can show that a given status quo benefits some people disproportionately (as I think we can for any real world status quo), such a demonstration falls short of showing that these beneficiaries created the status quo, act in any meaningful way to maintain it, or could, in the future, act effectively to deter changes in it. Every status quo distributes benefits that in at least some light can be construed as uneven. But different status quos may be created and maintained in vastly different ways, even when they throw off similar patterns of benefit.

There are such phenomena as people who benefit, but do not cause. Free riders are only one example. There are occasions when for one reason or another people oppose policies likely to benefit them—as was the case in the United States when organized medicine strenuously opposed Medicare, which, as predicted, has been a bonanza for doctors. Or people may cause, but not benefit, by advocating, enacting, or administering policies that subtract from or have no impact on their net value positions. Can we say that career civil servants, for example, who do not personally profit from decisions that they make, are *ipso facto* powerless?

None of this denies—or affirms—the following propositions: that ownership and control of economic assets is frequently split between different persons or types of persons, that people tend to work to improve their

45. James L. Payne, "The Oligarchy Muddle," *World Politics*, 20 (April 1968), 452.

long-run value positions, that over the long run people who have the power to do so arrange to receive benefits from the operations of the political or economic system, and so on. The extent to which any of these are true is a matter to be established empirically and not by defining who governs and who benefits as identical.

In all of these matters, we must look to the political powers and activities of variously advantaged groups, and not merely to the distributed outcomes of the pattern of advantages alone. This, of course, is what pluralists (and others) do when they study who governs. Who benefits? may, after all, be an interesting question—I argue here only that it is a different question from who governs? In any event, it is susceptible to empirical investigation by those genuinely interested in studying it.

To say this, therefore, is to admit that not all conceivable questions or important questions about community politics can be answered by correct answers to the question who governs? and, in that sense, no doubt a book that takes the question who governs? as its focus is "incomplete." In an article, Robert Dahl also concedes this, saying:

> Some of the links that a power analyst may take as "effects" to be explained by searching for causes are the outcomes of specific decisions; the current values, attitudes, and expectations of decision-makers; their earlier or more fundamental attitudes and values; the attitudes and values of other participants—or nonparticipants— whose participation is in some way significant; the processes of selection, self-selection, recruitment, or entry by which decision-makers arrive at their locations in the political system; the rules of decision-making, the structures, the constitutions. No doubt a "complete" explanation of power relations in a political system would try to account for all these effects, and others. Yet this is an enormously ambitious task. Meanwhile, it is important to specify which effects are at the focus of an explanatory theory and which are not. A good deal of confusion, and no little controversy, are produced when different analysts focus on different links in the chain of power and causation without specifying clearly what effects they wish to explain; and a good deal of criticism of dubious relevance is produced by critics who hold that an investigator has focused on the "wrong" links or did not provide a "complete" explanation.[46]

In short, the agenda of research that Professor Deutsch prescribes is well known and may be a fruitful one; his testimony on this point would,

46. Robert A. Dahl, "Power," *International Encyclopedia of the Social Sciences*, (New York, The Macmillan Co. and The Free Press, 1968), vol. 12, p. 412.

of course, carry greater conviction if he had taken the trouble to pursue the matter a short way himself. In that case, he might have come to the view that to counsel perfection is often easier than to achieve it. He might even concede that "correct" answers to the question who governs? may be as valuable for some purposes as insistence on (but not work on) answers to the question who benefits?

## REDEFINING THE SECOND FACE OF POWER: BALTIMORE

Because Bachrach and Baratz and their followers concentrate their fire upon pluralist researchers, it has not been much remarked that their misgivings about the neglect of nondecision-making and the underlying values and attitudes of all possible actors apply with equal force to all empirical studies of community power. Therefore, if we were to assert that a business elite "power structure" runs New Jerusalem, attention to the strictures of Bachrach and Baratz's argument about the "second face" of power would not permit us to let the matter rest there. Perhaps, we would have to say, the business elite rules overtly; but what about the values and attitudes of everyone else, the insidious effects, as Keynes once suggested, of "some long-dead economist" upon one or more of their minds, the undiscussed alternatives foregone, the restrictions of the New Jerusalem agenda that we do not know about?

Since all community studies, whatever their conclusions, fail to satisfy at least one of Bachrach and Baratz's criteria—the one that demands a canvass of nondecisions and all potential actors—does this not indicate the hopelessness of the enterprise of empirical study in community power? Strangely enough it apparently does not, by Bachrach and Baratz's lights, since after publishing their methodological recommendations and their critique they went forward to contribute a community study of their own. How well do they succeed in evading the pitfalls they have descried in the paths of others?

Much of the material in *Power and Poverty,* Bachrach and Baratz's book, consists simply of their reprinted articles. In one important respect, however, they move beyond their critique of pluralist research to specify the meaning of the term "nondecision" in a new way, a way singularly helpful to those undertaking empirical research. For in place of the hopeless task of studying all potential actors, past and future, and mapping the trajectories of their wants, expressed and hypothetical, onto a projection of an infinite number of alternate futures, Bachrach and Baratz suggest a far more practical substitute: For the purpose of their research, they redefine a nondecision as any observable act which has as its goal the suppression of conflict in the community. They write:

The primary method of sustaining a given mobilization of bias is nondecision-making. A nondecision, as we define it, is a *decision* [emphasis added] that results in suppression or thwarting of a latent or manifest challenge to the values or interests of the decision-maker. [N]ondecision-making is a means by which demands for change in the existing allocation of benefits and privileges in the community can be suffocated before they are even voiced; or kept covert; or killed before they gain access to the relevant decision-making arena; or, failing all these things, maimed or destroyed in the decision-implementing stage of the policy process.

Nondecision-making can take any of several forms. The most direct and extreme form is one in which force is invoked as the means of preventing demands for change in the established order from entering the political process. . . . The threat of sanctions against the initiator of a potentially threatening demand . . . one that invokes an existing bias of the political system . . . to squelch a threatening demand or incipient issue. . . . The fourth and most indirect form of nondecision-making involves reshaping or strengthening the mobilization of bias in order to block challenges.[47]

Of course to define "nondecision" as a certain sort of "decision" is to revive the very pluralist approach that these authors earlier deplored. Pluralists are already under a methodological injunction to observe acts. Nowhere are pluralists forbidden to seek or even discouraged from seeking information of the kind here described by Bachrach and Baratz as "nondecisions." Indeed, many do so. I have already quoted passages in *Who Governs?* for example, where Robert Dahl describes factors entering into the Mayor of New Haven's cautiousness in setting the political agenda. Edward Banfield makes a great deal of the strategic passivity of Chicago's Mayor Daley in avoiding commitments of his own power in situations where conflict might have harmed his future influence.[48] Sayre and Kaufman state that one of the central problems of their book is to explain the distribution of resources and services in the city of New York between the public and private sectors—i.e. they are asking what the overt acts and customs are that tend to put things on and take things off the political agenda.[49] Any industrious student can find much other information about "nondecisions," according to this new definition, in other "pluralist" studies.

47. Bachrach and Baratz, *Power and Poverty*, pp. 44–46.
48. Edward C. Banfield, *Political Influence* (Glencoe, Free Press, 1961), pp. 251–53, 271.
49. Wallace S. Sayre and Herbert Kaufman, *Governing New York City* (New York, Russell Sage Foundation, 1960), pp. 57–64.

The redefinition of the second face of power to coincide with the first face comes at a juncture at which Bachrach and Baratz might have been able to provide an example of actual empirical research meeting the stringent criteria they advance in criticism of pluralist studies. But their own study of Baltimore (reported in *Power and Poverty*) provides less in the way of context than many of the studies they criticize. Indeed, Bachrach and Baratz provide only a scanty general description of Baltimore politics, give nothing beyond thumbnail sketches (in appendixes to the book, apparently written by students) of the local scene, offer little justification at all for the selection of a single issue-area—poverty—as illustrative or indicative or emblematic or typical of the exercise of power in Baltimore, and conclude with no general evaluation of the state of community power in Baltimore.

If Bachrach and Baratz did not insistently describe what they were doing as in some sense responsive to, contributory to, and critical of the community power literature, claims that are evidently taken seriously, there would hardly be grounds for including their work in a survey of the literature. For what they have done is to erect extremely high hurdles for everyone else to jump, and then when their turn came to do some empirical work they removed the bar altogether, waltzing through the gap where the obstacle once stood. This exhibits a measure of self-indulgence unlikely to confer lasting benefit upon scholarship.

It will not do to defend this sort of enterprise as theoretically helpful although practically inconsequential. Even the "purest" and least "practical" theorist has entered the realm of research in the following two senses when he claims "we cannot exclude the possibility that there are burglars under the bed": (1) what is implied (weakly) by such a statement is some notion of the actual probability of burglars under the bed; (2) more strongly, this implies a recommendation about the deployment of finite resources to be devoted to investigation. Looking under beds for burglars precludes, at the margin, looking in some other places. Consequently the advocacy of "theory" carries responsibilities for research strategy and tactics that are inescapable. Theory of this sort can be—and should be— evaluated for its usefulness as a set of prescriptions not only about where to look but also ultimately about what possibilities are of sufficient empirical remoteness to be worth excluding.

Since "pluralists," who are at the focus of Bachrach and Baratz's criticisms, already study observable acts of a sort portrayed by Bachrach and Baratz as "nondecisions," one may conclude that under the research procedures that Bachrach and Baratz actually follow the second face of power in practice merges with the first face and they become identical. This is the consequence of redefining the "second face" of power so as to be observable in principle as acts directly affecting outcomes defined beforehand as significant for understanding the exercise of power in a given community.

## Nonissues: A Comparative Approach

Thus in my view Bachrach and Baratz utterly fail to contribute to the solution of the dilemma they posed so dramatically for the scholarly community. Are we therefore helpless to discover whether those things we cannot observe might, if known, drastically modify the common understanding of the locus of power in any community? And in particular, are we helpless with respect to the subtleties surrounding the question of which matters could arise in a community and which could not?

So long as this last proposition, this Elijah at the feast, is postulated as an ever-present possibility, nothing short of controlled experimentation, which introduces its own practical and methodological problems, can dislodge it. The fact, for example, that no shred of actual evidence in a given community points to Banker Sly's influence may be interpreted as showing that Banker Sly is so powerful he can cover up his tracks more efficiently than the human eye can detect—or better yet, make no tracks at all, as others in the community, behaving spontaneously or in response to cues (such as some human equivalent to inaudible dog whistles), avoid offending him or attempt to do what they surmise is his bidding. That Banker Sly should afford us our example is, as scholars addicted to this mode of discussion sometimes say, no accident. No evidence may be equally available to support the supposition that millionaires and bums are running the community; yet political theory, sometimes masquerading as common sense, sometimes unadorned, has provided a definitive choice among possible power elites where the evidence, unaided, could not.

In some quarters nagging doubts have remained. People have asked: Is there any empirically sound way of resolving a disagreement between someone who asserts that a lack of evidence in support of a particular proposition attests to its very plausibility and someone who says no evidence weakens a proposition rather than strengthens it? An optimistic view has brought forth the following proposed strategy: Suppose, instead of investigating issues that actually arise in a community, we attempt to study why issues do not arise. Perhaps something can be learned about power and its exercise by taking note of community problems which in some communities lead to action of various kinds but in others do not, and studying these problems in communities where they did not become issues.

Careful readers will note at this point that merely studying "nonissues" will not necessarily settle the disagreement posed above. Studying a particular set of nonissues in any given community or group of communities simply adds to the population of cases that one might investigate in determining how power is exercised. Conceivably the addition of these sorts of case materials in one or more communities will yield findings that contradict or modify findings gathered from issue-areas where there is something more overt to observe. But this is, presumably, an empirical question. Thus, studying nonissues may reinforce or may modify conceptions of power in any given community that arise from the study of more accessible materials.

*The Un-Politics of Air Pollution,* by Matthew Crenson, is a major attempt to grapple constructively with the problem of studying nonissues.[50] This book offers a study of the problem of air pollution, which, Crenson finds, when raised as a community issue, generally leads to pollution abatement measures of some sort.[51] Thus, whether or not the issue is raised at all is crucial in determining the disposition of the issue.

Crenson's empirical study of this problem proceeds along two tracks. The first track consists of two attenuated community studies in which Crenson describes in detail the politics surrounding the raising and disposition of the issue in the adjacent cities of Gary and East Chicago, Indiana. The second track consists of manipulating some statistics from an NORC opinion survey in 48 middle-sized American cities having known levels of air pollution.

With respect to his community studies, Crenson found that East Chicago addressed the problem of air pollution well before Gary did and enacted a more stringent law. He found that in both communities the steel companies that were causing significant levels of pollution were passive. In Gary it was believed that U.S. Steel would oppose stringent air pollution measures; and in East Chicago, the leading activist on the issue likewise "anticipated that ... businessmen would be unfriendly to his air pollution proposal." Crenson nevertheless concludes that "in spite of its political passivity, U.S. Steel seems to have had the ability to enforce inaction on the dirty air issue."[52] The conclusion is extravagant. In both communities the steel companies were inactive; in both they were assumed to be unfavorably disposed. If the results in the communities differed, as Crenson reports, why pick on the steel companies, which did not differ? There is a difference, furthermore, between passive and active; U.S. Steel, on Cren-

50. (Baltimore, The Johns Hopkins Univ. Press, 1971).
51. Ibid., p. 90.
52. Ibid., pp. 47, 78, 84–86, 114.

son's showing, "enforced" nothing whatever. Crenson makes the charge that "pluralists" dismiss as irrelevant and unfathomable information such as he turned up in Gary in which political actors testified to their beliefs about constraints in the community upon their behavior, and in a particularly confusing passage he asserts that this is what pluralists are attacking when they attack the reputational method of influence attribution.[53] In fact, as I have shown, there is plenty of discussion by pluralists of the beliefs of political actors, and the assertion that they ignore such data is false. The confusion of these beliefs with data uncovered by the reputational method, as the method is normally employed in community power studies, is Crenson's own original idea and is, so far as I can see, sustained by nothing at all in the literature.

We arrive, then, at the heart of Crenson's attempt to study air pollution as issue and nonissue. The data consist of questionnaires administered to 10 highly placed people in each of 48 middle-sized American cities. Among the questions Crenson sought answers to were whether the air pollution issue had come up and who had taken a position for and against. In general, Crenson found that as air pollution increased, actors in the community (labor councils, political parties, newspapers, chambers of commerce) were more likely to take a position on the issue. He found that whether or not they were held to be influential seemed to have no impact on the extent to which various actors took a position on the issue (controlling for actual air pollution). Crenson then threw away most of his cities and concentrated upon the 18 with high air pollution. Here, he found, when industrial influence was held to be high, the probability that certain other actors (chambers of commerce, newspapers) would take a position on the issue was lower than when industrial influence was held to be low. He also found, however, that the probability of other actors taking a position on the issue was positively correlated with their reports of having had conversations with industrial leaders on air pollution.

Crenson makes a great deal of these and a few other bits and scraps of findings. My view is that they will not support the burden he places on them. When he says, for example, "industrial influence does inhibit the growth of the air pollution issue,"[54] one must remember that Crenson is here referring to a *correlation* in which data from 18 cities are arrayed, some presumably showing high inhibition, some low, so that the actual incidence of inhibition at all may be quite slight; that "industrial influence" in this context means some aggregation of what 10 respondents in each

53. Ibid., p. 80.
54. Ibid., p. 120.

community said about whether local industry was influential on the air pollution issue (and does not mean communication between industrial leaders and others); and that the "growth of the air pollution issue" here means only whether or not certain specified other actors "took a stand" either for or against on the issue.

I do not think we can place very much confidence in Crenson's findings—and still less in Crenson's account of his findings, which is, on the whole, euphoric. Let us ask, nevertheless, whether this approach to the nonissue problem offers some promise. I believe in some respects it may, principally because Crenson follows a prescription occasionally propounded in the study of community power but not often taken: He is comparative in his approach. It is meaningful to ask why an issue in one community is not an issue in the next. It is sensible to control for the effects of nature, in this case by comparing cities with similar levels of air pollution. It is reasonable to search for relationships among questionnaire items in many cities, if only to uncover hypotheses that can be tested more rigorously against better data. The fact is, however, that Crenson's data are not terribly vivid and yield conclusions of questionable validity only after the most relentless pummeling by an investigator whose biases are busily engaged.

It cannot be said, moreover, that the study of nonissues such as Crenson attempted is capable of resolving the dilemma of Banker Sly's influence posed above. It could, in principle, tell us something about community power just as the study of innovations, of controverted issues, of routine decisions, and of what Dahl called "vetoes" presently does. But it is no mean trick, as Crenson's book illustrates, to make problems at the periphery of community attention accessible to the human eye.

The difficulty occurs not merely with Crenson's data and the way he manipulates them. There is a problem in the logic of the enterprise as well. If an issue is not raised in a community, there are at least two possible reasons why it is not: Either it is being suppressed or there is genuine consensus that it is not an issue. The problem is to discriminate between the two possibilities. The bare bones of Crenson's argument is as follows: that by matching communities alike in their levels of air pollution but unlike in the emergence of air pollution as an issue, it is possible to make this discrimination. Thus, communities with high air pollution but no issue can be said to be suppressing the issue because in some high air pollution communities the issue is raised. Nobody, presumably, wants air pollution so high that at least some communities find it intolerable.

Charles O. Jones shows, however, in his study of Pittsburgh, that this presumption is quite false.[55] Many people trade off air pollution against employment, and it iš not necessarily the case that they do so unwittingly. Therefore merely showing that in some communities a given issue is raised and tends to lead to a particular conclusion does not discriminate between the possibility in other communities that an issue is being suppressed and the possibility that a genuine consensus exists although that consensus is contrary to what an observer can find elsewhere. I have shown that it is precisely at this point—where it becomes necessary to discriminate between suppression and consensus—that Crenson's empirical account becomes forced and unreliable. There is still some work to be done before we can say that this sort of comparative approach has proven itself.

## CONCLUSION

It is not at all clear that Pluralists$_2$ have looked at the wrong data in coming to their conclusions about community power. Many of them have been attentive to the social and political contexts within which the decisions they studied were made. They do not in principle confine their investigations to instances of overt conflict nor do they neglect anticipated reactions, as has been charged. And of course they are under an injunction to look at actual "decisions"—even decisions not to expand the community

55. See Charles O. Jones, *Clean Air* (Pittsburgh, Univ. of Pittsburgh Press, 1975). This inconvenient fact may assist readers in parsing the following passage from Steven Lukes, *Power: A Radical View* (London. Macmillan, 1974), p. 45:

> Crenson's analysis is impressive because it fulfils the double requirement mentioned above: there is good reason to expect that, other things being equal, people would rather not be poisoned (*assuming, in particular, that pollution control does not necessarily mean unemployment*)—even where they may not even articulate this preference; and hard evidence is given of the ways in which institutions, specifically U.S. Steel, largely through inaction, prevented the citizens' interest in not being poisoned from being acted on (though other factors, institutional and ideological, would need to enter a fuller explanation). (Emphasis supplied.)

The relevance of the trade-off between air pollution and employment in Gary, Indiana, is clearly spelled out in William E. Farrell, "Closing of Last Steel Furnaces Alarms Gary, Ind.", *New York Times,* Jan. 5, 1975, p. 43. Or see Gregory Jaynes, "Pennsylvania Mill Town Prefers U.S. Steel to Clean Air," *New York Times,* May 27, 1979, p. 26. It is not necessary for my argument, however, that public opinion in Gary on the air pollution issue actually differ from opinion elsewhere, since many other things relevant to the crystallization and mobilization of opinion may also vary: party systems and consequently access to politicians; bureaucratic arrangements, such as the existence of appeals boards, and so on. These and other factors may determine what sorts of trade-offs are made in any given community; my point is only that we have ample evidence to reject the belief that people are unaware that trade-offs are involved in setting local air pollution standards.

agenda. For the reasons I have given, I do not think that data about who benefits is appropriately substitutable for data about who governs, and comparative study as ·a method of getting at nonissues, while in principle promising, evidently presents problems in execution.

One possible conclusion from this survey is that the problem of the mobilization of bias is either larger or smaller than is commonly believed: larger because of the enormous difficulties of studying it, smaller because of the probable empirical payoff from doing so. At their most powerful, findings about the second face of power do not erase findings about the first face. They may, at their most powerful, qualify, supplement, or amend these findings. But in order even to do this, an actual empirical inquiry must take place in which findings are made and the methods for making them explained and defended. The mere casting of aspersions, the manufacture of innuendos, the raising of possibilities will not substitute for competent empirical investigation whose results are reported and subjected to critical scrutiny.

The devising and the execution of a research strategy capable of discerning the mobilization of bias in a local setting, and relating findings about the mobilization of bias intelligibly to other sorts of propositions about the exercise of community power, turn out to be an extremely difficult set of tasks. Blind alleys and mistakes in conception or interpretation are not rare. And in the end, when these are cleared away, it may well be that the increment to knowledge about community power that the study of the mobilization of bias is likely to contribute will be quite modest. However, this remains to be seen.

# 12. Interests and Preferences

It was a part of my original intention to identify underlying presuppositions about human behavior and politics which were compatible with pluralist conclusions about community power and which could be contrasted with underlying assumptions of the stratification theory. I did not assert that these pluralist assumptions contaminated the results of community power research because I believed, and continue to believe, that an assertion about the contamination of research ought to be grounded in empirical evidence of contamination in the form of mistakes such as I have documented in chapters 2 and 3. I could find no justification for such an assertion in the case of pluralist studies, and no such empirical demonstration has in the intervening time been forthcoming. Scholars have in my view carelessly mistaken axioms for findings in their discussions of "pluralist theory" and have accused pluralist researchers of making claims about local communities that they have never made.

"[P]luralist theory," says Kenneth Newton, without citation, "tends to work on the assumption that each and every interest is equally capable of organizing and defending itself."[1] He goes on to show that of *some* groups in Birmingham, England, this is not so. And this, surely, is the point: Although pluralist "assumptions" may start from something like the axiom Newton suggests,[2] no pluralist researcher necessarily asserts that proposition as a finding of research or as a description of empirical reality. To "work on an assumption" is where research begins and not where it ends; to make a claim that an assumption is untrue—or, for that matter, as Newton does, "absolutely correct"[3]—is gratuitous, since its function is to facilitate, not to preclude or to substitute for, empirical investigation. If it can be shown that a set of assumptions has in fact precluded empirical study or has rendered it difficult or impossible for analysts to reach conclusions

1. Kenneth Newton, *Second City Politics* (Oxford, Clarendon Press, 1976), p. 228.
2. Not "each and every" but "many"; not "equally capable" but "frequently in some manner or another capable, and depending upon the availability of a variety of resources, the skill and intensity with which they are employed, and the legitimacy of the group" would be closer to the mark.
3. Newton, *Second City Politics*, p. 229.

compatible with their findings, this of course constitutes grounds for a recommendation that over the range of applications in which these contami-
nations occur, the axioms be discarded. Even here, however, we must
understand what we are doing. To say that the five propositions of the
stratification theory of community power made no sense in New Haven is
not to discredit an axiom from general stratification theory like "People
are organized for political action into classes" for all times and places. It
is merely to dispute the utility of such an axiom for studying local politics
in New Haven, especially in the light of the evident incapacity of researchers who entertain such axioms to describe the politics of other
American local communities intelligibly or accurately. What is discon-
firmed, however, is not axioms, which in the study of community power is
what propositions of general stratification theory, or Pluralist₃ assumptions
are; rather, Pluralist₂ propositions, or the five propositions of the stratification theory of community power that began this book, are the sorts of
propositions that are accessible to empirical test with evidence gathered
from the politics of local communities, and these therefore are the propositions that evidence of this kind can uphold or refute.

It is possible to have more than one opinion on the general question
of how closely linked the presuppositions of investigators are to the conclusions of their research. My view is that the original finding in this book
of a close and influential linkage between presuppositions and conclusions,
a linkage so close as to repel inconvenient facts, constitutes a finding of a
relatively rare phenomenon in social research. Far more common is reluctance or even antipathy toward the weaving of a consistent argument
out of disparate—or even of internally consistent—findings. But scholars
rarely invest so heavily in their presumptions as to become blind to their
own findings. Blindness to the *implications* of findings is not uncommon.
However, the linkage of this blindness to internally consistent doctrines
about the world, even when these scholars entertain such doctrines, is, I
suggest, infrequent, and cannot be presumed to exist without some empirical demonstration to that effect.

In short, while the outer boundaries of what we may perceive, compre-
hend, and therefore find are undoubtedly constrained in important ways by
the language we use and the conceptual luggage we carry, it is nevertheless possible to arrive at conclusions about the world that are in some sense
*not* comprehensively foreordained by general presuppositions. Even when
researchers can be shown to hold various sorts of general presuppositions
to be true—itself not a matter to be settled by fiat—such a showing is not
enough to sustain a claim that empirical findings or conclusions are predetermined by general presuppositions. In my opinion, the annals of social

research are not rich in such predeterminations, although no doubt there exist others than the one documented in these pages.

I offer this by way of preface to the discussion of one of the knottiest and most interesting disputes about the underpinnings of the community power literature, having to do with the problem of "interests" and "preferences." I think I can show that less is riding on the way in which this issue is resolved than students customarily assert, if we are to judge from the evidence of the community power literature.

The problem of "interests" arises in the first instance in this literature as an attempt to impugn pluralist descriptions of community power. The reasoning, as best I can reconstruct it, goes something like this. It may be true that pluralist methods are capable of monitoring individual and group activity of various kinds and of detecting the *overt* expression of dissatisfaction or complaints about unmet needs in a population which would ordinarily lead to the surfacing on the community agenda of an "issue". If this is so, then there are no grounds for postulating that in Pluralist$_2$ work a systematic bias arises from ignoring information about community politics that might come to an investigator's attention either through the unsuccessful political activities or the expressed dissatisfactions of losers or the disadvantaged or the expressively dissatisfied in community politics.

There is, nevertheless, a remaining possible source of systematic bias that arises from ignoring dissatisfactions that remain unexpressed, and these can only be postulated to exist by virtue of the observer's understanding of the way the political system is structured so as to gratify some political ends, but not others. One set of these other ends, excluded from gratification because of the normal operations of the political system, may be identified as unarticulated or unexpressed interests of those not especially favored by the operations of the system as it currently exists. As William Connolly says:

> Conceptual blinders of this sort help to explain the failure of liberal social scientists of the last generation to anticipate the political crises of the sixties and seventies ... to detect those troubles shuffled out of pluralist politics.[4]

Thus the search for a means to describe interests as something other than the revealed preferences or expressed desires of actors becomes an integral part of an argument about the adequacy of one or another description or generalization about the configuration of power in local communities. If such an effort is successful, presumably new data become available.

4. William E. Connolly, "On 'Interests' in Politics," *Politics and Society*, 2 (Summer 1972), 469.

Whether or not these new data confirm, undermine, supplement, or challenge conclusions about community power derived from more readily accessible data is, of course, an empirical question. The answers cannot be assumed to be known in advance, and, as would be true for the production of any data, reasonable care has to be taken to assure that these sorts of data are not defined into existence in such a way as to answer by definition questions that are ostensibly empirical.

It can certainly be stipulated that coming to an understanding of what the interests are of people in a community is not necessarily as easy as reading a gas meter. Two fundamental strategies appear to exist through which the interests of actors can be determined, and both presumably exist in pure and adulterated versions. One pure strategy, which I have identified as an axiom of Pluralists theory, accepts the choices or other revealed preferences of actors as defining their interests. The other maintains that observers are entitled to assert what conduct and what choices are in the interests of actors, regardless of the actors' own choice behavior. To both pure strategies very substantial objections may be raised. Recently, however, the latter approach has become fashionable and has had a number of advocates.

For example, Isaac Balbus says:

> A person may be affected by something whether or not he realizes it; hence evidence can be marshalled to demonstrate that an individual has an interest even if he is not aware of it or even that what an individual thinks is in his interest is in fact not in his interest.[5]

William Connolly, after stating objections to a number of alternatives,[6] settles upon a conception of interests as the choices actors would make after exposure to the results of various alternatives. "This does require," he concedes, "investigators to make different judgments, in many situations, about the choices a person would make if he had had the relevant experiences."[7]

5. Issac D. Balbus, "The Concept of Interest in Pluralist and Marxian Analysis," *Politics and Society,* 1 (Feb. 1971), 152.

6. One of which he attributes to me (despite my efforts in private correspondence to dissuade him) rather than to the pluralist writers whose views I was attempting to formulate.

7. Connolly, "On Interests," p. 472. Connolly gives an illuminating example on p. 475: "Thus the worker who changes his preference scale as between more income and a more creative work life after having experienced benefits produced *by the latter* [emphasis supplied] can be said to provide solid evidence in support of the view that the policies promoting a more creative work life were more fully in his interest after all." We may wonder in passing why Connolly would not want workers to make their choices after also experiencing higher incomes.

STRATEGIES FOR DETERMINING "INTERESTS" OF ACTORS

I. Pure choice by observer (who judges "enlightenment" of actor's choices) (Lukes, Connolly)

II. Adulterated choice by observer, constrained by prior specifications of:
  - "needs" (Bay)
  - obligations to maximize specified values
    e.g. "equality"
       "democracy"
       "autonomy"
       etc.
  (Sharpe, Dunleavy, Abell)

III. Adulterated choice by actor, constrained by
  - actor's prior specification of his "wants" (Barry)
  - actor's prior specification of his "ultimate goals" (Oppenheim)
  - widespread agreement on instrumental rationality

IV. Pure choice by actor
  (some Pluralist₃ writers?)

Steven Lukes rather mysteriously applies honorific labels such as "three dimensional" and "radical" to this particular conception.[8] He says: "The radical... maintains that men's wants may themselves be a product of a system which works against their interests, and, in such cases, relates the latter to what they would want and prefer, were they able to make the choice."[9] But Lukes is in error in thinking this strategy belongs to radicals alone; authoritarians of any stripe can make use of it with equal facility. For example, in what was probably his most reactionary book, Walter Lippmann defines "the public interest" as "what men would choose if they saw clearly, thought rationally, acted disinterestedly and benevolently."[10]

"Enlightened" choice resembles the other pure conception, one I have

Connolly characterizes as authoritarian people who worry that analysts who say actors are mistaken about their interests may jam their views down actors' throats, and offers the following reassurance: "I might simply try to persuade you or to bribe you." Ibid., p. 474, n. 31.

8. Steven Lukes, *Power: A Radical Approach* (London, Macmillan, 1974), passim. Lukes is not sparing in self-congratulation; he also finds his preferred approach "deeper" (pp. 38, 42, 57) and "serious" (p. 38).

9. Ibid., p. 34. See also Frank Cunningham, "Pluralism and Class Struggle," *Science and Society*, 39 (Winter 1975–76), 391.

10. Walter Lippmann, *The Public Philosophy* (Boston, Little, Brown, 1955), p. 42. Barry Hindess makes a similar point, mentioning Ortega y Gasset and Martin Heidegger: "On Three-Dimensional Power," *Political Studies*, 24 (Sept. 1976), 330.

said many pluralists entertain, in that both refer to choices made by political actors. One, however, refers to actual choices and the other to choices people "would" make if they possessed certain sorts of knowledge. But that knowledge, according to theorists of enlightened choice, is evidently not available to choosers. If it were, then presumably the first conception of interest—actual choices—would suffice to account for the interests of actors. Where, then, is the relevant knowledge to be found that permits people not merely to choose but to choose *in accordance with* their interests? If such knowledge exists at all, we must conclude it is in the possession of self-proclaimed "radicals" or third-dimensionalists (or even reactionaries) who know enough to be able to tell when it is appropriate to reject the choices of ordinary citizens as insufficiently enlightened to reflect their real interests.

A definition relying upon "enlightenment" in some form or other amounts to an argument that actors would choose differently if they knew what analysts knew; in short, it consists of a substitution of analysts' choices for actors' choices. The difficulty with this sort of definition is not simply that in some cases analysts are less able than actors to discern what the correct choices should be from the actors' own perspective. Rather, the problem is that there is no method for determining when analysts are choosing better than actors in the actors' behalf and when they are not. It is not always clear, for example, that long-run benefits are to be preferred to short-run benefits, or vice versa, although analysts and actors may choose quite differently between these alternatives.[11]

Thus analysts who define interests in this fashion create for themselves a self-fulfilling universe of data in which the choices actors make can be arbitrarily invalidated. In principle, this objection might be overcome if analysts were willing to commit themselves to criteria less arbitrary than their own unadorned preferences are likely to be, so as to help others to distinguish between the valid and invalid choices of actors.

This moves us back a step to an adulterated strategy of interest determination in which the choices observers make in behalf of actors are constrained by criteria to which observers commit themselves in advance as relevant to the welfare of actors. Such a strategy might stipulate a value

11. Casual observation suggests that observers are more likely to criticize actors for neglecting long-run than short-run considerations. Thus people who gratify their (short-run) craving for nicotine—i.e. smokers—are likely to be criticized for indulging a (long-run) self-destructive habit. Another less defensible but perfectly real case would be the denial of painkilling drugs to terminally ill patients on the grounds that the drugs are addictive. Those patients might be better off if Keynes had said, "In the short run we are all dead."

to be maximized, such as "democracy" or "equality"[12] or "freedom" or "autonomy"[13] or "human dignity," and weigh alternative courses of action or policies according to the observer's assessment of the capacity of these policies to deliver the stipulated values to actors. Policies ranking high in this capacity would be regarded as in actors' interests, even if actors did not choose them. Third parties could weigh the claims observers make in behalf of actors by adducing independent evidence of the means—ends relations argued by observers, but presumably are estopped from arguing that observers have made the wrong choices of goals to be maximized.

An example of this strategy is the attempt to discover a list of human "needs" against which policies can be tested. It can be argued that there must be a not impossibly long set of human needs that people will agree upon. If the choices people make trespass in some fashion upon this short list, then they can be said to be choosing against their own interests. An example of a method of generating such a list would be Christian Bay's definition of a need as "any behaviour tendency whose continued denial or frustration leads to pathological responses."[14]

Presumably, then, the reciprocal of anything which in Bay's analysis "leads to" pathology counts as a need. Problems with this approach include difficulty in achieving widespread agreement about how to diagnose pathological behavior, how to identify the specific needs that specific pathologies frustrate, how to distinguish greater from lesser needs, or how to identify need-regarding from need-disregarding behavior. Nor is it easy to tell how to analyze the vast bulk of choice behavior, which bears only trivially on the satisfaction of basic needs. Under the circumstances, it is no wonder that some scholars who identify interests with needs neglect to say further what needs are.[15]

Difficulties of this sort make the conception of interest as preferences and as overt choices made by actors in their own behalf look more defensible. It is, I argued, compatible with other pluralist beliefs to assert, at least *a priori*, that what an individual or group wants, or what they say they want, or in some way indicate they want, is, by definition, what their political interests are.

12. This is roughly what L. J. Sharpe advocates in a forthcoming book on democracy in Britain and America.
13. See Peter Abell, "The Many Faces of Power and Liberty: Revealed Preference, Autonomy, and Teleological Explanation," *Sociology, 11* (Jan. 1977), 3–24.
14. Christian Bay, "Needs, Wants and Political Legitimacy," *Canadian Journal of Political Science, 1* (Sept. 1968), 242.
15. E.g., Patrick Dunleavy, "An Issue Centred Approach to the Study of Power," *Political Studies, 24* (Dec. 1976), 432–33.

Whatever the advantages of this formula, and I believe they are not insubstantial, it entails at least one clear cost. It makes it extremely difficult to raise directly as an issue the relationships between preferences and interests defined otherwise. For example, if choices become available to actors by virtue of their access to resources, then a lack of resources may preclude choices that they otherwise would make. Hence an analyst's knowledge of the existence or the intensity of a preference may regularly depend upon, and be limited by, the resourcefulness of actors. This weakens the reliability of various actors' choices as a measure of their interests, and implies that in many circumstances it will be necessary to find criteria other than the overt choices of actors alone in order to determine if their interests are being expressed.

In earlier chapters I held that for a strict dyed-in-the-wool Pluralist₃ it would verge on nonsense to say of a community actor, "He acted against his interests," or "He was unaware of his best interests." How are we to reconcile this claim of mine with the apparent fact that when the chips are down researchers whose findings make them Pluralists₂ have nevertheless discussed issues of this kind? They have had to grapple, for instance, with the failure of retail merchants who knew they would be put out of business by urban renewal plans to oppose these plans in a timely or effective manner.[16] It is obviously unsatisfactory, and quite contrary to common usage of the concept of "interest" in ordinary language, to say that the failure of these businessmen to fight urban renewal was in their interests because had it not been in their interests they would have fought. And, as a matter of fact, no Pluralist₂ researcher has to my knowledge made such a statement, although such a statement would, I believe, have been strictly entailed by full acceptance of one Pluralist₃ axiom as I earlier formulated it.

It seems to me we are faced here by the following difficulty. I have not claimed, nor do I believe, that the source of Pluralist₂ conclusions is Pluralist₃ axioms; only that these conclusions are generally compatible with these axioms. But in the case of this axiom (and conceivably others) even the loose linkage I have traced is evidently incorrectly specified, because Pluralist₂ researchers apparently do entertain a conception of interest other than interest as preference, manifested in overt choice behavior.

Here are two possible supplementary axioms, that state the existence of something like instrumental rationality on a limited scale: (1) The relationships between causes and effects are frequently well and generally understood in a large number of situations in which human beings are

16. This occurred both in New Haven and Chicago. Wolfinger, *Politics of Progress,* pp. 320–38; Peter H. Rossi and Robert A. Dentler, *The Politics of Urban Renewal* (New York, The Free Press, 1961), pp. 91–95.

faced with choices that have direct consequences for their overall value positions. (2) People generally try to maintain or improve their overall value positions. When people choose not to maintain or improve their overall value positions in situations where causes and effects are clearly specified and well known, they can be said to be acting against their interests. This more or less corresponds to an adulterated conception of interests as actors' choices—constrained by an observer's right to override these choices in the event actors do not choose in such a way as to get what they "want." What actors "want" must in these circumstances be understood in advance. A formulation that is for our purposes equivalent would be that actors' choices, to be rational, must be compatible with their ultimate goals, as specified in advance by the actors themselves.[17]

So stated, these axioms do not seem to me to rest upon bedrock, since lengthy discussion would probably have to precede agreement on precisely what cause and effect relationships, what situations, what choices, what direct consequences, pertaining to which wants and which goals, would count as instrumentally rational. As a practical matter, moreover, many of these features of the real world are quite sharply controverted. Recall the earlier example of the wealthy Americans who voted against Franklin Roosevelt for President in 1932. Were they acting in their interests? Obviously, many of them thought so at the time, but not all did. Others have since taken the view that Roosevelt, by preserving American capitalism, improved the overall value positions of well-off Americans over the long run.[18] In order to constitute a satisfactory application of the axiom I have proposed, agreement about the causal relationship between adoption of a given alternative and the value position of an actor must be far more general and widespread than indirect evidence of the contemporary evaluation of the majority of the actor's social group.

Paul Meehl gives an excellent rundown of features that tend to build confidence in statements about human affairs (for our purposes cause and effect statements bearing upon the instrumental rationality of a given course of action) not established by strict scientific means—statements that he refers to as "fireside inductions":

17. Cf. Brian Barry, "The Public Interest," *Proceedings of the Aristotelian Society*, Supp. 38 (1964), 1–18; and Felix E. Oppenheim, "Self-Interest and Public Interest," *Political Theory*, 3 (Aug. 1975), 259–76. Barry and Oppenheim are for our purposes similar, but in some other respects disagree.

18. This, among other things, is what is inconvenient about C. Wright Mills's definition of false class consciousness as statistical deviation from the political attitude of one's social group (defined as class). Suppose the minority makes a better calculation of class interest?

Hardly anyone entertains serious doubts about the induction. Persons of different theoretical persuasions agree about the fireside induction almost as well as persons holding the same theoretical position. There is a consensus of the fireside that cuts across demographic variables such as education, occupation, social class, religious belief, ethnic background, and the like. Within the legal profession prosecutors, defense lawyers, law professors, and judges are in substantial agreement. Personality traits (e.g., dominance, social introversion, hostility, rigidity) are not appreciably correlated with adherence to the induction. The particular fireside induction involves an observation of actions, persons, or effects that occur with sufficient frequency so that most qualified and competent observers will have had an extensive experience as a generalization basis. The fireside induction deals with relatively objective physical or behavioral facts rather than with complicated causal inferences. The policy implications of the induction are such that nobody's political, ethnic, religious, moral, or economic ideology or class interest would be appreciably threatened or mobilized by its general acceptance in the society or by lawmakers' or administrators' reliance upon it in decision-making. Sophisticated armchair considerations do not reveal a built-in observational or sampling bias that would operate in the collection of anecdotal support or refutation of the induction. The induction is qualitative rather than one that claims to make quantitative comparisons despite the lack of a reliable measuring device.[19]

This formula, stressing common opinion about causes and effects, falls well short of the stipulation that the interest of an actor can be defined as what an actor "would" choose, given his values and adding only a greater degree of enlightenment. When there is a difference between what actors choose and what, from the standpoint of observers, seems to be in their interest, the first question should not be what causes actors in these situations to choose "wrongly" but rather what causes observers to believe that a wrong choice has been made. To establish that observers have a suitable warrant for such a belief, I think it is desirable to specify criteria having empirical reference, which can be shown to be met in any case where observers want to claim that actors are behaving against their best interests. Once this is shown, the discussion of reasons for the divergence between analysts' expectations and actors' choices can add up to more than the arbitrary substitution of one preference schedule for another. There is then

19. Paul E. Meehl, "Law and the Fireside Induction," *Journal of Social Issues,* 27 (no. 4, 1971), 94.

some basis for giving serious consideration to the possibility that the information available to actors has been manipulated or their alternatives artificially restricted in some other manner. Or other explanations may be
invoked, such as the stubbornness or craziness of actors (we must concede,
after all, that some actors—like some analysts on whom we admittedly
have better data—are crazy) or involvement in a complex set of trade-offs
that for one reason or another are of more interest to a given set of actors
than to a particular analyst.

How can we choose among these various possibilities in any individual
case? I have no special insight to offer; the problems involved seem to me
in principle no more intractable than any difficult situation calling for
analysis of causes and effects, weighing evidence, and so on.

What is the general applicability of axioms such as I have suggested?
Pluralists$_3$ are, I think, likely to apply them far more circumspectly than
social analysts who have more tightly articulated or more comprehensive
beliefs about causes and effects that affect the value positions of political
actors. Nevertheless, it makes one uncomfortable to load so much baggage
on the axiomatic end of a social theory. But it seems to me that in their
analyses of concrete social and political phenomena Pluralists$_2$ behave as
though something like an assumption that people will act to maintain their
value positions was operating as an underlying axiom of their political
theory, in addition to a conception of interest as choice behavior.

Critics will no doubt observe, and with justification, that it is a rather
messy and unsatisfactory political theory which embodies axioms leading to
contradictory theorems, as seems to be the case here. Certainly as loosely
stated these axioms could readily lead to contradiction. What would be
required to meet this objection would at a minimum be a specification of
the conditions under which actors would be expected to reveal their interests by their explicit choices and the conditions under which common
knowledge about the causes of maintained or increased value positions for
political actors would be held to indicate the interests of actors.

I am not going to attempt any such specification here. Such a task ranges
far beyond my central purpose, which is to discuss only those ideas which
appear to have proximate consequences for research and empirical description, and not to give an exhaustive account of those ideas which seem
to underlie alternative depictions of power in American communities.

It appears to be true that Pluralist$_2$ researchers are not much concerned
with one particular set of problems that would suggest that axioms such as
I have proposed are in play. I am referring to problems of "false consciousness," a term often employed by admirers of Karl Marx to denote precisely
those political situations in which the explicit choices of actors are different

from those the analyst believes are in the actor's best interests. I believe that a heavy responsibility rests upon analysts in such situations to justify the claim that actors are in fact unaware of what they are doing and are genuinely misguided by their own lights, rather than simply involved in trade-offs disagreed with (or not understood) by analysts. For it remains a lively possibility that the connections between cause and effect that an analyst perceives in a given situation are not perceived by actors because the connections are not there, or are overridden by connections that actors themselves find more compelling—some significant subset of which might even be justified as "enlightened" choices. How are we to distinguish between nonexistent connections and those that only a particular set of actors are unable to see? Here, I think, it is necessary to appeal to very widely shared agreement about cause and effect in the political world, agreement shared, for example, by many other actors situated similarly to those held to be falsely conscious, and also shared by analysts who disagree about what constitutes the good society, or good policy. Short of such agreement, it seems to me unlikely that we shall be able to resolve whether false consciousness in any given instance is in the behavior of actors or in the eye of a beholder.

It is possible to carry an argument about trade-offs and false consciousness a step or two further. It can be said, for example, that for a system to exist in which there are trade-offs involving unwholesome or unpleasant alternatives constitutes evidence for the idea that people making such trade-offs within the system are falsely conscious. That is, they do not realize that such trade-offs are unnecessary. How do analysts know they are unnecessary? Because they observe that wherever possible the rich buy their way out of many trade-offs that scarce resources impose on the less rich. While this is no doubt sometimes true, it is an argument that raises difficulties. It cannot, I think, be empirically established that the rich are exempt in their lives from all trade-offs entailing tragic choices, or that rich people can escape all the consequences of trade-offs made in communities in which they live. They can, for example, avoid bad local school systems by sending their children away to school, but not everyone finds it an unmitigated pleasure to live apart from their children.

Of course to be rich in a capitalist economy—that is, in an economy where goods and services are for sale, where individuals may influence the deployment of goods and services by their individual decisions to purchase backed by their individual access to resources—is to have more alternatives than to be poor, more or less by definition. This does not imply that if everyone had equal access to money that trade-offs entailing difficult or unpleasant choices would disappear. In fact, it can be maintained that on the margins the encouragement of productivity and economic efficiency rather than equality in the distribution of wealth is a more effective way of reducing the net influence of unpleasant trade-offs in society.[20] The argument that rich is better does not imply that promoting equality is a method for getting rich—it may be a device merely to impoverish everybody. And insofar as this is true, it is clearly not a device for escaping unpleasant trade-offs and hence it fails as an argument in support of the notion that people in the community are falsely conscious when they make these trade-offs.

Thus we can not argue successfully that the choosing among unpleasant alternatives within a community indicates per se that a given description of power relations in a community is invalid. Nor, as I have tried to show, given the variety of motives that actors may legitimately have, is the choice of any particular alternative.

The foregoing cannot be read, I think, as a concession to the view of Lukes that the vocabulary with which we discuss these matters, and in particular the term "power," is "essentially contested," in that what I am here asserting has nothing to do with the definitions of terms; rather, I suggest that there are sure to be many instances where observers disagree among themselves, as well as with actors, over the instrumental rationality of actors' choices, even when they agree on the meaning of the concept of instrumental rationality.[21] It seems to me that reaching a conclusion that agreement is unlikely to occur in all cases does not excuse analysts from making attempts to find ways to increase the area of agreement. That was my purpose in suggesting that well-established "fireside inductions," meeting strong criteria of impartiality, might helpfully constrain observers' notions of instrumental rationality and give us a handle on the problem of actors behaving against their interests—without granting plenary powers to observers to invalidate actors' choices.

Insofar as observers are willing to accept this sort of constraint, it becomes possible to use the actual choices of actors as data in determining whether or not the interests of actors are expressed in policy-making, and

20. For interesting discussions of this and related issues, see Arthur Okun, *Equality and Efficiency: The Big Trade-Off* (Washington, D.C.: Brookings, 1975); Okun, "Further Thoughts on Equality and Efficiency" in Colin D. Campbell, ed., *Income Redistribution* (Washington, D.C.: American Enterprise Institute, 1977), pp. 13–34, and Stanley Lebergott, *Wealth and Want* (Princeton, Princeton Univ. Press, 1975).

21. See Lukes, *Power*, p. 9; K. I. MacDonald, "Is 'Power' Essentially Contested?" *British Journal of Political Science*, 6 (July 1976), 380–82; Barry Clarke "Eccentrically Contested Concepts," *British Journal of Political Science*, 9 (Jan. 1979), 122–26; W. B. Gallie, "Essentially Contested Concepts," *Proceedings of the Aristotelian Society*, 56 (1955–56), 167–98. I consider myself agnostic on the issue Lukes raises of the essential contestedness of power terms.

analysts can ward off the problem of infinite regress that so often plagues this field of study. According to the standard implied by this method for identifying interests, I do not think the Pluralist₂ studies of community power can be shown to have so neglected the study of relevant actors' interests as to have biased their account of the distribution of power in a local community.

Observers must be prepared to accept that opportunity costs are imposed on all courses of action, and hence the choice of any option implies that some actors' interests will be disadvantaged. Those who undertake to plead for actors or groups disadvantaged by a given set of choices will have reason to complain of systematic neglect of the interests of the groups for whom they hold a brief; but I doubt that such complaints constitute a valid indictment of the accuracy of a description of policy-making processes that produce or maintain any given status quo. It is mistakes of this sort that lead some observers to the conclusion that Pluralist₂ descriptions constitute an endorsement of such disparate enterprises as wife-beating, the persecution of gypsies, and the economic exploitation of the very poor.[22] It is obviously possible to have political systems that are more and less humane with respect to the least fortunate members of society, but it is not possible, at least not in any real world system I can readily call to mind, to have an ongoing political enterprise of any size or scope that does not, by virtue of its very continuity (regardless of other reasons), create a status quo of some sort which in turn allocates opportunity costs systematically and hence tends toward at least some sorts of inequalities among those differently situated. I think this is very generally what it means to assert that systems are conservative by nature, that a healthy system is one that tends to maintain itself—i.e. resists breakdown. Observers may properly reserve judgment as to whether they like the results, but their opinions on this question ought to be capable of formulation without prejudice to the question of whether or not a given account of community politics is accurate.[23]

22. I draw—tendentiously—upon examples furnished by Kenneth Newton, *Second City Politics*, p. 231.

23. This, more or less, is the argument I would make against the charge that Pluralist₂ descriptions encode the preferences of scholars about decision-making. See Kenneth Newton, "A Critique of the Pluralist Model," *Acta Sociologica*, 12 (No. 4, 1969), 221; and Colin Bell and Howard Newby, *Community Studies* (London, George Allen and Unwin, 1971), p. 238, for examples of confusion on this point.

# 13. In Conclusion: Brief Epistemological Reflections

The preceding pages are meant to convey a notion of the proper uses of theory and theorizing in social science. My idea of theory, a widely held but evidently not universally shared view, is that it exists primarily for the purpose of facilitating the storage and recall of information about objects of empirical inquiry, and for producing new knowledge by confronting scholars with the results of the order into which information is organized. Thus theorizing consists of acts of scholarship that seek to encode empirical information, to make distinctions and identify similarities, to explore analogies and contrasts, to accumulate instances and spin out deductions, to formulate laws and sentences explaining why laws are true, all for the purpose of providing illumination about a world that has some existence independent and apart from the language in which scholars palaver.

One consequence of this epistemological preference is that assertions purporting to be theoretical contributions ought to be inspected for their empirical consequences. Those distinctions, analyses, and so forth that appear not to be especially useful in ordering empirical experience, or which unexpectedly fail to take account of some range of empirical experience that they claim to, are, to scholars sharing the epistemological preference I have identified, less satisfactory than assertions, pretending to theory, that help in converting some of the disorderly noisiness of the world into some sort of coherence, interpersonally communicable and more easily recognized as "information."

In the last analysis, I suggest, information—if possible, new information—that remarkable artifact of human ingenuity and effort, is what we are, or ought to be, seeking when we read and write theory about community power. The introductory section of this book states the belief that all those who inaugurated the study of community power subscribed to this preference. To claim or to demonstrate some shortfall in the empirical usefulness of the explanations in an early community power study was to invoke a standard mutually shared among all participants in the enterprise.[1]

Such an assumption cannot be entertained with confidence today. One

1. See above, p. 7.

of the most remarkable features of the progress of the community power literature since 1960 has been the explicit detachment of a goodly portion of this literature from empirical constraint. Assertions having empirical import continue to be made. In earlier times the address to central questions having to do with the strength of the warrant for one or another empirical statement might appear to raise issues of mistakenness or even, *in extremis,* incompetence; today such issues sometimes seem to be resolved by a flat rejection of the commitment to the establishment of "scientific" knowledge by adherence to shared norms of investigation.[2] There are no means at my disposal for compelling the return to the fold of scholars so minded. I can only signal explicitly what is undoubtedly clear enough in any event: these pages are written under the old dispensation and are meant neither to contribute to nor intrude upon the religious experiences of people contrarily oriented to social inquiry.

Neither are they meant to assert some overarching explanation for world events, "national power structures," or other earthshaking entities. I should be disappointed if it were to prove to be the case that the principles of investigation that appear to produce relatively reliable information about one domain—community politics—should prove utterly barren in guiding research into other domains. But it seems to me obvious—as it evidently was not to some readers of the first edition of this book—that assertions purporting to summarize evidence from one empirical domain ought not to be attributed to some other empirical domain. Some readers have made this point ostensibly against the New Haven study;[3] whether an explicit

2. A forthcoming book on urban politics by Peter Saunders promises to be helpful and illuminating on this point. See also, Shin'ya Ono, "The Limits of Bourgeois Pluralism," in C. A. McCoy and J. Playford, eds., *Apolitical Politics* (New York, Crowell, 1967), 99–123. On pp. 104–05, Ono says:

> As a general model of politics in American society, the theory . . . cannot be challenged on a purely empirical basis. . . . [A]s long as we remain within the framework of purely "empirical" and "descriptive" analysis, we can never clarify the fundamental limitations of this general conception.

In *Class, Crisis and the State* (London, NLB, 1978), Erik Olin Wright says, p. 9:

> As a graduate student in sociology I constantly confronted the hegemony of an empiricist, positivist epistemology in the social sciences. In virtually every debate over Marxist ideas, at some point I would be asked, "prove it!" . . . Marxists in the social sciences reacted to these pressures in several distinct ways. Perhaps the dominant response was to dismiss the attacks of non-Marxist social scientists as reflecting bourgeois ideology and/or a positivist methodology. It was common in Marxist student circles to argue that the very enterprise of formulating "testable hypotheses" was inimical to a Marxist methodology. . . . The demand that we prove theoretical claims through empirically testable propositions, therefore, was treated as purely ideological.

3. See, for example, Claude Burtenshaw, "The Political Theory of Pluralist Democracy," *Western Political Quarterly, 21* (Dec. 1968), 577.

disclaimer will do any good in helping them read this second edition more accurately I do not know.

In summary, I should simply acknowledge that the alternative strategy for studying community power explicitly recommended in the first edition of this book and exemplified in the New Haven study has proven highly controversial. As I have indicated, objections to the recommended strategy that I have been able to identify have depended heavily upon statements about the strategy that are often flatly false. In some cases counterrecommendations have been forthcoming that do not add up to a program of research so much as to, variously, a little word magic (such as redefining "nondecision"), a newer, more complex method of bootlegging prejudices into conclusions ("anticipated reactions"), or a vacuous counsel of perfection. In one case, a comparative approach was suggested that seems to me promising, regardless of its disappointing execution in the instance in which it was first attempted. I remain unconvinced that answers to the question who benefits? are readily substitutable for answers to the question who governs? and skeptical that the interests of actors can be easily discerned entirely without regard for their revealed preferences. A satisfactory theory would, no doubt, take explicit account of the fact that who benefits from a political arrangement or decision or system is not a negligible question, but that has never been disputed. What is at issue is whether it is the same nonnegligible question as who governs. Likewise there is room for differentiation between revealed preferences and instrumental rationality as commonly understood in some situations; whether more dogmatic assertions of disagreements by analysts with the revealed preferences of actors ought to be admitted to serious discussion hangs, as I have suggested, on the resolution of some points that have not yet been adequately clarified in the literature, despite serious efforts to address the issues involved.

In light of all the difficulties, the false starts, the blind alleys, misunderstandings, misquotations, and misinterpretations to which this literature has given rise is there anything of sufficient value in community power studies to justify still another set of recommendations about future research? Some scholars have rushed into aggregate comparative work without a careful assessment of what sorts of things they were comparing.[4] Elaborate but not very successful simulations of common sense have been the best product of this enterprise; tautology and double-talk have been the worst. But not all aggregate studies suffer from a lack of clarity about the actual distribution of their dependent variable or the meaning of their independent vari-

4. A plethora of illustrations occurs, e.g., in Terry N. Clark, ed., *Community Structure and Decision-Making*, esp. pp. 15–126.

able. Fried's work on municipal budgeting,[5] which, among other things, found that Socialist-controlled city governments in West Germany did not spend especially heavily on the poor, is a good example. So is Paul Peterson's work on patterns of local expenditure in which he elaborates a notion of local specialization within a diversified national competition among American cities for economic well-being, civic amenities, and influence at higher levels of government.[6] The work of Raymond E. Wolfinger and others on factors tending to promote and retard ethnic solidarity in local voting,[7] and the somewhat inconclusive work by Banfield, Wilson, Wolfinger, Field, Lineberry, Fowler, and others on the development of civic subcultures[8] are other examples of studies of interest and importance about politics in American communities.

It has been argued that since none of these studies—and other good studies like them—makes use of the characteristic vocabulary of community power, a case can be made for the thought that the whole apparatus of community power studies, with its heritage of disagreeable wrangling, ought simply to be dismantled and forgotten.[9] I will pick no quarrel with researchers who adopt the view that it is a better use of their time to ask fresh questions and seek fresh answers about urban or local or community politics than in some sense to take account of the disorderly literature we have been examining. Insofar as they reach for a global assessment of

5. Robert C. Fried, "Party and Policy in West German Cities," *Am. Pol. Sci. Rev.,* 70 (March 1976), 11–24. A good overview of this and other studies is contained in Robert C. Fried, "Comparative Urban Policy and Performance," in Fred I. Greenstein and Nelson W. Polsby, *The Handbook of Political Science,* 8 vols. (Reading, Mass.; Addison-Wesley, 1975), 6:305–79.

6. Paul E. Peterson, "A Unitary Model of Local Taxation and Expenditure Policies in the United States," *British Journal of Political Science,* 9 (July 1979) 281–314; or Peterson, "Redistributive Policies and Patterns of Citizen Participation in the Local Politics of the United States," in L. J. Sharpe, ed., *Decentralist Trends in Western Democracies* (London, Sage, forthcoming).

7. Raymond E. Wolfinger "The Development and Persistence of Ethnic Voting," *Am. Pol. Sci. Rev.,* 59 (Dec. 1965), 896–908; "Some Consequences of Ethnic Politics," in M. Kent Jennings and L. Harmon Ziegler *The Electoral Process* (Englewood Cliffs, N.J., Prentice Hall, 1966), pp. 42–54.

8. James Q. Wilson and Edward C. Banfield, *City Politics* (Cambridge, Mass.: Harvard Univ. Press, 1963), esp. chaps. 3, 16; James Q. Wilson and Edward C. Banfield, "Public-Regardingness as a Value Premise in Voting Behavior," *Am. Pol. Sci. Rev.,* 58 (Dec. 1964), pp. 876–87; Raymond E. Wolfinger and John Osgood Field, "Political Ethos and the Structure of City Government," *Am. Pol. Sci. Rev.,* 60 (June 1966), 306–26; Robert L. Lineberry and Edmund P. Fowler, "Reformism and Public Policies in American Cities," *Am. Pol. Sci. Rev.,* 61 (Sept. 1967), 701–16; James Q. Wilson and Edward C. Banfield "Political Ethos Revisited," *Am. Pol. Sci. Rev.,* 65 (Dec. 1971), 1048–62.

9. See Raymond E. Wolfinger, "Nondecisions and the Study of Local Politics: Rejoinder to Frey's Comment," *Am. Pol. Sci. Rev.,* 65 (Dec. 1971), p. 1104.

power relations in their research site, however, students will almost certainly have to confront the sorts of issues raised by this literature. And despite the notable lack of consensus displayed in this literature about what the right answers are to these issues, it will almost certainly save a researcher much time and painful digression to be able to follow these issues through a literature that already exists rather than to have to reinvent *de novo* an approximation of even the rather squarish wheel that we are presently using.

The state of the literature today does not immediately suggest a research agenda fundamentally different from the sorts of problems that could have been tackled fifteen years ago. It still seems to me a good idea to proceed comparatively, first specifying a set of dependent variables that makes more sense than pluralism vs. power elite and *then* seeking causal variables. If American communities lacked autonomy in many things fifteen years ago, as I believed, it seems even more so today, so that a specification of intracommunity influence relations is bound to be even less comprehensively revealing about outcomes than was true then. Major forces of urban growth and decay, affluence and bankruptcy, are as difficult to pin on the explicit choices of individually powerful local actors today as they were fifteen years ago. Some decision-makers, to be sure, give the appearance of riding the tiger of demographic trends whereas others fall off; in the end it may well be that limited comparisons of the sort implied by this metaphor will be all one can legitimately claim one is making when one studies community power. How, for example, can inner cities built for nineteenth-century population densities survive the explosion in the number of automobiles, regardless of the wisdom or the power of local leaders? When a technological innovation like air conditioning becomes widespread, what sort of political decisions, deploying finite resources, made in northern cities can stem the southward redistribution of the population?

It is still true of course that significant functions remain in most communities and likewise some degree of freedom in managing resources and achieving outcomes. As students gain experience in analyzing the scopes and styles of community politics, propositions that are promising candidates for general application will no doubt continue to emerge and be subjected to critical scrutiny. One continues to hope that these in turn will tutor our expectations and shape our conclusions about power in local communities.

# Index

Abell, Pater, 223, 225n.
Abercrombie, Nicholas, 197n.
Abu-Laban, Baha, 45n., 51n., 63n., 66n., 68
*Action* (urban renewal group), 173, 174
Adams, John Quincy, 183n.
Agger, Robert E., 45n., 125–26, 156n.
Aiken, Michael, xn., 143n., 146n., 149
Allen, Ivan, 161n.
"And-also" fallacy, 24, 59, 67
Anderson, C. Arnold, 106n.
Anderson, Elin, 133n.
Anticipated reactions, rule of, 202, 235
Anton, Thomas J., xiin., 156n., 157n., 163n., 168n.
Apcar, Leonard M., 160n.
Atlanta, Ga., 160–62, 177; Cleveland study of, 12n. *See also* "Regional City"

Babchuk, Nicholas, 67n.
Bachrach, Peter, 142, 151, 189–218
Bahr Corporation (New Haven, Conn.), 187
Bailey, Stephen K., 81n.
"Bakerville," Miss., 126
Balance of power assumption, 67
Balbus, Isaac, 222
Ball, Terence, 197n.
Baltimore, Md., 210–13
Baltzell, E. Digby, 8n., 9n., 10n., 42–44, 68, 104n., 107, 150
Banfield, Edward C., 12n., 119n., 122n., 211, 236n.
Banker Sly's influence, dilemma of, 213, 216
Baratz, Morton, 142, 151, 189–218
Barber, Bernard, 24n., 99n., 103n.
Barbieri, Arthur T., 82, 83
Barry, Brian, 223, 227n.
Barth, Ernest A. T., 45n., 51n., 63n., 66n., 67n., 68
Baton Rouge, La. *See* "Bigtown"
Bauer, Raymond, 128n.

Bay, Christian, 223, 225
Belknap, George, 12n., 45n., 112n., 113n., 114, 115n., 118–19, 120, 124, 149n.
Bell, Colin, 232n.
Bell, Wendell, 7n.
Bendix, Reinhard, 8n., 51n., 99n., 109n., 116n.
Beneficiaries (of political system), 132, 206–10
Bennington, Vt., 114
Bensman, Joseph, 13n., 116, 128, 129, 133n.
Bentley, Arthur, 112n., 117n.
Bias, mobilization of, 189–218
Bierstedt, Robert, 3n., 109n.
"Bigtown," 56–59
Birmingham, Ala., 159n.
Birmingham, England, 194–95n., 219
Blackwell, Gordon, 45n.
Blau, Peter, 77n.
Bloom, Harold, 147n.
Bloomberg, Warner, Jr., xiin., 142
Blumberg, Leonard U., 15n., 45n., 51–52
Blumer, Herbert, 117n.
Bolce, Louis H., 172n.
Bonjean, Charles M., xn.
Boston, Mass., 12n.
Braybrooke, David, 112n.
Buckley, Walter, 99n., 100n.
Bunzel, John H., 113n.
Burtenshaw, Claude, 234n.
Bush, Prescott, 181, 182, 185
Business class: in Bigtown, 56–58; in Cibola, 59–63; in Elmtown, 31; in Middletown, 15–24; in Pacific City, 63–66; in Philadelphia, 42–44; in Regional City, 46–47; 54–55. *See also* Economic elite; Social-economic position

Caen, Herb, xvi, xviin.
Campbell, Angus, 116n.
Campbell, Colin D., 231n.